WILEY **CPA** Examination Review ®

YOU CAN PASS THE
CPA EXAM

G E T
M O T I V A T E D

WILEY **CPA** Examination Review

YOU CAN PASS THE
CPA EXAM

G E T
M O T I V A T E D

Knowledge and
Confidence-Building
Techniques

 *Includes Audio CD*

Debra R. Hopkins

PERMISSIONS

Library of Congress Cataloging in Publication Data:

Hopkins, Debra R.
   You can pass the CPA exam: get motivated/Debra R. Hopkins
      p.cm.
   Includes index.
   ISBN 0-0471-37010-X (pbk: alk. paper)
   1. Accounting--Examinations. I. Title.
HF5661 .H58 1999
657'.076–dc21   99-051619

Printed in the United States of America

10 9 8 7 6 5 4 3 2 1

Dedication

This book is dedicated to the thousands of CPA candidates who have motivated me to believe in myself. Special recognition goes to my two favorite CPA candidates, Joyce H. and Jenny W.

CONTENTS

PREFACE

Over the last 15 years, I have witnessed thousand of CPA candidates attempt to pass the Uniform Certified Public Accountant's (CPA) examination. While there are many manuals and courses which outline the CPA exam's technical material, there is not much available to help CPA candidates manage the entire preparation process.

With so little information available about managing the entire CPA journey from start to finish, it is no wonder that hundreds of CPA candidates find themselves overwhelmed by the whole experience. With a pass rate of 12-16%, I know it is crucial that candidates not only possess the technical knowledge, but also understand how to use and display that knowledge in a format that the CPA exam graders can understand and will reward with points.

Whether you enroll in a formal CPA review course or self-study, this book will help you deal with the emotional side of the exam. You have made a considerable investment in your career by the time you decide to sit for the exam. Why waste time and money in the last leg of the journey. Passing the exam is the crowning glory of the accounting degree. Save yourself time, anxiety, and stress by doing the right things to increase your chances of passing the exam.

Over the last 15 years, I have helped over 1,200 CPA candidates per year prepare for the exam. I have put all my experience as a professor and director of one of the highest-achieving review courses in the nation into this book. I want the information and guidance made available to as many people as it can reach. I believe that candidates from all over the world have made a considerable investment of time and money in preparing for the exam and they deserve the best guidance when it comes to the preparations process. Enjoy the book, the CD recording, and even enjoy taking the actual exam. It's much easier when you know what to expect and how to handle difficult areas.

I am grateful to those who have inspired me to help people all over the world pass the Uniform Certified Public Accountant Examination. Gratitude is expressed to Ms. Carol Denton for her expert typing assistance and to Ms. Mary Hamell for her strong belief in my abilities. Special thanks go to my mentors, Drs. Richard Baker, Patrick Delaney, and John Simon, for their support has been crucial to my career development and understanding of the CPA exam. I am also grateful to John Wiley & Sons' staff for their careful and timely efforts. Finally, a heartfelt thank you to Lorraine, Roger, Tony, and Megan. Without their loving support, nothing would be accomplished.

Good luck in achieving the worthwhile goal of becoming a CPA!

Debra R. Hopkins, CPA, CIA

ABOUT THE AUTHOR

Debra R. Hopkins directs the nationally acclaimed Northern Illinois University (NIU) CPA Review course in the Chicago, Illinois area. For over 15 years she has taught auditing and financial accounting.

As director, she assists over 1,200 CPA candidates each year. She has skillfully combined her education, experience, and enthusiasm into a format that is easy to follow and understand. She attends the Chicago CPA exam every 6 months, and knows firsthand just how frustrating the experience can be for a person who is not aware of the entire CPA process. She has seen and heard directly from the candidates.

1 BELIEVE THAT YOU CAN PASS!

Passing the Uniform Certified Public Accountant (CPA) examination is not easy. Every 6 months, over 60,000 people throughout the United States attempt to pass this difficult 2-day exam. With a first-time passing rate of 12-15%, it is assumed that most people will fail upon their first attempt. That's right, the odds are against you. Yet, CPA exam candidates keep on trying. Completing the exam is one of the greatest accomplishments an accountant can achieve. Without the three initials "CPA" you are just another accountant. How could three initials mean so much?

Being a CPA sends certain signals. People know that you have achieved a very difficult goal--you have passed the Uniform Certified Public Accountant exam. In the business world, working with a CPA instills confidence and trust. Compared to an accounting graduate who has not yet attained certification, CPAs command higher salaries, are in greater demand in the workforce, and are given greater respect by the general public. Who wouldn't want more money, more job choices, and more respect? The desire to become a CPA should be yours. You must believe that you have the skills and knowledge necessary to pass this exam. If you can look at yourself in the mirror and say, "I can pass the CPA exam," you are ready to proceed. Believing that you can pass the exam is the first step. Now, how do you proceed?

STEPS TO SUCCESS ON THE CPA EXAM

In today's information age, it is amazing how many people take the CPA exam without knowing much about the process. Perhaps this is the reason that the majority of the people sitting for the exam, roughly 88%, fail upon their first attempt. To successfully complete the CPA exam you must understand much more than just technical material. The 3 to 4 hours that it will take you to read this book will save you countless hours of study time. *Get Motivated* is designed not only to keep you "pumped" throughout the study process, but also to help you

- Increase your memory power
- Design a personalized study plan that fits your situation
- Eliminate the fear of failure by understanding the exam process
- Decrease text anxiety
- Improve your study habits
- Maximize the efficiency and effectiveness with which you study

Taking the CPA exam is a costly venture. When you add up the cost of a review course, textbooks, software, the exam sitting fee, the time off work, and the cost of travel to and from the exam, the total investment can easily exceed $2,000. Yet many exam candidates have the attitude that they will just "go try the exam to see what I can learn." If you were running a business, would you waste time and money just to understand the process? I doubt it. You would hire a consultant who not only understands the process but who can quickly teach you how to make the most out of the experience. This book provides you with just such tips and strategies. For over 15 years, I have helped thousands of people from all over the world pass the CPA exam. I have witnessed firsthand what it takes to pass. I know why people fail. Why take chances? Learn how to attack the CPA exam and beat the odds of failure. Learn from other people's mistakes. Learn from other people's successes. Why reinvent the wheel? Utilize a best practice management plan--use a consultant to help you.

You are ready to proceed. You have the desire to pass the CPA exam. The next step is to understand why so many people fail.

FAILURE

Failure is the act of nonperformance. Failure means you were not successful at this attempt. Failure is temporary. Failure does not last forever. If you did not pass the exam, you are not awful, stupid, or careless. You just did not perform in the manner that was required. There is no need to provide excuses as to why you did not or will not pass the CPA exam. Making excuses takes time, bores the person who is listening to you, and reminds you that you were not successful. Thinking about failing the exam is the wrong focus. Spend a brief amount of time analyzing why others have failed. Then use your knowledge to move on. Learn from other people's mistakes.

Why do so many people fail? About one-third of the people pass each exam section each time. The overall pass rate for first-time takers passing all four parts is about 12-15%. What makes this exam so difficult?

First, the exam is not similar to any other exam you have probably ever taken. The total exam time is 15½ hours, spanning a 2-day time period. Most exams you took in college were much shorter, perhaps 1 to 2 hours. A 4-hour exam would be considered very long. Take 4 hours and multiply it by four and you have the CPA exam.

Next, the exam is not usually given in a place that is familiar to you. The exam site is often in a large city to which you must travel. You will not know most of the exam takers; you will probably not know the exam administrators and proctors. You will be given no choice as to the exam day; the dates and time are set for you. No matter how you feel or what crises you might be undergoing, the exam will go on. The exam will proceed under the rules set by the American Institute of Certified Public Accountants (AICPA). Most CPA candidates are not informed about the exact exam-taking rules. They are only told that the rules must be followed.

Finally, the exam covers material you learned over a 4- to 5-year time period. The amount of material is overwhelming. If you stack up your college textbooks that support the subjects on the CPA exam, you will have about a 3-ft high pile. Dealing with such breadth of material is enough to destroy your confidence.

After the exam, you must wait 3 months for your scores. Your kind college professor will not be grading the exam. Accounting professionals who do not personally know you will be grading your essays and problems. They will use a predetermined grading guide. You will be expected to achieve at a certain level. The level is often established well before the exam is given. When the scores are released, you will not see your answers. You will only see your overall grade for each section and a brief summary of your performance called a "Candidate Diagnostic Report." Yes, the uncertainty of the content, the exam environment, the grading process, and the sheer volume of material are enough to make you want to give up. Don't give up! If you give up, you will never become a CPA. Read this book and learn how to develop a customized study plan to maximize your study effectiveness. Learn how to remain motivated and confident during both the study process and the exam-taking process. On exam day, learn how to attack and control the exam. Learn step by step how to remember concepts, apply exam strategy, and achieve a passing score. Don't think about what you can't or don't know how to do. Believe and it can happen. Believe that you have what it takes to become a CPA. If you don't believe in yourself who else will? You must convince the exam graders that you possess the necessary knowledge to have earned the right to call yourself a CPA. If you keep saying, "I can't pass the CPA exam," you are probably correct. A successful candidate does not accept an "I can't" attitude. If you so easily discount your ability to perform, imagine what the exam graders are going to do! From now on, even when you are feeling low or doubtful about your abilities, you are to remind yourself that you can pass the CPA exam. You will believe in yourself.

The CPA exam is not a new experience. Since 1917, people just like you have been passing this exam. You aren't the only person in the world who will struggle from time to time in your exam preparation. You are not the only person in the world who will have distractions, crises, and problems during your study process. You are not the only person in the world who is anxious, fearful, or worried about the exam. You are not alone. If you dwell on your troubles, you will become distracted and lose focus. Take a lesson from people who have failed.

Failure on the CPA exam occurs because of:

- Fear of failure--not believing in yourself
- Lack of technical knowledge
- Lack of knowledge about the exam environment
- Loss of focus on the task on hand

It's easy to see from the list above that people fail because of both a lack of knowledge about the exam and of themselves. Unfortunately, some people even fail after hours of studying. They study the wrong material. Using out-of-date study materials is one of the biggest mistakes a person can make. Material that is more than 6 months to 1 year old is out of date. If a person spends hours studying their old college textbooks, they are probably not only using out-of-date material, but are also studying material meant for a college class. The exam has its own unique method of testing material. A person can arrive at the exam and find no correlation between the material they studied and the material tested upon. Why study just to study? Your time is too valuable. Spend your time learning and using the concepts that are tested on the real exam.

A well-studied person can fail because they allowed themselves to be overcome with test anxiety. Taking an exam with strangers in a strange place can be very upsetting. What a shame to have spent months preparing for something and then to be overcome with fear just because the setting was not what you had expected.

If you have attempted the CPA exam and did not pass, you are not a failure. You have just hit a temporary setback. You have the power to turn failure into success. Once you have passed the CPA exam, no one is going to ask you how many times you sat for the exam before you passed. The question is always: "Are you a CPA?"

What can you learn from other people's mistakes? It takes more than just technical knowledge to pass. The successful candidate will do the following:

- Prepare an organized study plan
- Use the proper study materials
- Learn about the exam environment, the grading process, and the exam requirements
- Remain motivated throughout the study process
- Use knowledge about the exam process to control the exam
- Remain confident throughout the entire 2 days

• Always believe that he or she can pass the CPA exam

Enough talk about failure. You must focus on obtaining positive results. Use your energies towards achieving a positive outcome. Believe that you are a successful person. Your focus is to pass the exam. Your focus should never be failure. Once you abandon the failure focus, you can begin to work on the steps to success. Success is easier to talk about than failure. However, success does not come overnight. Wouldn't it be nice if someone could develop a CPA knowledge potion that you could purchase at a fast-food restaurant? You could drive through the drive-up window, order one large CPA success drink, drink it, and then be prepared to take the exam. The inventor of the CPA success drink would be one very rich person. No, it is not that simple. There is no fast track to success. You must go one step at a time. Slowly, step by step, you learn the concepts. Slowly, step by step, you gain exam confidence by learning more about the exam process. Slowly, step by step, you understand how the exam is graded, what the graders are looking for, how to attack the machine-graded exam questions, and how to keep yourself calm during the exam-taking process.

HOW TO USE THIS BOOK AND THE CD

Each chapter is designed as a separate informational unit. Feel free to skip around. If at the moment, family, friends, and coworkers seem to be your biggest problem, read Chapter 11, " Coping with Family, Friends, and Coworkers." If you know how to apply to sit for the exam in your jurisdiction, skip Chapter 3, "Applying to Sit for the Exam." Closer to the exam, read the chapters dealing with the actual exam day and exam-taking procedures again. As you read along, tab and label certain pages to refer to frequently, such as the time-management chapter.

This book serves as a useful reference source to supplement your actual review materials. Often, review materials just cover the technical issues: Who's going to help you with the emotional side of passing the exam? What should you wear to the exam? How do you apply to sit for the exam? What study techniques really work to help improve long-term memory? This book will walk you through the complete CPA journey, from the moment you think you want to be a CPA to the moment when you receive your results that say: "Congratulations, you are a CPA."

At the end of every chapter, you will find a section entitled "Personally Speaking." Here I speak firsthand to you about the fears, mistakes, and successes that I have witnessed over the years. Let these real-world situations teach you how to be successful.

Use the CD to motivate yourself. When you are feeling totally overwhelmed, listen to a friendly voice reminding you that passing the CPA exam is an achievable goal. Enjoy your preparation process. If you begin your studies with a positive outlook, you might be surprised. You could actually enjoy studying.

As you read, listen, and study, always keep the end result in mind. Picture yourself walking across a stage receiving a certificate that names you as successfully completing the Uniform Certified Public Accountant exam. You are now a CPA. Don't lose hope. Visualize yourself as a CPA. Believe that you can pass!

PERSONALLY SPEAKING

At the beginning of every CPA Review course I have ever conducted, the most common statement made by the candidates is: "I am not your typical CPA candidate. Do I have a chance to pass?" The answer is simple--are you willing to dedicate yourself to the study process? Are you willing to remain focused and at all times to believe in your abilities? In other words, the answer to passing is not being a typical CPA candidate. The key to passing is the willingness to work. There is no magic age to sit for the exam. The youngest candidate I have ever worked with was a child genius who received his college degree early and sat for the exam at age 18. The oldest candidate was a 71-year-old grandfather who sat for the exam with his 26-year-old granddaughter. They both passed. They both worked very hard.

Part-time college students who picked up their accounting hours over a 10-year period have the same chance of passing the exam that a new college graduate has as long as both are willing to work for it. If you received all "A's" in your college courses versus the person who received a "C" average, you are not guaranteed a better chance to pass. You may be very bright, but perhaps you will not be able to handle the stress and pressure of taking a 2-day, 15 ½ hour exam where you will never be able to know everything.

Let's face it, when we look around we can always find someone who seems to be brighter, younger, thinner, richer, and better-looking than ourselves. What do these things have to do with passing the CPA exam? Don't worry about other people and other situations. Use your time and energies to assess where you are and what you can improve. My age is out of my control, and I am not going to worry about it. I am going to be concerned with what I can control and improve. Focus on what you can do to improve your chances of passing the exam. All other concerns are not important now. Understand that you are the typical CPA candidate no matter how old you are, where you went to college, or what grade-point average you earned. The typical CPA candidate is just like you--concerned about passing the exam. Believe me and believe in yourself. No matter who you are, you are the kind of person that with hard work and dedication can pass the CPA exam! To begin planning a successful CPA exam event, complete the checklist in Exhibit 1 to determine your basic knowledge level about the CPA exam.

Exhibit 1: Questionnaire

Complete the following questionnaire to begin assessing your knowledge level about the CPA exam.

Knowledge Level Check About the CPA Exam

Statement	Yes	No
1. With hard work and dedication I believe I can pass the CPA exam.		
2. Candidates must apply to sit for the CPA exam several months in advance as the exam is given only twice a year.		
3. Candidates must prove certain educational and/or experience requirements to qualify to sit.		
4. Candidates should obtain current study materials that are designed to assist them in understanding and testing the concepts tested on the exam.		
5. Passing the CPA exam takes a great deal of time and commitment.		
6. If I plan ahead, budget my study time, and stick to a study plan, I will greatly increase my chances of passing.		
7. The CPA exam tests a candidate's writing skills as well as their technical knowledge.		
8. Today's CPA exam tests more analytical and critical thinking skills and less memorization.		
9. The CPA exam is a pencil and paper exam. The computerized exam format is scheduled for no earlier than 2003.		
10. By passing the CPA exam, I could increase my salary, earn the respect of others in the field, and increase job mobility.		

"Yes" was the correct answer to all of the above questions. If you checked "No" to question number 1, please stop here. You are not ready to attempt this difficult, 2-day exam. You do not believe in yourself. If you checked "No" to questions 2-10, use this book to learn more about the exam and how you should prepare for it. Learn how to manage your time. Learn how to control your fears by controlling the exam. Someday you, too, will sign your name and add the three initials "CPA." Go for it--the results are well worth it.

2 A TIME AND PLACE FOR EVERYTHING

Are you really ready to work toward the goal of becoming a CPA? Is this a good time in your life to do this? Are you hoping to find a time period in your life when everything will be operating smoothly, and you will have no conflicts with people and time? Think again. There is never an ideal time to sit for the CPA exam. A better way to phrase the question is: "Are you ready to make the commitment it takes to become a CPA?" If your answer is "YES!" then read on to find out when you should begin the study process, what materials and/or courses you should use to study, and where you should study. If you are unsure about making a commitment to the hard work it will take, at least read the next section about selecting the CPA exam date that fits your life. Maybe you will find a way to make the goal of becoming a CPA important to you.

SELECTING A DATE TO SIT FOR THE CPA EXAM

Begin preparing for the exam as soon as possible. The CPA exam is given every May and November--usually the first Wednesday and Thursday of the month. To obtain an exact schedule of dates, check the AICPA website at www.aicpa.org/exams or order the *AICPA Information for Uniform CPA Examination Candidates* current booklet by phoning the AICPA order department at (888)777-7077. This booklet not only lists all 54 jurisdictions that administer the exam, but also provides the candidate with exam dates and valuable information about the exam and its content. Five factors to think about before choosing the exact date when you will sit for the exam are as follows:

1. Have you fulfilled the necessary educational and degree requirements? Check the AICPA website for the requirements in your jurisdiction, review Chapter 3 in this book (entitled "Applying to Sit for the Exam"), and call your state board of accountancy to verify the requirements and to examine your credentials.
2. Are you currently under the pressure of losing your job or being overlooked for a promotion if you don't pass the CPA exam? This is not a scare tactic. Public accounting firms do not promote staff auditors to manager until they have successfully completed the exam. This is part of the quality control element of the accounting profession.

3. Have you recently graduated from college or recently completed your accounting hours?
4. Do you see becoming a CPA as a priority in your life?
5. Do you believe that passing the CPA exam will give you greater job stability, job mobility, and a higher salary?

Obviously you must be able to answer question number one with a yes. You won't be allowed to sit for the exam until you meet the established requirements in the jurisdiction where you plan to register your scores.

An affirmative answer to question number two indicates that you are under considerable pressure. Spend additional time researching CPA review programs. Find a very disciplined schedule to keep you focused and motivated. You are at risk of overreacting to the pressures and finding yourself giving up. Your boss is not being unreasonable. Whether you have attempted the exam or not, the rules of the profession are the rules. Don't look for someone or something to blame. Make up your mind to do it right this time. A helpful chart is shown in Exhibit 1--this should guide you as you make your decision.

Question number three is not meant to discourage people who have completed their college work some time ago. However, we can't overlook the obvious fact: the CPA exam is an exam that tests an accountant's entry level skills and competencies. There are frequent changes made to accounting, auditing, and income tax rules. As a recent college graduate you are used to taking exams, the material is fresher, and your work load is not yet as demanding as it will be when you advance within the company. The best time to take the CPA exam is as soon as you meet the requirements to sit, which is usually upon your graduation.

What about those of you who completed your coursework several years ago? Don't give up! You too can pass. There is something to be said for work experience, especially in the area of tax and auditing. Work experience helps you to quickly analyze situations, to write better, and to read with greater understanding. Your advantages will be discussed later.

Questions four and five are important to your decision. You must take becoming a CPA seriously. It just doesn't happen--it takes hard work. Are you concerned that you will never be able to make such a commitment? Don't be! You must not lose sight of the fact that people do pass this exam. The point is to understand what they did to become successful. Admitting to yourself that this is going to require a great deal of work that only you can do is a key element. It's not easy, and that's why those three initials mean so much. If becoming a CPA were easy, many more people would be CPAs and the value of the title would be greatly diminished. Are you ready? Good, now let's start the process of obtaining the necessary study aids and finding the proper places to study.

STUDY AIDS

CPA candidates might think the very best study aid would be their college textbooks. Think again. Today's CPA exam is quick to test new topics. In fact, candidates are responsible for knowing accounting and auditing pronouncements 6 months after a pronouncement's **effective** date, unless early application is permitted. When early application is permitted, candidates are responsible for knowing the new pronouncement 6 months after the **issuance** date. In the tax area, candidates must know the tax laws in effect 6 months before the examination date. In the area of Business Law and Professional Responsibilities, you are responsible for knowing federal laws 6 months after their effective date and uniform acts 1 year after they have been adopted by a simple majority of the jurisdictions. Over the past 10 years there have been many changes in all areas. Changes to income tax and federal tax laws are common. The accounting profession has been changing pronouncements to keep up with the rapidly developing financial instruments' area and the increase in global investments. Every time the accounting profession changes a pronouncement, the auditing profession must respond with changes in audit techniques and procedures. On the average, textbooks are revised every 2 years. Therefore, many of the testable topics are not even presented in the text. It is very dangerous to rely solely upon your textbooks. Not only could they be out of date; they also present much more material than is tested on the exam. You don't have time to study extraneous facts. Your studies must be focused on the concepts that are tested on the CPA exam, not all of the concepts that were ever developed.

Another problem occurs with presentation style and use of language. Textbooks can present a topic in a different method than it is tested on the exam. Also, language usage may vary. Your center of concentration should always be on the test methods and language used on the CPA exam. Your task is to learn what is required to pass--no more. There is not enough time to learn more concepts than are required to pass. That is not to say that you should never refer to your old accounting book. Realize that textbook knowledge is not going to show you what and how concepts are tested on the actual CPA exam. Keep your accounting books and refer to them when you want a different approach to something that your CPA review manuals or CPA review course materials don't clearly explain. Your primary study materials should be CPA examination-based.

Where will you find CPA examination-based materials? One source is the AICPA itself. After all, they write the exam don't they? For about $100, you can purchase the AICPA "Candidate Kit." This kit includes three study aids:

1. *Information for Uniform CPA Examination Candidates* referred to above. The booklet is a must-read for all candidates. You will find the state addresses of the boards of accountancy, the content specifications for exam sections, sample questions, and a discussion of exam-grading procedures. Separate order price is about $8 and could be included in your CPA exam application in some states.

2. The Uniform CPA Examination calculator to use when you practice your financial accounting and your tax, governmental, and managerial topics. At the real exam, the AICPA will give you a calculator for the above sections that looks just like the one you will receive with this kit. Practicing on a calculator like the one you will be using is a smart thing to do. You will know how it works ahead of time. Separate order price is about $10.

3. The *Uniform CPA Examination Selected Questions & Unofficial Answers Indexed to Content Specification Outlines.* These are actual CPA exam questions that the AICPA Examinations Team has prepared and used on previous exams. The AICPA makes it clear that these questions will **not** appear on **future** examinations. The idea here is for you to see actual questions to learn the depth, type, and format of what might be tested. If you don't take the time to work real CPA questions, you may fool yourself into believing the exam is easier than it really is. Separate order price is about $90.

Stop! If you plan on registering for a CPA review course, don't order the above kit until you know what materials are included with your CPA review. Most CPA review courses include not only the information booklet and the calculator, but also software and manuals that contain actual CPA exam questions. A quality review manual will explain the answers by stating why one answer is correct and why the others are incorrect. The AICPA manual just lists the correct letter answer and does not include an explanation. Since manuals are often a part of the CPA review course program, your next decision is about taking a CPA review course versus self-study.

SHOULD YOU ENROLL IN A CPA REVIEW COURSE?

Whether to enroll in a CPA review course is not a decision to make quickly. Review courses are costly at an average price of about $1,200.

Price is only one of the many variables to consider. A quality CPA review course should offer you the following:

- A focused study plan
- Exam-taking strategy
- Up-to-date review materials
- Support materials such as software, flash cards, and an AICPA calculator
- Confidence-building techniques
- Simulated examinations
- Assistance in obtaining and completing the CPA exam application

If the price is less than the going rate, maybe it is because the course has omitted one or more of the above features. Now that you know what a quality review course should offer, ask yourself if you need or want this type of assistance. To help answer this question, think about how you learn best. Exhibit 2 can aid you in the decision-making process. If you learn better by working out the questions on your own, checking the answer, and learning from what you got wrong, you might not want to take a review course. Don't get too excited about saving money yet. If you choose to self-study, you must be a very disciplined person. Do you have the ability to prepare a study plan and stick to it? A disciplined person can skip to the next section entitled "CPA Review Manuals for Self-Study." Be honest; if you are a procrastinator, you would benefit greatly from the structure that a review course provides.

Are you a visual learner? An on-line interactive review course might work for you. Like self-study, an on-line course puts the responsibility on the learner to stay on track. On-line reviews are a good choice for busy people who work well on their own. Candidates save commuting time and energy and can study whenever and wherever they are. Before you enroll in an on-line course, or any review course, be sure to preview the presentation. Your computer must be compatible with the course medium. Stay away from a course that does not allow you to attend or preview a few sessions. Some courses will require full payment up front and then refund the full amount within a specified time if you decide the course is not a good fit for you. This is a positive policy that shows the candidate that the review people are willing to let you determine what works for you. They are not trying to coerce you into taking their course. Avoid pushy sales representatives that call you at home or work and promise you the world. The decision is yours to make. Take the time you need to clearly evaluate your choices.

Live lecture courses should be just that--lectures presented in person. Some courses advertise live when they really are playing audio or videotaped lectures in a classroom setting. Live lectures have the benefit of keeping the candidate in a structured environment that is motivational because the presenter is a real person who cares about the audience. Be sure to read the qualifications of the instructors before you enroll. Are they part-time people who work at full-time accounting jobs during the day? If they work all day in a job that is not related to the CPA exam, how much time do they take to learn new concepts and to understand the CPA exam? In the last 10 years, the CPA exam has changed considerably. Beware of the professor or review instructor who is relying only on personal experience. Their experiences are not going to be similar to what you will face today. Some college professors haven't kept up to date with the format changes on the exam. If the professors teach the review course the same way they teach their college courses, they might not be presenting the material in a manner that will help you understand and master the exam concepts. Most college professors are good teachers, but for this situation, being a great lecturer or teacher is not enough. They must understand and teach you the CPA exam.

Are you a traveling auditor or accountant? If you are, be sure to find a course that is flexible. This doesn't rule out live lectures as long as the candidate is given a recording of the lectures or offered an alternative makeup date.

Audio or videotaped lectures are great for those candidates who learn by listening. If you are in the comfort of your own home, you can repeat sections of the lecture as many times as you wish. Audio or videotaped lectures presented in a classroom setting can be very boring. Previewing classes is crucial, as many people find it difficult to remain attentive while staring at a television or computer monitor. Find out what presentation medium fits you. Like live lectures, audio and videotaped classroom settings will provide the candidate with a structured environment to keep them learning at the proper pace. At-home taped lectures offer little or no structure, so procrastinators beware.

Should you select a review course based on exam-passing percentages? This is almost impossible to do. Externally published data on CPA exam-passing percentages is compiled by the National Association of State Boards of Accountancy (NASBA) every August. The booklet is entitled *Candidate Performance on the Uniform CPA Examination* (about $130) and can be ordered by accessing the NASBA website at www.nasba.org. If you consult the NASBA manuals you will see that the statistics are given by colleges and universities, not proprietary CPA reviews. External verification of private CPA review course pass rates is not available. Be wary of any review course that promises a 70-90% pass rate. They might be referring to a select group of people who passed one section, which may or may not get you any closer to your goal of becoming a CPA.

In addition to previewing the various course types, talk to those who have passed. Ask your friends and colleagues who have recently passed about the study aids they used. Recommendations from satisfied customers are powerful statements. Keep in mind that the methods used to pass the exam even 5 years ago may now be out-of-date. Survey those who have passed within the last 3 years.

CPA review courses are most beneficial in the following situations:

- You are a procrastinator and need the structure of a course to keep you disciplined
- It has been a long time since you have taken your accounting courses
- Your university or college program was deficient in providing you the necessary coursework
- You faked your way through your classes and never really learned the material the first time through
- You learn best when guided
- You are an international student whose first language is not English. A review course helps you to equate terms to your language.
- You want to give yourself every possible advantage to pass this exam the first time through

There are some situations where you simply should **not** enroll in a review course. If you know you won't be able to attend several sessions, why pay? Don't fall for the 100% guaranteed pass rates. There are usually stiff requirements to meet, such as nearly perfect class attendance and a high percentage of homework completion. Take the time to investigate just how those guarantees work. Remember, it is not the review course alone that will get you closer to your goal, it is your hard work and dedication. There is no magic CPA potion.

CPA REVIEW MANUALS FOR SELF-STUDY

At the very least, all CPA candidates should purchase a high-quality set of CPA review manuals. Acquaint yourself with the question types, breadth, and depth by practicing the actual concepts tested. Lack of practice time can set you up for failure. Since this exam is unlike any other that you have ever taken, time must be spent on understanding what is tested and how it is tested. Don't let the price be your sole influence. Some manuals cost as little as $20 per exam section, while others are as high as $50. Go to your university or college bookstore and examine what they have to offer on the shelves. Watch the publication dates since anything over 1 year old is probably unsafe to use. Again, personal recommendations from friends and colleagues are invaluable. If a friend offers to give you the manuals they used, use the 1-year rule--have they been published within the year? If not, do not use them at any price. You will be wasting your time studying old material. If the bookstore is stocking an old manual but you like the format and style, ask them to order you the most recent publication. High-quality review manuals include

- Discussion and presentation of multiple-choice questions, essays, and other objective and problem-type questions. Some manuals only include multiple-choice question formats. This is dangerous because even if the candidate scored 100% on the multiple choice, he or she would not be guaranteed a passing percentage since multiple-choice account for 60% of the total exam score.
- Complete explanations for all answers. It is not enough to know the correct answer. The well-trained candidate should understand why the other answers were incorrect.
- A detailed index. When you are studying and run into a problem, a detailed index can quickly guide you to the discussion section. Some manuals are over 300 pages long, and you don't want to waste your time searching for a concept.
- A look and feel that suits you. If the color of the ink or the feel of the pages doesn't suit you, it won't get any better after you spend hours studying. If it doesn't look good to you now, it won't improve later. Look for a manual that is easy to read. Long complex sentences are very difficult to read and translate when you have studied for several hours.

The time you spend investigating review courses and manuals will pay off in the future. Using materials that are not a good fit for you can actually serve as a deterrent to your studies. Find what works for you.

OLD CPA EXAMS

Your college library or your friend may have actual copies of old CPA exams. These exams are very old, since the CPA exam has been a "nondisclosed" exam since 1996. In other words, the questions remain secure and entire exams have not been published since 1995. The only value old exams have is to allow you to preview the question formats. Most of the content has been changed or revised. Refrain from using old exams as a study aid.

SOFTWARE

Computer software containing old exam questions is readily available. Many candidates say they can review material quicker by using a computer. It has been difficult for vendors to program exam essays and problems. Software containing only multiple-choice question formats requires you to supplement your studies with review manuals. Again, make sure that the software has been updated within the last year, that you enjoy the look of it, and that you can easily maneuver through the content. The CPA exam is not yet computerized. The year 2003 is the projected date for a computerized exam. Until that time prepare to take a pencil and paper exam.

FLASH CARDS

Purchased flash cards present definitions and lists for you to memorize. There are two problems with this method.

1. The idea behind a flash card is not only that you can use it as a quick review tool, but also that you have prepared and summarized the information on it. You want to learn not only by reviewing the card, but also by preparing the card.
2. Purchased flash cards list data and definitions. Today's CPA exam seldom asks you to prepare a list. The questions require you to analyze, think, and evaluate the situation. Memorized lists taken out of context leave the candidate with no sense of where, when, and how to use the knowledge. You could invest a great deal of time mastering flash card concepts only to find out at the real exam that you don't know how to apply what you have memorized.

A properly prepared flash card will prompt you to remember concepts and how those concepts are used. Don't look to the cards for a quick fix. There is no substitute for working problems and obtaining the knowledge by learning it.

STUDY AID SUMMARY

Your choices of study aids are numerous. The essential characteristics of any study aid are as follows:

- Up-to-date--no older than one year
- CPA exam focused
- User-friendly -- easy to use, easy to read
- Comprehensive--demonstrating all question format types and giving complete answer explanations

Take your time to preview a variety of materials. Try previewing different courses 6 months to 1 year before you plan to enroll, giving yourself time to clear your thoughts and escape any high-pressure sales tactics. Once you have made your choice(s), remain confident in your selection and use the materials daily. The plan has always been to purchase study aids that benefit you. Spending money for courses and materials only to leave them in a pile collecting dust is foolish. Find a place to keep your study aids handy and ready for use.

FINDING A SUITABLE STUDY PLACE

The ideal study location is a place that is handy, well-lit, comfortable, and easily accessible. Spending time driving to a faraway location, with the risk that you might forget most of your materials at home, can waste valuable time. Usually your home is your best study area. This does not require you to have a large secluded home office. Something as simple as a card table set up in your bedroom will suffice. Having a neat home is not your primary goal. Making it easy for you to study by keeping everything you need at your fingertips is far more important. Try not to use a place like the kitchen or dining room table. Here you must take the time to pack up your materials daily. Keeping your study area visible will serve to remind you about the importance of studying. The more visible your area is, the less chance you have of forgetting about the primary task at hand. Find an area that you can claim as your spot and where you can leave your materials out.

Do you really need a phone close by? It is better to get up and go to the phone when it rings. You don't want to be tempted to waste time calling friends and family. A far more important item is a good lamp. Good lighting will keep you alert and prevent your eyes from tiring quickly. Lamps should be placed over your right shoulder. Keep pencils and highlighters handy. A coffee cup or glass makes an ideal holder. Blank note cards can be stacked on the floor nearby. Completed note cards can be filed in plastic boxes by exam section and then further divided by exam topic. Keep your study area well organized so you won't waste time searching for the proper study aid.

The visibility issue is vital. After all, what if you can't sleep at night because you are suffering from exam anxiety? The best cure for insomnia brought on by exam anxiety is to work through it--literally. Get up out of bed and begin answering CPA questions. You will be amazed at how quickly you will want to go back to bed and sleep after completing a few questions. If you must open drawers or cabinets to find your books before you begin studying, you will waste time. Out of sight, out of mind. A visible study area invites you to study.

Your plan of attack is beginning to take shape. The exam date has been selected; you have purchased your study aids and readied a study area. Your next step is to develop a personalized study plan of what to study based upon an assessment of your strengths and weaknesses.

PERSONALLY SPEAKING

Are you scheduled to get married and to take a 1-month honeymoon to Europe a few months before you plan to take the CPA exam? Think again! Maybe this is not the best time to sit for the exam. A realistic person will know that planning a wedding and taking time out for a long honeymoon are not conducive to the study process. Another common scheduling mistake candidates make is hurrying to fulfill the CPA exam requirements by taking only the bare minimum of required coursework. What's the big hurry? Understandably, you want to graduate, get a job, and begin working so you can pay back those school loans. Taking the time to do the job right the first time requires a certain maturity level. Think before you rush into something. It's far more difficult to backtrack and start over again after a rushed attempt has failed.

As the director of one of the most successful CPA review courses in the world, I bet you think I am going to tell you that you have little or no chance of passing the exam without a review course. Actually, I chose the self-study routine for the same reasons I stated earlier--I would have spent too much time traveling to and from the city where the course was located. Now, I am not going to tell you that self-study was the easiest method. I am a procrastinator and always operate best when there is an immediate dead-line. The problem here is that the exam scope is too broad to think you can pull an all-night review and be successful. To be prepared for the CPA exam you must start early. I did have some positive things going for me--I was a recent college graduate from a reputable accounting program where I had achieved honor-roll status every semester. Four-hour nightly examinations were the norm for all accounting tests. My professors had done their best to provide a transition to an exam as difficult as the CPA exam. I had been taught CPA material and had already learned it. To successfully complete a review, the person must truly be reviewing the material instead of learning the material for the first time. Sure, there will always be some concepts that your college courses did not cover. For me, that was governmental accounting. We spent one week at the end of the advanced accounting course studying governmental funds. I knew from the questions in my review manual that I was not adequately prepared for this area and budgeted more time to study the material. When you read the chapters that discuss the content for each exam section, ask yourself if you ever learned the material. For example, if you have never had a corporate income tax class, you must learn up to 40% of the Accounting and Reporting exam on your own. This is new learning for you. I also benefited from the excellent firm training I received, especially in auditing. I was working long hours at a CPA firm, mostly assigned to out-of-town jobs, and I took the time to study at the hotel instead of going out to party. I chose to sacrifice some fun to achieve my goal. Self-study worked for me, but recall what I have been telling you--it is up to you to assess your situation and to make a decision based upon what works best for you.

The greatest advantage that a review course gives you is the discipline. A quality review will cover all areas tested. You will be encouraged to study all exam content areas, even if you already know the material. A good review never hurt anyone. The schedule should keep you somewhat on track. At least you will know what you have to accomplish before the exam. Another real advantage to a review course is the motivation you receive from your review instructors and the people you attend the review with. It helps to associate with others who are undergoing the same activity and can relate to your frustrations, fears, and concerns.

Regardless of the method of study you choose, the worst mistake you can make is to study out-of-date material. Notice how often I have discussed the fact that your study aids should not be older than 1 year. I cringe when I receive a call from a very nice candidate telling me they are studying with books or handouts that are 2 years old. What a waste of time! Up-to-date study materials can mean the difference between receiving a score of 74 or a score of 75. There is much more than just one point difference between those two scores. It is the difference between failure and success. Yes, new materials are costly. Every time you buy new materials you are crediting cash, but you are also debiting a unique asset called "investment in the future." This asset known as investment in the future will give you great paybacks. I suggest you forgo a few dinners out and purchase current materials. Your time and self-esteem are too precious to be floundered away by making a bad decision to save money and study old concepts. Give yourself every advantage you can.

Although there are a number of study aids available, my favorite textbooks are the *CPA Examination Review* published by John Wiley and Sons and written by Dr. Patrick R. Delaney. These books are the most current because they are updated annually. Another positive feature is the complete answer explanations; even incorrect answers are explained so you can learn the tricks and distractions that the examiners use.

In the discussion of the study area, why didn't I suggest to you that the area must be a quiet place? The exam site usually is not very quiet. In large states like California and Illinois, several thousand candidates take the exam in the same room, leaving no chance of perfect silence. I encourage you to get used to some noise. If you are the type of person who requires total silence, you could try earplugs, but by all means try them during your study process because they take some getting used to. Earplugs are great if you prefer your own body sounds to some background noise.

Obviously, there are other desirable places to study other than in your home. Varying your study places keeps you motivated but places such as the library, your university, or retail establishments may provide too many distractions and take too much time to travel to and from, not to mention that you must haul your materials with you.

I urge you to carefully evaluate your choice of exam dates, study aids, and study areas. Do everything possible to minimize failure and to maximize success.

Exhibit 1: CPA review comparison chart

Use the following chart to record responses from the various CPA review courses that you are considering. Upon completion, decide which factors are most important to you, for example, location, live instruction, and price. Select the course that best fits your needs.

Factors to consider when comparing CPA reviews	*Course name and response*	*Course name and response*	*Course name and response*
1. Course price			
2. Price for textbooks			
3. Other materials included in course such as software, calculator, flash cards, and additional fees charged, if any			
4. Number of hours class meets			
5. Price per hour (Add dollars given in questions 1-3 and divide total by number of hours shown in question number 4)			

Factors to consider when comparing CPA reviews	Course name and response	Course name and response	Course name and response
6. Type of instruction: • Live with real CPA faculty covering the points • Live, with person showing video or playing tapes • All video • All tape recorded • CD-ROM, On-line			
7. Refund policy			
8. Repeat policy if parts not passed			
9. Policy on tape recording live sessions			
10. Extra assistance provided such as completion of application, passport photos, review sessions at exam, e-mail and phone support			
11. Policy for making up missed sessions: • Travel to other site • Receive video or audio tape recording of missed session			
12. Location: • Number of miles from home or work • Time to commute to site			

Exhibit 2: Decision Table--Self-study or enroll in CPA review

Read through the following table and check the situation that best describes you.

Factors to consider when choosing to self-study or enroll in a CPA review course.	*Self-study*	*CPA review*
• I prefer to work on my own.	xx	
• I am a disciplined person who can stick with a schedule.	xx	
• I learn best by listening and watching another person solve the question.		xx
• I am a procrastinator who needs a deadline to help me complete tasks.		xx
• It has been some years since I have taken my accounting courses.		xx
• I had a wonderful time in college and received below average grades.		xx
• I have taken the CPA exam within the last year, and I received scores of 70 or better.	xx	
• I have taken the CPA exam within the last year, and I received scores in the 60s or below.		xx
• My family, friends, and coworkers are very supportive of my study process and will leave me alone to study.	xx	
• I travel frequently for my job to small towns and cities.	xx	
• I need to be motivated during the study process. My confidence level tends to slip.		xx
• I am a parent who has difficulty finding adequate childcare for evenings and weekends.	xx	
• I will begin my exam preparation 4 to 5 months ahead of time and will continue to study every week.	xx	
• I enjoy working with another person who is also studying.		xx

3 APPLYING TO SIT FOR THE EXAM

Before you sit for the exam, you must meet certain requirements. Although the exam itself is a national exam, written by the AICPA Examination's Task Force in New Jersey, approval to sit for the exam is given at the state level. Obtain approval from the state or United States territory where you plan to physically sit for the exam. Fifty-four United States jurisdictions administer the CPA exam which includes the 50 states, the District of Columbia, and the following 3 United States territories:

1. Guam
2. Puerto Rico
3. Virgin Islands

Each jurisdiction has specific requirements to sit for the exam and to become licensed as a certified public accountant. For a complete listing of the jurisdictions, consult the American Institute of Certified Public Accountants (AICPA) website at www.aicpa.org/exams. The requirements always include proof of education. Some states require as little as 120 semester hours of college to qualify to sit for the exam. More and more states are requiring 150 semester hours. Some states list specific accounting, auditing, and business law courses that the candidate must complete before sitting for the exam. Others just count hours and not specific coursework. An official sealed transcript from your college or university is the usual method used to prove the hours earned.

When should you begin the application process? As soon as possible, usually 6 months before the exam date in which you plan to sit. (See Exhibit 1 at the end of this chapter for a sample timetable.) Suggested questions to ask the board when you request an application to sit are as follows:

- Do I have to be a resident in the state where I plan to sit?
- If a residency requirement is in place, how many months do I have to live in the area before I am considered a resident?
- What are the course and hour requirements to sit for the exam? Are the hour requirements measured in semester hours? If so, how does the board convert quarterly or trimester hours into semester hours?
- Are there specific courses that I must take?
- Do grades of "D" or better count?

- Do pass/fail courses count?
- Must I obtain a college degree before I sit for the exam, or can I sit by just completing a prescribed number of semester hours?
- May I apply for approval before I complete the necessary course-work? If so, what special forms will I need to complete?
- How long does the approval process take?
- How much is the fee to sit for the exam?
- If I earned my college hours outside of the United States, must I obtain a special foreign transcript evaluation before I apply to sit? If so, how long will the process take, who do I contact, and how much does the evaluation cost?
- If I plan to sit in one state and have my scores transferred to another state, what is the process for this procedure? How much does this cost?
- Must my college transcripts be officially sealed or will a copy or unofficial set suffice? May I enclose my transcripts along with the application, or must I ask that my university or college submit the transcripts directly to the state board?
- Must I obtain pictures to prove my identity? If so, how many must I submit? Should the pictures be official passport-type or taken with an instant camera? Do the pictures have to be in color or will black and white be acceptable? Do the pictures have to be just head and shoulders or may the entire body be shown?
- What is the application deadline? Must the application be received by the due date, or may it just be postmarked by the due date?

Many times you will be able to answer these questions by calling the appropriate board or by consulting their website. Begin early and leave nothing to chance.

COMPLETING THE APPLICATION

When you receive your application, make a copy of it. Use the copy to pencil in your information. Take the application process seriously. Read the instructions carefully. An incomplete or incorrect application can lead to delay in acceptance. Wouldn't it be awful if you studied hard and were very prepared for the upcoming exam, only to find out a few weeks before you sit that your state board has denied you admission to the exam site? If you are not clear as to the information required, clarify it with your board immediately.

Common application mistakes include

- Leaving requested information blank

- Illegible handwriting
- Questions answered incorrectly
- Missing signatures
- Inappropriate fee enclosed or check made payable to the incorrect party
- Improper attachment of necessary photographs
- Missing supporting information such as college transcripts
- Returning the application to the wrong address
- Mailing too late to qualify for the application deadline

Ask a friend or family member to review your application copy. Then, carefully transfer the information to the original application. Use the appropriate writing instrument (usually a blue or black ink pen). Avoid the use of markers that smear. Don't try to be fancy by typing the information unless it is clearly stated to do so. You can make numerous mistakes when typing an application. Watch the address section. Many application forms ask you to list a temporary and a permanent address. If you list an address such as your parent's home, and your parents are going to be on vacation for two months in Europe, who will be home to give you any mail you might receive from the board? If you have made an error or left out important supporting documents, the board will probably contact you via the mail. Be sure your address is one where people check the mail frequently and understand the importance of promptly dealing with a request from the Board of Examiners.

PHOTO IDENTIFICATION

Some jurisdictions require that photos be attached to the actual application form. Some simply ask that you bring a picture ID such as a driver's license to the exam. When the board requests that the photo be sent with the application, read the instructions carefully. Does it require an official passport photo? If it does, you must go to a photo establishment that you know takes passport photos. Having your picture taken in a photo booth at the local discount store will not suffice. If a regular photo will do, be sure you follow the directions and take the head and shoulders at a close range. Remember that the purpose of this photo is to verify your identity.

Be sure to affix your application photo(s) in the correct area. Before you attach your photo, write your name on the back so if the photo falls off, the board will know to whom the photo belongs. Use rubber cement to attach the photo. Tape, staples, and paper clips often do not remain attached and could result in your photo or application form becoming torn.

TRANSCRIPTS

Exercise special care when providing the state board with transcripts. Some states require that the university mail the transcripts directly to the board. Other states will allow the candidate to obtain official sealed transcripts and include them with the exam application form. Note that transcripts are no longer official and sealed after they have been opened. To be safe, request two (2) copies of the official sealed transcripts. Open one set to check that the information is complete and will serve as the necessary proof to meet the requirements to sit. Send the second, unopened set to the board.

Some colleges have differences between official sealed transcripts and those transcripts mailed to the student themselves. It is wise to request transcripts from all the colleges you have attended to insure that all classes are listed. If your jurisdiction requires specific courses, you must be sure the transcript provides enough information so that an outsider looking at the form can tell the course subject and the number of credits granted. Beware, repeated courses will only count once, not twice. The good news, however, is that usually grades of A to D will count and there is no time limit on how recently the courses must have been taken.

If you are unsure whether you will qualify to sit for the exam, call your board and ask if you can mail or fax a copy of your transcripts for review. Sometimes the board will perform what is called a preliminary evaluation just to let you know how close you are to meeting the requirements.

Don't ask a professor or friend to evaluate your transcripts. Even a CPA Review course manager or director is not qualified to conduct a transcript evaluation. Your state board is the only group that approves candidates to sit for the CPA exam.

FOREIGN TRANSCRIPT EVALUATION

For degrees or college credit earned outside of the United States, many jurisdictions require that a foreign transcript service evaluate your transcripts. Always check with your jurisdiction. Obtaining a foreign evaluation of your transcripts may take an additional 2 to 6 weeks at an extra cost over and above the regular exam application fee.

International schools may not send transcripts to outsiders. If this is your situation, be sure you send the original documents that the evaluation service requires. Spend the extra money to send your documents one-day mail using a service such as Federal Express, United Parcel Service, or DHL. You wouldn't want to lose the only proof you have of your educational credentials.

Follow up with the evaluation service every 2 weeks. After the foreign evaluation is completed, forward all of the information to the board. Ask your board if they also need the original documents. Don't count on receiving an extended deadline just because the foreign transcript evaluation has not been completed. Most jurisdictions will not extend deadline dates. It is up to you to start the process early enough to obtain all of the necessary paperwork.

EXAM APPLICATION DEADLINE

The deadline date means just that--the board must receive your materials by the deadline date or you will probably be denied a seat at the exam. Waiting 6 more months will only make it harder for you to get motivated to study and pass. Don't assume that the deadline date means the application can be postmarked on that date. Some jurisdictions allow postmark dates to count while others state that the materials must be received on or before the specified deadline. Why wait? Make your life less stressful by completing and mailing your application early. Tell yourself the date listed as the deadline is the day that the board must receive all materials. You won't be disappointed if you are conservative--after all, isn't conservatism an accountant's motto?

MAILING THE APPLICATION

Verify the mailing address. If you have any doubts about the correct address, consult the board. If the board includes an envelope to return the application in, use it. Clearly indicate a complete return address in case delivery problems occur. Again, avoid the use of markers that can smear if the application address gets wet. Don't guess on the postage. Take the time to go to the post office and have your envelope weighed.

Spend the extra money to mail your application certified mail or use a method that allows you to track the delivery. Don't assume that using one-day services such as Federal Express or United Parcel Service are the best. One-day services are expensive and should be used only when you are close to the application deadline or if international documentation is enclosed. Usually, the United States post office will meet your needs. Ask for the mail process that allows you to check the delivery date on the Internet. It is an effective and inexpensive method of assuring that your application arrives on time. When you use a method where the receiving person must sign for the application, you will have a name and department to show you not only when the application was delivered, but also who received it.

Don't throw away the instructions and unused forms. Prepare a file folder labeled "CPA Exam Application." Put the application instructions, unused forms, and a copy of your actual application in the folder. Copy all supporting documentation that you enclosed, even your check.

If you accidentally omitted a required form, you can consult your file, quickly complete the form, and promptly return it. Keep your mailing information in the same folder.

APPLICATION FOLLOW-UP

Don't leave the receipt of your application materials to chance. Wait 2 to 3 weeks after you mail your application. If you do not receive an acknowledgment from the board, phone them to inquire about your application status. Always be calm and courteous. Most board members are not CPAs. They often license many groups within the state such as electricians, lawyers, barbers, and plumbers. Explain to them that you are just making sure that **you** followed the necessary procedures. You are not checking on them, you are checking on the status of your application.

When transcripts have been mailed directly by your college or university, be sure to verify with the board, not the university, that the transcripts have been received. The university or college may have sent the transcripts to the incorrect address or may not have sent them as they promised. You will be sure of meeting the requirements only if the board has received your documents on time.

SPECIAL CONSIDERATION FOR CANDIDATES
WITH DISABILITIES

All 54 jurisdictions recognize their responsibilities under Title II of the Americans With Disabilities Act to provide reasonable, appropriate, and effective accommodations, including auxiliary aids, to qualified examination candidates with disabilities. A disability is defined as a physical or mental impairment that substantially limits one or more of the major life activities of an individual. Disabilities are usually of three types:

1. Physical
2. Mental
3. Learning

Mental impairment includes any mental or psychological disorder such as organic brain syndrome, emotional or mental illness, and specific learning disabilities. A learning disability is further defined as individual evidence of significant learning problems that substantially affect or limit one or more major life activities and that are not primarily due to cultural, conditional, or motivational factors. Typical impairments include:

- Difficulty to attend and concentrate
- Reception, perception, and/or verbal comprehension difficulty
- Problems in the areas of memory, cognition, and/or expression

It is your responsibility to request special consideration for any disability. You are required to provide the necessary documentation which often includes performance on reliable standardized tests and a doctor's or other qualified person's certification of the disability. Keep in mind that for security reasons the CPA exam is given within a two-day time frame. When a candidate needs additional exam time, a special facility is often used. Sometimes disability candidates take the exam in a room by themselves with one proctor timing and monitoring their exam-taking experience.

Don't be afraid. The laws are established to provide you with the same opportunities as others. Communicate with your state board of accountancy well before the exam date. Obtain all of the necessary forms and complete them carefully. When in doubt, call the board to clarify areas of uncertainty. The policies and procedures for reasonable accommodation of exam candidates with disabilities are there to help you.

REQUESTING AN EXAM LOCATION

Some states have more than one exam location. Include a letter to the board asking them for the city of your choice. List your reasons, such as you have relatives in the area that you want to stay with to help decrease exam costs. Be honest and polite; the board will do their best to meet your request. Again, the earlier you apply to sit, the better chance you have of being granted your special request.

Candidates may sit for the CPA exam in one state and have their scores mailed to another state. This process is called "being proctored." You would want to request this if perhaps you were in the armed forces and stationed away from the state where you normally reside. Begin your application process with the state where you want your scores to be recorded. Additional fees will apply.

REFUND OF FEES

Examination fees vary considerably from about $75 to $300 or more to sit for the exam. Usually, the more candidates who take the exam, the higher the exam fee, as the board of accountancy must rent a larger facility and pay for more proctors and security. Before you pay, be sure you understand the refund process. The hope is that you won't need to request a refund. However, such situations do arise. When you pay, note the refund deadline on your calendar on the actual day and one week before the refund deadline to serve as a reminder to you to reevaluate the situation as the refund deadline approaches.

COMMUNICATE WITH THE STATE BOARD EARLY AND OFTEN

The best words of advice for all application procedures: **Begin the application process early, at least 6 months before the exam date.** Call your state board of accountancy and ask questions. You will never know the answers unless you ask.

PERSONALLY SPEAKING

It always amazes me when people do not take the time to carefully complete the CPA exam application. If you are unable to complete the application, should you even attempt to become a CPA? The fact of the matter is that most people get very nervous about completing the application correctly and make mistakes. TAKE YOUR TIME! Read everything carefully and double check that you completed all of the necessary pages and forms. One of my brightest CPA candidates had to incur the cost of flying to another state over 1,000 miles away just because he forgot to complete the second page of the application. He had mailed in the application on the last day. By the time the Board opened the application to process it and realized that is was incomplete, the deadline date had expired. I helped him find another state that did not have a residency requirement and that would accept his application at a later date. He did sit for the exam, and he did pass; however, it was at a much greater cost than if he had taken the time to do things right the first time around.

Please keep the necessary funds in your checking account until you are sure that the board has processed your check. Every year I have about 20 people who assume that their exam application check is immediately cashed upon receipt. Ideally, every organization should deposit checks daily for effective internal control, but that is not always how things work. After a check has bounced, a state board often requires that you drive to the location and pay cash or deliver a money order. Who needs this additional stress? Yes, sitting for the CPA exam is costly, so begin saving now. If it's your birthday or the holidays, ask family and friends to give you items such as notecards, textbooks, or money that you will put to good use in your exam preparation.

Watch that photo ID! The picture I sent in with my CPA exam application showed me with a hair color that was very different from the color that I had when I arrived to sit for the exam. Adding to the hair color change, I wore my contacts for the picture and my glasses to the actual exam. I was almost denied access to the site. They thought I had paid someone to take the exam for me. Try to take the picture looking as close as possible to how you will probably look at the real exam. Just in case, bring several other forms of identification. Luckily I had my driver's license and other identification to prove who I really was.

Women should always list a maiden name on the application, even if it is not required. Don't use a married name until you really have been married. Use your last name as it is at the moment that you complete the application. If your name changes at a later date, call the board and inform them of the change.

My final words of advice about the exam application process are plain and simple:

- Begin early (at least 6 months before the exam date)
- Have a friend check your completed application before you mail it to the board
- When in doubt, don't assume--call the board to ask questions
- Be polite and kind, never demanding. After all, the board decides whether to allow you to sit for the exam.

Exhibit 1: Timetable checklist applying to sit for the CPA Exam

Use the following timetable and checklist to monitor the exam application process.

Task to complete:	Due date	Date completed
1. Check the AICPA website www.aicpa.org/exams for the exam dates and the requirements to sit in the jurisdiction where you want your scores registered.	6 to 7 months before the exam	
2. Obtain the CPA application from your jurisdiction. Prepare a file folder to keep all application materials.	6 to 7 months before the exam	
3. Send international transcripts to the appropriate office for foreign transcript evaluation.	6 to 7 months before the exam	

Task to complete:	*Due date*	*Date completed*
4. Obtain transcripts to prove your education. Determine if the board of examiners allows you to mail in official sealed transcripts. If the answer is yes, obtain official sealed transcripts. Do not open them. Save them to mail in with your completed exam application.	6 to 7 months before the exam	
5. Obtain the necessary identification photos.	5 to 6 months before the exam	
6. Complete the application. Have a friend check it over for completeness. Copy all supporting materials, even your check.	5 to 6 months before the exam	
7. If necessary, complete any special need or disability verification.	5 to 6 months before the exam	
8. Verify that the Board of Examiners has received all of the necessary application materials.	4 months before the exam	
9. Verify that you have received your official exam permit to sit for the exam.	4 to 6 weeks before the exam	
10. Pack your permit and supporting documentation to take to the exam.	2 weeks before the exam	

4 CONTENT AND GRADING OF THE CPA EXAM

The Uniform CPA Examination is just that, uniform. The AICPA examination's task force writes the exam. All candidates take the same exam on the same 2 days every 6 months. The state boards of accountancy in each jurisdiction uniformly administer the exam. The AICPA Board of Examiners' Advisory Grading Service grades the examination. The more the CPA candidate understands about the content and grading of the exam, the better his or her experience will be. The purpose of this chapter is to help CPA candidates learn more about the exam. This is important, since the exam is **nondisclosed.**

NONDISCLOSED EXAM QUESTIONS AND ANSWERS

Since 1996, the CPA exam has been nondisclosed. This means the candidates no longer have access to exam questions and answers after each exam. What are the implications of this change? Because the candidates do not see actual exams, it is more difficult for candidates to learn about exam changes, areas tested, and the form of the exam. Now more than ever, it is important that CPA candidates purchase a proven source, such as quality review manuals or an up-to-date CPA review course to help them learn about the exam.

Review course directors, accounting professors, CPA candidates, and other interested parties may purchase released questions from the AICPA. This is the only source of current questions used on the exam. Candidates are encouraged to obtain the *Information for Uniform CPA Examination Candidates* booklet from the AICPA order department by phoning (888) 777-7077. The cost of the booklet is about $8 for nonmembers of the AICPA. Understand that this booklet contains very few questions. These are for sample purposes only and the chances of one of these sample questions being used on the actual exam are slim to none. These questions are for demonstration purposes only.

To keep the nondisclosed exam secure, the candidates are asked to sign a statement of confidentiality. This statement reads as follows:

> I hereby attest that I will not divulge the nature or content of any question or answer to any individual or entity, and I will report to the board of accountancy any solicitations and disclosures of which I become aware. I will not remove, or attempt to remove, any Uniform CPA Examination

materials, notes, or other unauthorized materials from the examination room. I understand that failure to comply with this attestation may result in the invalidation of my grades, disqualification from future examinations, and possible civil and criminal penalties.

The AICPA means business. Do not violate the nondisclosure exam policies by discussing the exam with anyone, even someone who you know just took the exam. If someone overhears your discussion you could be reported, and it is difficult to prove that no one could have overheard you. It is just best to avoid the problem by not discussing the exam with anyone. This will benefit most candidates as they will not become discouraged by discussing the exam with other exam-takers.

CPA review providers are allowed to solicit information about their products. However, the information must be requested in such general terms as, "How was our coverage on auditing with the computer?" The candidate may respond in very general terms by indicating whether the coverage was poor, adequate, or overly detailed. This type of questioning provides guidance to interested parties without divulging the exact question content, format, or type. A wise CPA candidate will purchase current materials from a trusted source that is current and knowledgeable about the nondisclosure rules. Being current is critical, because the focus of the exam continues to change.

CPA EXAM STRUCTURE

The examination consists of four distinct sections, each worth a total of 100 points. The exam is administered over a 2-day period, with two sections tested each day. The sections and times tested are as follows:

- Wednesday, 9:00 a.m.--noon, **Business Law & Professional Responsibilities**
- Wednesday, 1:30 p.m.--6:00 p.m., **Auditing**
- Thursday, 8:30 a.m.--noon, **Accounting & Reporting (ARE)-- Taxation, Managerial, and Governmental and Not-for-Profit Organizations**
- Thursday, 1:30--6:00 p.m., **Financial Accounting & Reporting (FARE)**

Notice that the total testing time is 15½ hours. Wednesday is the shorter day, testing only 7½ hours compared to 8 hours on Thursday. On Wednesday the candidate works the exam without a calculator. On Thursday morning, the exam proctors distribute an official AICPA calculator for the candidate to use the entire day.

CPA EXAM DATES

The CPA examination dates are set well in advance. Beginning with the new millennium, the dates are as follows:

May 3 and 4, 2000	May 8 and 9, 2002
November 1 and 2, 2000	November 6 and 7, 2002
May 2 and 3, 2001	
November 7 and 8 2001	

The AICPA has not released exam dates after 2002 because it hopes that by 2003 the new computerized exam will be fully developed and ready to go. For now, the formats, dates, and structure of the exam remain a 2-day, 15½ hour exam, administered the first Wednesday and Thursday of every May and November.

CPA EXAMINATION FOCUS

The focus of the exam is on a broad range of knowledge and skills that an entry-level CPA needs to practice public accounting. As reported in the *Information for Uniform CPA Examination Candidates,* a candidate's knowledge and skills are assessed using three cognitive levels of ability.

1. Understanding--the ability to recognize or recall learned materials and grasp the meaning.
2. Application--the ability to use learned materials in novel situations by relying on the principles that underlie the material.
3. Evaluation--the ability to extract relevant information from a context, draw conclusions, make appropriate decisions, and communicate judgments to a variety of audiences.

Presently, greater than 60% of the exam assesses the candidate's knowledge using level 2, application knowledge, and level 3, evaluation skills. This means most of the material is tested above the pure definitional level. The candidate must know how to apply and evaluate all areas. Just knowing definitions will not be enough to pass.

The essay and problem sections of the exam require candidates to evaluate situations, formulate conclusions, make recommendations, and present the information in a written report format. Several questions require the application and analysis of real-world business information. For sample AICPA questions, see Chapter 5, "Assessing Your Strengths and Weaknesses," or check the most current examples on the AICPA website at www.aicpa.org/exams.

GENERAL EXAM CONTENT

The overall content of the exam is based on studies conducted by the AICPA about the entry-level skills required in the early years of public accounting. Practitioners and educators participate in the content revision process. To date, two studies have been conducted and a third is underway.

The exam is written and administered only in English. Essays and problem responses are graded only if they are written in English. In addition to testing technical skills, 5% of three exam sections are graded for writing skills. Only ARE is excluded, since that exam section is all multiple-choice and other objective answer format questions that can be machine graded. See Chapter 9, "Writing a Beautiful Essay Answer," for a discussion of the required writing skills. Specific content detail is provided for each exam section. Check your exam review materials against the current content specifications. If you see holes or areas not mentioned in your review material, be careful. Your materials might be out of date or simply too condensed. It is better to be aware of what is tested and to attempt to learn something about it than to ignore areas that are listed on the content specifications. The AICPA is serious; the material is tested as outlined in the content specifications. Unfortunately, the candidate has no way of knowing how much each section could be tested. It is a guessing game. Attempt to learn something about everything listed. Always check the AICPA website for the most current specifications at www.aicpa.org/edu/candspec because the specifications are revised as the accounting profession makes changes.

LAW SPECIFICATIONS

Of all the content specifications, the Law section is the most detailed. See Exhibit 1 for the most current content specifications available at the time of printing. Use the detail to help you allocate study time. For example, debtor-creditor relationships account for 10% of the total points, while professional and legal responsibilities account for 15% of the point total. The smart candidate will spend more study time on professional responsibilities than debtor-creditor issues.

Candidates seem to think that contracts is a major part of the CPA exam. Ten percent of the points are allocated to contracts. This is not as heavily tested as you might think. Most college law courses spend a great deal of time on contract issues. That's because most law professors spent at least one of their college courses just dealing with contract topics. While contract knowledge does permeate many exam areas, you can cut your knowledge short by spending too much time learning contracts and skipping other areas. Don't overdo contracts--it's only 10%.

A must-know area for business law is the 1933 and 1934 Securities and Exchange (SEC) Acts. The SEC acts are most often tested via other objective and essay questions. Be sure to practice these question formats for this topical area. Make sure your review materials include an easy-to-understand discussion and many practice questions for the SEC acts, including the Private Securities Reform Act of 1995. This Act, which became effective in 1997, helps to limit a CPA firm's legal liabilities.

Devote adequate time to the area of professional responsibility; it is 15% of the Law exam. It is not necessary to memorize or learn the various court cases. Court case **names** are not tested. The Law exam tests the concepts arising out of a court case, not the actual name of who fought whom. For example, the issue of confidentiality is tested by asking the candidate to demonstrate that they know what information must be kept confidential and why. The questions usually do not refer to specific court cases.

It is also not necessary to learn the code section references of the Uniform Commercial Code (UCC). Just like confidentiality, UCC questions deal with the meat of the law, not the specific code sections. If your law review instructor enjoys citing code references, tell the instructor it is not necessary to clutter you brain with such detail. You would rather learn the relevant issues, because that's what is tested.

Watch for a crossover of law and audit topics. More and more candidates are claiming that some law issues are tested on the Audit exam and some audit topics are tested on the Law exam. For those candidates who must take both Law and Audit, this should not create a problem. Since these areas are tested on Wednesday, it is easy to prepare for both. Stay flexible and use your knowledge whenever you need it. It's dangerous to stick to a compartmentalized, rigid plan of when to use your knowledge. Be flexible by using your knowledge of all topics whenever you believe it to be relevant.

Condition candidates, those who have met the jurisdiction requirements by passing one or more parts of the exam, might experience problems with the crossover of law and audit knowledge. The area where one could expect the most crossover is professional and legal responsibilities, which includes the 10 generally accepted auditing standards (GAAS). Just to be safe, candidates sitting only for the Law section might want to review the audit discussion of the 10 GAAS, and Audit-only candidates might want to review the law discussion of professional and legal responsibilities, which includes the AICPA *Code of Professional Conduct*. The AICPA code has national acceptance, whereas other codes may only apply in certain jurisdictions of the United States.

AUDIT SPECIFICATIONS

The audit content specifications cover the entire audit process from start to finish. Several types of nonaudit situations are also tested, such as reviews and compilations of nonpublic entities. As a rough guideline, expect that about 70-80% of the exam tests the knowledge needed to audit a medium-sized public entity. The other 20-30% tests nonaudit situations such as review and compilations for nonpublic entities, use of an internal auditor, and other attestation and assurance services. The candidate cannot count on just audit knowledge to carry him or her through the exam. A well-prepared person must be ready to answer questions about nonaudit services that a typical public accounting firm would provide. There are some exceptions. Tax preparers' responsibilities are now tested on the ARE exam and consulting services are tested on the Law section. Exhibit 2 lists the auditing AICPA content specification outline available at the time of printing. Be careful, as changes are expected. Always refer to the AICPA website to obtain the most current outline.

A few topics are tested on the Law section that you might think are tested in the Audit section. Accountants' legal liability is tested on law, making up as much as 15% of the Law exam. Independence issues can account for as much as 5% of the Law exam. Again, check your review materials to see that this distinction is made.

The suggested list of audit study material includes several AICPA publications. Purchase publications only if your review materials do not include coverage of the areas. For the average CPA candidate who has audited for only a short time or never performed an audit at all, reading these materials is almost impossible. It takes a trained auditor to read, understand, and interpret how the examiners will test this material. This is why it is so hard for CPA candidates to prepare for the exam on their own just by using their college texts. Get some help here. The money will be wisely spent and most important, you will save valuable time by knowing what to study.

The Audit exam requires the candidate to demonstrate some practical audit skills. If you have never audited for a public accounting firm, it is wise to enroll in a quality review course to help give you the knowledge to deal with real-world issues. Of all the exam sections, Audit is the most attuned to real-life experiences. You will be expected to respond to the essays like a person who has actually performed auditing.

A very useful study source for audit is the AICPA *Audit Risk Alerts and Compilation and Review Alerts*. These can be purchased at the AICPA. Another item to purchase is the AICPA *Technology Series*. Audit technology is the latest addition to the content specification list of publications to study. The AICPA even publishes some computer-related questions dealing with technology issues in an appendix to the *Information for Uniform CPA Examination Candidates*. As much as 10-15% of the exam could deal with computer and information technology issues, so be sure to check that your study materials assist you in learning and reviewing this important new area.

ARE SPECIFICATIONS

Income tax issues make up 60% of the topics tested, governmental and not-for-profit accounting account for 30%, and managerial topics currently test only 10% of the total points. As you examine the ARE content specifications shown in Exhibit 3, note that the tax area tests much more than just the individual tax form 1040. Candidates make a big mistake by forgetting to study partnership and corporate taxation. Other important areas include S Corporations, estate and trust taxation, and exempt organizations. Your review materials should encompass a study of all of the mentioned areas. Being current for tax is more important than in any other CPA exam area. The United States Congress frequently changes our tax laws. The general rule for determining which laws are tested is to use the tax laws in effect 6 months before the examination date. This usually means the **previous** year's laws are tested on a May exam, while the **current** year's laws are tested on November exams. As a practical matter, the examiners generally avoid testing recent tax law changes. Some questions specify the year of the law to use when answering the question. If no period is given, use the **current** *Internal Revenue Code and Tax Regulations.*

As in law, don't be impressed with a review instructor's use of the code sections. Again, the code section numbers aren't tested; the content of the tax code is tested. Some say the May exam is likely to contain another objective format question concerning individual taxation, while the November exam contains another objective question testing corporate taxation. Don't count on the examiners to follow a pattern. Just study and learn all of the tax concepts. It does not matter whether a candidate must demonstrate the concepts in a multiple-choice or other objective answer format question. What matters is that the candidate knows and can apply the concept.

Governmental and not-for-profit accounting is tough since most candidates have never studied this area in college. Use a review manual to help you at least learn the basic funds, their use, and how to account for and prepare governmental financial statements. It is also wise to obtain some general knowledge about accounting for universities. Recall that the best study method to learn a new area is by actually attempting the questions and then learning from the answers. It is probable that you will prepare many index cards for constant review of this area. You can't afford to neglect 30% of the ARE exam. Study governmental and not-for-profit questions.

A word of warning to candidates who will be preparing for the November 2000 and after examinations--there is a major governmental revision underway. Avoid using review materials that have not been updated for this change. Almost all college texts will be out of date. Beginning with the November 2000 exam, use only those college texts with a copyright date of 2000 or after.

The 10% managerial area tests topics at a basic level. The efficient and effective CPA candidate will skip reading about managerial topics and will dive right into the questions. Learn from what you get wrong. Perhaps you will remember more from your cost accounting class than you think. There has been some talk of increasing the managerial content and decreasing the governmental percentage. Check the AICPA website every 6 months for specification percentage changes.

FARE SPECIFICATIONS

Financial accounting topics change more than one might think. The latest change includes the addition of a new financial statement, the Statement of Other Comprehensive Income. Not knowing a new financial statement can hurt greatly. This area was tested shortly after the Financial Accounting Standards Board (FASB) issued the statement. Consider a topic to be testable 6 months after a pronouncement's **effective** date unless early application of the standard is allowed. If early application of the standard is permitted, candidates are responsible for knowing the new pronouncement 6 months after **issuance** date. Examining the FARE content specifications in Exhibit 4 won't give the average candidate much of an idea of what is tested in this area. The basic topics come from your intermediate accounting classes and your advanced accounting class coverage of business combinations and consolidations. Candidates should not even attempt the exam until they can proficiently prepare the basic five financial statements in fine form using all classifications when required. The five financial statements are as follows:

1. Balance Sheet
2. Income Statement
3. Statement of Retained Earnings
4. Statement of Cash Flows
5. Statement of Other Comprehensive Income

Proper headings must be used. Please note that the balance sheet is the only financial statement that is prepared "as of " a particular date. All other statements are prepared "for the period ending." Know how to prepare a single- and a multiple-step income statement. Know the five sections of a classified balance sheet and which accounts go under which section. The five sections are as follows:

1. Current Assets
2. Long-Term Investments
3. Property, Plant, and Equipment
4. Intangible Assets
5. Other Assets

Be able to list several accounts that would be included under the first four sections. The other asset section includes accounts that don't fit under any of the above areas.

Let's face it, candidates must be super number-crunchers when it comes to FARE. Of course you will have your AICPA calculator to help you with the math, but before you can punch numbers, you must know the formula and which data to use. Application of concepts is very important. Be able to compute the dollar amounts of specific items. Bonds, investments, financial instruments, pensions, leases, and deferred taxes will always be **big areas.** A candidate might get lucky and not be required to demonstrate much combination and consolidation knowledge, but you are always required to know the financial statements and the big areas just listed. Don't fool yourself into believing that you can pass by just knowing general terms and definitions. Prepare to analyze, calculate, and identify the issues. Know something about everything listed, and learn much about the big areas. Yes, there is so much information to absorb, but don't give up. People do pass the CPA exam. Continue to believe that you can pass and take some comfort from the fact that the CPA exam graders do curve the exam.

EXAM GRADING PROCESS

The AICPA Board of Examiners' Advisory Grading Service grades the exam uniformly and fairly. Yes, it is a fair process. Graders are carefully selected and well-trained. The AICPA applies strict quality control checks that include additional reviews if needed. See Chapter 21, "The Waiting Game," for a detailed discussion of first and second grade reviews and what to do if you receive a score that is close to the passing score of 75. Scores of zero to 99 are issued for each exam section. The magic number is 75. A candidate seldom needs a raw score of 75, since the exam is curved.

CURVING THE CPA EXAM

The CPA exam is curved, but not using the same technique that most college professors use. On the CPA exam, the passing standard is based on the modified Angoff passing standard studies conducted in 1996. A process known as **equating** is used to statistically relate the difficulty of the current exam to previous exams. A complete understanding of the Angoff method is not necessary. What is important is to trust that the CPA exam is fairly graded. Time has proven that few mistakes have been made.

The grader will not know the candidate. All papers are graded maintaining total anonymity. Candidates are not given a chance to talk to the grader. All answers must be complete enough for the grader to understand without interpretation. When a candidate's presentation is unclear, the graders will simply not award points.

All grading is done on a positive basis. In other words, every candidate begins the exam with a score of zero and then goes on to earn points by correctly answering questions. You will not be penalized for guessing on multiple choice and other objective formats. For problems and essays, it is in the candidate's best interest to go ahead and state the concept, even when he or she is not sure. If the graders don't like it, they will ignore it. However, a candidate must provide only relevant information. It is a waste of time to talk about irrelevant topics since the graders will only ignore them and the candidate could be wasting valuable time needed to answer the rest of the exam. Utilize the tips for writing essays discussed in Chapter 9, "Writing a Beautiful Essay Answer." Go for the 75 points to pass.

CONDITIONAL STATUS

Some jurisdictions grant conditional status for passing some parts of the exam. For example, in the state of Illinois, candidates may earn conditional credit by passing two or more sections with a score of 75 or more, and earning at least a 50 in the part(s) not passed. As condition candidates, they are entitled to six additional trials on the subject or subjects not passed. The candidate must write all failed sections at the same time. In other words, if you pass Law and Audit with scores of 75 and receive a score of 65 in ARE and 52 in FARE you have conditioned in the state of Illinois. Illinois candidates are given six attempts to write off their condition. The attempts count whether you sit or not. If you decide to take the next exam off, you have lost one of your trials and now have 5 exams to write off your condition. The candidate must attempt ARE and FARE each time until one or more are passed. Say at the next exam, the candidate receives a 76 in ARE and a 47 in FARE. Will the candidate earn a pass in ARE? No, because the FARE score was less than 50. The good news is the candidate will not lose the previous condition on Law and Audit. Those sections have been earned. The only way a candidate can lose the condition sections is by not passing the exam before the six trials expire. Let's say that upon earning condition status, the candidate was too busy to sit for the next exam. The next exam would count as one of the six trials. If trial number two was unsuccessful, the candidate would have four more exams to try to pass. Time to study. At the third try, the candidate passes ARE with a 78 and gets a 52 in FARE. With one more section complete, the candidate now has only three more attempts to pass FARE. This example describes the condition rules in the state of Illinois. Call the Board of Examiners in your jurisdiction for the particular condition rules.

CHEATING

Forget about cheating; don't even try it. After all, a CPA's professional reputation is built upon integrity and trust. Some of the actions the AICPA define as cheating include:

- Falsifying credentials
- Copying answers from another person's paper
- Using crib notes
- Talking to and/or helping another person in the exam room
- Using unauthorized materials or equipment like rulers or handheld computers
- Divulging examination information in violation of the nondisclosed policy

Trained proctors watch candidates enter the exam room and complete the exam sections. Proctors may even be stationed in the restrooms or in the hallways outside of the examination room. Act like a professional at all times. After all, you are hoping that by passing the CPA exam you will become part of a profession that is known and trusted for its commitment to ethical behavior. Perform well on your own and you can be proud of your accomplishment. Believe that you can pass on your own, without applying any devious methods.

PERSONALLY SPEAKING

Why is it that such a diverse base of knowledge is required to pass the CPA exam? One look at the content specifications for each section and it's enough to make you give up. Of course that's not an option. This exam is greatly respected and much of that respect comes from the rigor. Nothing that's easy commands much respect. Accomplish what others can't do and you are respected. No need to panic. Arrive prepared by studying the topics to the best of your ability. Leave no stone unturned. Know something about everything and believe in the power of the curve.

How many times do I mention that your materials must be current? I can't stress that enough. The AICPA is quick to test new auditing and accounting standards. Tax questions are quickly changed to reflect the new laws. Pay attention to the 6-month rules. New concepts are generally tested within 6 months.

The AICPA used to publish the curves. They no longer do. However, I would guess that a raw score of a 62 might qualify for a curved score of 75 for ARE and FARE. These areas are so diverse, technical, and computational that most candidates are going to need some help to pass. Law and Audit require little or no curving. It is not your job to figure out how many curve points will be awarded. Your job is to provide answers to the exam questions. As you're working the exam, just complete one question at a time. Don't think about what your overall score is going to be. The AICPA pays graders to grade your paper. Don't take their job away from them.

Fortunately, I have not witnessed cheating, as most candidates are well versed in the rules. However, I have overheard candidates discussing exam questions in the halls, at restaurants, and in the elevators. Don't discuss exam topics after the exam. Not only does this violate the nondisclosed exam rules, it can also really upset you.

When I took the exam, you could talk about it. In fact, they mailed you your actual question booklet. Immediately after my first section, a candidate began asking me about how I answered a particular essay. After I explained my approach, she went on to tell me that my approach was incorrect. She answered the question using another method. I will never forget how I felt. I began to doubt my abilities. I wanted to give up and go home. Fortunately, I found the courage to regroup, by telling myself that I could be right and so could she. Maybe there were two methods. In the end, when I saw the unofficial answer from the AICPA, I noted that my approach was correct and hers was incorrect. Most accountants tend to be more critical of themselves and willing to believe that others must be correct. She passed that section. I passed that section. It's a good thing that you have the excuse not to talk about the questions. When a candidate begins to query you about the test, say, "Quiet please, we are not allowed to discuss the exam." This will keep you from comparing answers. A "postmortem" approach never helps. Discussing the exam after each section is a waste of time and energy and could give you the idea that you did not pass. Leave the exam with the proctors and forget about it. Let the graders do their job. Your job is to continue with the exam, providing relevant answers, and believing that you can pass. Continue your job by preparing for the next exam area by doing some last minute reviewing. Don't look back; always look forward to the next event. You can't change your answers once you have turned your booklet in. Don't worry about what you can't change. Proceed with confidence and the belief that you can pass the CPA exam.

Exhibit 1: AICPA Content Specification Outline: Business Law & Professional Responsibilities (LPR)

I.   Professional and legal responsibilities (15%)
   A.   Code of professional conduct
   B.   Proficiency, independence, and due care
   C.   Responsibilities in other professional services
   D.   Disciplinary systems imposed by the profession and state regulatory bodies
   E.   Common law liability to clients and third parties
   F.   Federal statutory liability
   G.   Privileged communications and confidentiality
   H.   Responsibilities of CPAs in business and industry, and in the public sector

II. Business Organizations (20%)
   A.   Agency
      1.   Formation and termination
      2.   Duties of agents and principals
      3.   Liabilities and authority of agents and principals
   B.   Partnerships, joint ventures, and other unincorporated associations
      1.   Formation, operation, and termination
      2.   Liabilities and authority of partners and owners
   C.   Corporations
      1.   Formation and operation
      2.   Stockholders, directors, and officers
      3.   Financial structure, capital, and distributions
      4.   Reorganization and dissolution
   D.   Estates and trusts
      1.   Formation, operation, and termination
      2.   Allocation between principal and income
      3.   Fiduciary responsibilities
      4.   Distributions

III. Contracts (10%)
   A. Formation
   B. Performance
   C. Third-party assignments
   D. Discharge, breach, and remedies

IV. Debtor-creditor relationships (10%)
   A. Rights, duties, and liabilities of debtors and creditors
   B. Rights, duties, and liabilities of guarantors
   C. Bankruptcy

V. Government regulation of business (15%)
   A. Federal securities acts
   B. Employment regulation
   C. Environmental regulation

VI. Uniform commercial code (20%)
   A. Negotiable instruments
   B. Sales
   C. Secured transactions
   D. Documents of title

VIII. Property (10%)
   A. Real property including insurance
   B. Personal property including bailments and computer technology rights

Suggested Publications to Study--Business Law & Professional Responsibilities

- AICPA *Code of Professional Conduct*
- AICPA Statements on Auditing Standards dealing explicitly with proficiency, independence, and due care
- AICPA Statement on Standards for Consulting Services
- AICPA Statements on Responsibilities in Personal Financial Planning Practice
- Pronouncements of the Independence Standards Board
- Books covering business law, auditing, and accounting

Exhibit 2: AICPA Content Specification Outline: Auditing (AUDIT)

I. Plan the engagement, evaluate the prospective client and engagement, decide whether to accept or continue the client and the engagement, and enter into an agreement with the client (40%)
    A. Determine nature and scope of engagement
        1. Generally accepted auditing standards
        2. Standards for accounting and review services
        3. Standards for attestation engagements
        4. Compliance auditing applicable to governmental entities and other recipients of governmental financial assistance
        5. Other assurance services
        6. Appropriateness of engagement to meet client's needs
    B. Assess engagement risk and the CPA firm's ability to perform the engagement
        1. Engagement responsibilities
        2. Staffing and supervision requirements
        3. Quality control considerations
        4. Management integrity
        5. Researching information sources for planning and performing the engagement
    C. Communicate with the predecessor accountant/auditor
    D. Decide whether to accept or continue the client and engagement
    E. Enter into an agreement with the client as to the terms of the engagement
    F. Obtain an understanding of the client's operations, business, and industry
    G. Perform analytical procedures
    H. Consider preliminary engagement materiality
    I. Assess inherent risk and risk of misstatements
        1. Errors
        2. Fraud
        3. Illegal acts by clients
    J. Consider internal control in both manual and computerized environments
        1. Obtain an understanding of business processes and information flows
        2. Identify risks in business processes and information flows
        3. Document an understanding of internal control
        4. Consider the effects of information technology on internal control
        5. Assess control risk
        6. Consider limitations of internal control
        7. Consider the effects of service organizations on internal control
    K. Consider other planning matters
        1. Using the work of other independent auditors
        2. Using the work of a specialist

       3.   Internal audit function
       4.   Related parties and related-party transactions
       5.   Electronic evidence

L. Identify financial statement assertions and formulate audit objectives
       1.   Accounting estimates
       2.   Routine financial statement balances, classes of transactions, and disclosures
       3.   Unusual financial statement balances, classes of transactions, and disclosures

M. Determine and prepare the work program defining the nature, timing, and extent of the auditor's procedures

II. Obtain and document information to form a basis for conclusions (35%)
   A. Perform planned procedures including planned applications of audit sampling
       1.   Tests of controls
       2.   Analytical procedures
       3.   Confirmation of balances and/or transactions with third parties
       4.   Physical examination of inventories and other assets
       5.   Other tests of details
       6.   Computer assisted audit techniques, including data interrogation, extraction, and analysis
       7.   Substantive tests prior to the balance sheet date
       8.   Tests of unusual year-end transactions
   B. Evaluate contingencies
   C. Obtain and evaluate lawyers' letters
   D. Review subsequent events
   E. Obtain representations from management
   F. Identify reportable conditions and other control deficiencies
   G. Identify matters for communication with audit committees

III. Review the engagement to provide reasonable assurance that objectives are achieved, and evaluate information obtained to reach and to document engagement conclusions (5%)
   A. Perform analytical procedures
   B. Evaluate the sufficiency and competence of audit evidence and document engagement conclusions
       1.   Consider substantial doubt about an entity's ability to continue as a going concern
       2.   Evaluate whether financial statements are free of material mis-statements
       3.   Consider other informaion in documents containing audited financial statements
   C. Review the work performed to provide reasonable assurance that objectives are achieved

IV. Prepare communications to satisfy engagement objectives (20%)

A. Prepare reports
   1. Reports on audited financial statements
   2. Reports on reviewed and compiled financial statements
   3. Reports required by Government Auditing Standards
   4. Reports on compliance with laws and regulations
   5. Reports on internal control
   6. Reports on prospective financial information
   7. Reports on agreed-upon procedures
   8. Reports on other assurance services
   9. Reports on the processing of transactions by service organizations
   10. Reports on supplementary financial information
   11. Other special reports
   12. Reissuance of reports
B. Prepare letters and other required communications
   1. Errors and fraud
   2. Illegal acts
   3. Special reports
   4. Communication with audit committees
   5. Other reporting considerations covered by Statements on Auditing Standards and Statements on Standards for Attestation Engagements
C. Other matters
   1. Subsequent discovery of facts existing at the date of the auditor's report
   2. Consideration of omitted procedures after the report date

Suggested Publications to Study--Audit

- AICPA Statements on Auditing Standards and Interpretations
- AICPA Statements on Standards for Accounting and Review Services and Interpretations
- AICPA Statements on Quality Control Standards
- AICPA Statements on Standards for Attestation Engagements
- US General Accounting Office Government Auditing Standards
- AICPA Audit and Accounting Guides:
  - *Audit Sampling*
  - *Consideration of Internal Control in a Financial Statement Audit*
- Textbooks and articles on auditing and other attestation services
- AICPA Auditing Procedure Studies
- AICPA Audit and Accounting Manual
- AICPA Audit Risk Alerts and Compilation and Review Alerts
- Single Audit Act, as amended
- Textbooks and articles on the information technology topics that CPAs need to understand in order to perform auditing and other attestation engagements in a computerized environment
- AICPA Technology Series

Exhibit 3: AICPA Content Specification Outline: Accounting & Reporting--Taxation, Managerial, and Governmental and Not-for-Profit Organizations (ARE)

Federal Taxation Content Specification Outline

I. Federal taxation--individuals (20%)
   A. Inclusions in gross income
   B. Exclusions and adjustments to arrive at adjusted gross income
   C. Deductions from adjusted gross income
   D. Filing status and exemptions
   E. Tax accounting methods
   F. Tax computations, credits, and penalties
   G. Alternative minimum tax
   H. Tax procedures

II. Federal taxation--corporations (20%)
   A. Determination of taxable income or loss
   B. Tax accounting methods
   C. S Corporations
   D. Personal holding companies
   E. Consolidated returns
   F. Tax computations, credits, and penalties
   G. Alternative minimum tax
   H. Other
      1. Distributions
      2. Incorporation, reorganization, liquidation, and dissolution
      3. Tax procedures

III. Federal taxation--partnerships (10%)
   A. Basis of partner's interest and bases of assets contributed to the partnership
   B. Determination of partner's share of income, credits, and deductions
   C. Partnership and partner elections
   D. Partner dealing with own partnership
   E. Treatment of partnership liabilities
   F. Distribution of partnership assets
   G. Termination of partnership

IV. Federal taxation--estates and trusts, exempt organizations, and preparers' responsibilities (10%)
   A. Estates and trusts
      1. Income taxation
      2. Determination of beneficiary's share of taxable income
      3. Estate and gift taxation
   B. Exempt organizations

      1. Types of organizations
      2. Requirements for exemption
      3. Business income tax
    C. Preparers' responsibilities

Governmental and Not-for-Profit Organizations Content Specification Outline

V. Accounting for governmental and not-for-profit organizations (30%)

    A. Governmental entities

      1. Measurement focus and basis of accounting
      2. Objectives of financial reporting
      3. Uses of fund accounting
      4. Budgetary process
      5. Financial reporting entity
      6. Elements of financial statements
      7. Conceptual reporting issues
      8. Accounting and financial reporting for state and local governments
         a. Governmental-type funds and account groups
         b. Proprietary-type funds
         c. Fiduciary-type funds
      9. Accounting and financial reporting for governmental not-for-profit organizations (including hospitals, colleges and universities, voluntary health and welfare organizations and other governmental not-for-profit organizations)

    B. Nongovernmental not-for-profit organizations

      1. Objectives of financial reporting
      2. Elements of financial statements
      3. Formats of financial statements
      4. Accounting and financial reporting for nongovernmental not-for-profit organizations
         a. Revenues and contributions
         b. Restrictions on resources
         c. Expenses, including depreciation

Managerial Accounting Content Specification Outline

VI. Managerial accounting (10%)

    A. Cost estimation, cost determination, and cost drivers
    B. Job costing, process costing, and activity-based costing
    C. Standard costing and flexible budgeting
    D. Inventory planning, inventory control, and just-in-time purchasing
    E. Budgeting and responsibility accounting
    F. Variable and absorption costing
    G. Cost-volume-profit analysis
    H. Cost allocation and transfer pricing

I.   Joint and by-product costing
J.   Capital budgeting
K. Special analyses for decision making
L.   Product and service pricing

Suggested Publications to Study--Federal Taxation
- Internal Revenue Code and Income Tax Regulations
- Internal Revenue Service Circular 230
- AICPA Statements on Responsibilities in Tax Practice
- Income tax textbooks

Suggested Publications to Study--Governmental and Not-for-Profit Organizations
- Governmental Accounting Standards Board (GASB) Statements, Interpretations, and Technical Bulletins
- Financial Accounting Standards Board (FASB) Statements of Financial Accounting Standards and Interpretations, Accounting Principles Board Opinions, AICPA Accounting Research Bulletins, and FASB Technical Bulletins
- FASB Statement of Financial Accounting Concepts 4, *Objectives of Financial Reporting by Nonbusiness Organizations*, and FASB Statement of Financial Accounting Concepts 6, *Elements of Financial Statements*
- AICPA Statement on Auditing Standards 69, *The Meaning of Present Fairly in Conformity With Generally Accepted Accounting Principles in the Independent Auditor's Report*
- AICPA Audit and Accounting Guides and Statements of Position relating to governmental and not-for-profit organizations
- Government Finance Officers Association, *Governmental Accounting, Auditing, and Financial Reporting* (the Blue Book)
- Governmental and not-for-profit accounting textbooks and other accounting textbooks containing pertinent chapters

Suggested Publications to Study--Managerial Accounting
- Managerial accounting textbooks and other accounting textbooks containing pertinent chapters
- Accounting periodicals

Exhibit 4: AICPA Content Specification Outline: Financial Accounting & Reporting (FARE)

I.   Concepts and standards for financial statements (20%)
     A. Financial accounting concepts
     B. Financial accounting standards for presentation and disclosure in general-purpose financial statements
         1. Consolidated and combined financial statements
         2. Balance sheet
         3. Statement(s) of income, comprehensive income, and changes in equity accounts
         4. Statement of cash flows
         5. Accounting policies and other notes to financial statements
     C. Other presentation of financial data
         1. Financial statements prepared in conformity with comprehensive bases of accounting other than generally accepted accounting principles
         2. Personal financial statements
         3. Prospective financial information
     D. Financial statement analysis

II. Recognition, measurement, valuation, and presentation of typical items in financial statements in conformity with generally accepted accounting principles (40%)
     A. Cash, cash equivalents, and marketable securities
     B. Receivables
     C. Inventories
     D. Property, plant, and equipment
     E. Investments
     F. Intangibles and other assets
     G. Payables and accruals
     H. Deferred revenues
     I. Notes and bonds payable
     J. Other liabilities
     K. Equity accounts
     L. Revenue, cost, and expense accounts

III. Recognition, measurement, valuation, and presentation of specific types of transactions and events in financial statements in conformity with generally accepted accounting principles (40%)
     A. Accounting changes and corrections of errors
     B. Business combinations
     C. Cash flow components--financing, investing, and operating
     D. Contingent liabilities and commitments
     E. Discontinued operations
     F. Earnings per share

G. Employee benefits
H. Extraordinary items
I. Financial instruments
J. Foreign currency transactions and translation
K. Income taxes
L. Interest costs
M. Interim financial reporting
N. Leases
O. Nonmonetary transactions
P. Quasi reorganizations, reorganizations, and changes in entity
Q. Related parties
R. Research and development costs
S. Segment reporting

Suggested Publications to Study--Financial Accounting & Reporting (FARE)

• Financial Accounting Standards Board (FASB) Statements of Financial Accounting Standards and Interpretations, Accounting Principles Board Opinions, and AICPA Accounting Research Bulletins
• FASB Technical Bulletins
• AICPA Statement on Auditing Standards 69, *The Meaning of Present Fairly in Conformity With Generally Accepted Accounting Principles in the Independent Auditor's Report*, and Statement on Auditing Standards 62, *Special Reports*
• AICPA Personal Financial Statements Guide
• FASB Statements of Financial Accounting Concepts
• AICPA Statements of Position
• Books and articles on accounting

5 ASSESSING YOUR STRENGTHS AND WEAKNESSES

To successfully prepare for the CPA exam, the candidate must conduct an honest assessment of strengths and weaknesses. Physical, mental, and technical preparedness should be considered. This chapter assists the candidate in assessing all three areas, beginning with the candidate's physical well-being.

PHYSICAL WELL-BEING

It is not necessary to be a famous bodybuilder to pass the CPA exam. What's important is that the candidate takes some time to think about what physical attributes can be improved during the study process. Improve what you can, deal with the other problems later.

One of the first questions that comes to mind is, "Do you smoke?" If you do, then physically you are damaging your body. No, this is not a sermon about the perils of smoking. Smoking is mentioned here to inform you that smoking is not allowed during the CPA exam. For the 15½ hours of exam time, you must be smoke-free. Is this going to bother you? If it is, begin dealing with the problem now, as you prepare for the exam. Cut back or better yet, go to the doctor for help. Wouldn't it be wonderful if you could quit smoking while you were studying for the big event?

You can't study while you are under the influence of alcohol or other dependent drugs. Think about the seriousness of the situation. If you need guidance, seek professional help. The pressure and stress of the CPA journey is likely to increase your reliance on chemical substances. Take care of these problems before you begin the study process.

Think about what you must do to take the exam. Candidates sit for 2 days, about 8 hours each day. How's your back? Are you pregnant? Has poor circulation been a problem for you? Sitting for 2 days is going to be tough. If propping your feet up on a footstool might help, call your board of examiners and inquire if it is possible to bring a footstool into the exam room. Pregnant women may want to bring cushions in for their backs. Just call the board and obtain permission to do so.

How's your eyesight? Has it been awhile since you tested and upgraded your glasses or contacts? Contact lenses are not recommended for the study or exam process. Long and late hours of study can cause dry eyes that may make you rub them. Infections can spread from your hands. Get new glasses well before the exam, and practice with them when you do your homework. Be assured that you are reading the numbers properly.

Are your prescriptions current? May and November can be prime allergy months. Prepare in advance by renewing all prescriptions. Make your doctor appointments before you begin the CPA journey. Later, you will be too busy and you don't want the risk of having an allergic reaction to new medication. Experiment well before the exam dates.

What about that extra weight? Candidates can easily gain 5–20 pounds over the 4-month study period, as chips, cookies, and ice cream seem to be the preferred study snacks. Overeating can make you drowsy. Try eating assorted fresh vegetables and fruits instead. Drink 8 to 10 glasses of water every day.

It is not necessary that you become a new person before you pass the exam, but it is helpful to spend a few minutes reflecting about your physical well-being. If you can easily correct the weakness, do it right away. You will benefit by your actions.

MENTAL STATE

There is no need to get a psychiatric evaluation. Mental preparedness involves clearing your mind by resolving as much conflict in your life as you possibly can. Are you going through a divorce? Do you have a medical problem that causes you discomfort? Does someone you know need your help? Think about the situations in your life that could distract you. Attempt to resolve these conflicts before you begin the study process. The human brain is ready to help you as long as you aren't constantly sending out signals asking for help. Contemplate waiting until the next exam to sit. Sometimes delaying the exam is a wise idea. Proper preparation requires focus. If you are preoccupied with many thoughts, wait until some of these issues have been resolved.

Child care is often a concern. It's almost impossible to study while children need your care and attention. Work with a family member or trusted friend to establish a schedule of child care that will meet the demands of a lengthy and time-consuming study process. Tell it like it is--you will need a great deal of babysitting assistance. Arrange for your day care well before you begin studying.

Attempting the CPA exam isn't going to simplify life--quite the contrary. The pressures will only fuel the existing fires. Get yourself ready by clearing your mind to the best of your ability. Ignoring mental pressure, or believing that once you begin studying the stress will lift, is very dangerous. Face reality, admit your weaknesses, and correct what you can.

TECHNICAL ABILITIES

There is no doubt that your technical ability is the most important element in passing the exam. Upon reviewing the content specifications shown at the end of Chapter 4, "The Content and Grading of the CPA Exam," it is evident that the required technical knowledge encompasses many areas. Take some time to think back to your college days. Ask yourself if you even remember a discussion of these areas. Use the checklist in Exhibit 1 to evaluate how much you remember. Admit that if you can't recall anything about the area, you must be weak. If you took the course many years ago, more than likely you are weak for two reasons.

1. The longer the time between the coursework and the CPA exam, the more the candidate is likely to forget
2. The content has probably changed greatly over time

Evaluate your technical strengths and weaknesses individually by exam section, taking into account the possibility that the material might have changed.

OVERALL CHANGES BY SECTION

Business law is usually taught over two semesters. Ask yourself if your college course included a detailed discussion of commercial paper. Negotiable instruments are difficult to understand. Legal concepts have changed the least of any of the four exam sections. While there has been little change, some areas have been added. For example, the government regulation of business has been expanded to include environmental and employment laws. Federal securities acts are a "must know." It is difficult to pass the exam without knowledge of the Securities and Exchange Commission (SEC) 1933 and 1934 Acts, including the Private Securities Reform Act of 1995. Property issues now deal with the rights to computer technology, a new area within the last year.

Audit is always changing. In just 5 years, about 30% of the content has been revised. Be careful if your audit knowledge is out of date. Admit the weakness. Many college graduates complete only one audit course. Consider yourself fortunate if you took two courses. Even with two courses, areas such as review and compilation services and assurance and attestation standards are not covered. Statistical sampling is seldom covered in enough detail. Information technology topics are the hot new area on the audit exam. See Exhibit 2 for the list of topics that CPA candidates need to understand in order to perform auditing and other attestation engagements in computerized environments. Use review materials that include a separate unit on just audit technology. This is the AICPA's latest addition to the audit area. Expect a constant evolution of topics. Information technology could be as much as 15% of the Audit exam and would make a great essay topic.

Candidates are weak in the ARE section if they have never studied governmental and not-for-profit accounting and corporate income tax. Beginning in November 2000, a major change will occur in the governmental area. The Governmental Accounting Standards Board (GASB) is issuing two new statements, 33 and 34, which will almost completely change the format of the required financial statements. Beware--do not study the old material, since it could cost you almost 30 points!

Candidates who take only one income tax class have probably learned only individual taxes. Estate and trust taxation concepts are most often taught in the corporate tax class. Completion of two semesters of income taxation is preferred. Understand that the United States Congress frequently changes tax laws. If your knowledge is over 1 year old, you are probably out-of-date.

One semester of managerial accounting is enough. Very few changes have occurred in the cost-accounting area. A solid understanding of such basic issues as variances, process costing, and activity-based costing is sufficient.

New financial accounting standards are frequently issued. The Financial Accounting Standards Board (FASB) is not shy about changing accounting methods. In recent years we have seen the addition of a new financial statement, the statement of other comprehensive income, a change in segment reporting, and many changes dealing with investments and financial instruments. A candidate who does not know what a derivative is will have great difficulty in passing FARE.

How will you ever know if you are strong or weak in an area? In addition to the assessment of your strengths and weaknesses listed in Exhibit 1, why not attempt some real CPA exam questions? Be cautious, as your question bank must be current. Using current materials, go ahead and preview your knowledge.

KNOWLEDGE PREVIEW

To preview your knowledge, you simply go to an area (bonds, for example) and work some multiple-choice questions. A good suggestion is to work on 10 to 15 multiple-choice questions. Skip around, doing some of the first questions listed in the area, and some of the later questions. For example, if your review manuals contain 40 questions on bond accounting, you might work on every fourth question. You may want to go to a bookstore and use the review manuals on the shelves to do your previewing. Of course, when you answer the questions, you can't write in the book. Use a few different manuals to see which one you prefer. The more detailed the answer explanations are, the more effective and efficient your studies will be. Detailed answer explanations help you learn why a particular answer is incorrect. The next time through, you will know how the examiners trick you and what words they use to distract you.

Don't let your knowledge preview scare you. It is natural to forget technical subject matter such as accounting. The whole idea behind CPA exam preparation is to do just that--prepare. If you knew everything already, there wouldn't be anything to improve. Admit your weaknesses and begin correcting them. Don't fear them.

CORRECTING WEAKNESSES

The total extent of a candidate's weaknesses is not evident until the person begins the study process. It is by listening to lectures, working software questions, and answering questions in review manuals that the candidate will become painfully aware of weaknesses. It is one thing to identify weaknesses; it is another to correct them. The whole focus of the study and review process is to correct weaknesses. Chapter 7, "Study Strategies to Improve Your Memory," lists methods to help you learn new areas, correct old habits, and remember material that has been forgotten. Take the time to correct your weaknesses to the best of your ability. Perhaps you may never totally understand foreign currency hedges and translation. However, you have at least studied the area so that you can define terms, do some accounting, and recite the financial statement disclosure issues. If you ignore weak areas, you might be sorry, as the areas you ignore always seem to be highly tested. Work to correct your weaknesses and utilize your strengths.

USING YOUR STRENGTHS

Yes, there will be many areas where you remember the material and can still demonstrate, work, and discuss the area. This is wonderful news. It is especially exciting to know that your knowledge remains in your brain, ready for use. Still, candidates seem to continue to study what they know. Halt! This is a major mistake. There is no time to waste studying what you know. If you know it today, you will know it 4 months from now when the examiners test the area. Candidates like to study their strong areas because it makes them feel good about their progress. It is a comfort zone. Study to correct your weaknesses and use your strengths to build from.

PERSONALLY SPEAKING

Small changes yield big results. When it comes to correcting weaknesses, practice and effort to learn what you don't know will yield huge results. If you work to correct some areas, you will see benefits in other ways. Each time you conquer another technical area, you are not only adding to your technical base, but you are also increasing your confidence level by decreasing the number of subjects that you fear. A confident person is willing to take risks. The more confident you are, the more willing you are to take a risk and write down concepts for the graders to grade. I always say you can't win the lottery until you buy a ticket. You can't earn points on problems and essays until you write something down. Don't be afraid. Keep on studying. Every weakness corrected is another point for you.

Don't give up too early. I have worked with candidates who ask me a question about a large area the night before the exam. I spend a few minutes explaining some of the basic concepts, the candidate goes off to study, and later comes back to inform me that they now understand the area. The greatest payoff comes when the area is tested in an essay the next day. If the candidate had given up and said that they just couldn't absorb any more knowledge, they would have missed a great opportunity and many points. Some weaknesses take only a minute to correct, while others may take several hours of study. If you have the time, why be lazy? Utilize every minute to make progress toward correcting your weaknesses and continue to believe in your strengths.

Trying to be the perfect person while you are preparing for a difficult event such as passing the CPA exam is tough. I can talk all I want about eating carrots and drinking water, but as I wrote this book I found I could think more clearly when I ate chocolate covered raisins and drank gallons of coffee. You don't need the extra pressure of trying to be perfect. Relax and admit your shortcomings. Do your best to cope with the stress.

Technically, the best advice I can give you is to study current materials. Study to learn something about everything. Follow a detailed study plan to correct your weaknesses, not to reinforce your strengths. Study to be your best, not to be perfect. With practice, what you learn today you will remember in the future at the CPA exam.

Exhibit 1: Checklist of Strengths and Weaknesses

You will have some strong areas and some weak areas. The key to passing the exam is to accept your strengths (don't keep studying what you know) and to work to correct your weaknesses (you don't need to be perfect to pass). Take a moment and think about your strengths and weaknesses. Check the box that best fits your situation.

COURSE	TOOK COURSE AND DID WELL	TOOK COURSE AND DID POORLY OR DON'T REMEMBER	NEVER TOOK COURSE
First Semester of Business Law			
Second Semester of Business Law			
First Semester of Auditing			
Second Semester of Auditing covering statistical sampling			
Individual Income Tax			
Corporate Income Tax			
Governmental Accounting--separate course			
Managerial Accounting--one semester			
Intermediate Accounting, first semester			
Intermediate Accounting, second semester			
Advanced Accounting--study of combinations, consolidations,partnerships			
YOUR TOTAL			

Exhibit 1 cont'd.

If you have taken the exam before, a second tool to help analyze your strengths and weaknesses would be the candidate diagnostic report. Use this as a tool to identify your weak areas--particularly in Business Law and ARE. The most important thing you can do is keep track of areas you struggle with and allow extra time to carefully review the multiple-choice questions and problems.

Your Personal Weaknesses:

Exhibit 2: Information technology topics

CPAs need to understand the following technology topics in order to perform auditing and other attestation engagements in computerized environments. See the AICPA *Information for Uniform CPA Examination Candidates*, for a detailed discussion and sample technology questions.

- Role of information systems within business
- Hardware such as memory, communication devices, physical storage, and file servers
- Software operating systems, applications, and security
- Data structure including file organizations, types of data files, and database management systems
- Networks including LANs, WANs, and VANs
- Transaction processing modes such as batch, on-line, real-time, and distributed processing
- Electronic commerce such as data interchange, electronic fund transfers, and point of sale transactions
- Application processing phases including edit routines, master file maintenance, and transaction flow
- IT control objectives such as integrity, timeliness, and authorization
- Control activities and design
- Physical access controls and security
- Roles and responsibilities within the information technology department
- Disaster recovery and business continuity
- Audit tests of general and automated controls
- Computer-assisted auditing techniques
- Risks of auditing around the computer such as insufficient paper-based evidence and insufficient audit procedures

6 DEVELOPING YOUR PERSONAL STUDY PLAN

It's time to get down to the business of studying. Just talking and reading about the exam does not give you the technical edge. Chapter 4, "Content and Grading of the CPA Exam," explains what concepts are tested. Using the techniques in Chapter 5, "Assessing Your Strengths and Weaknesses," you have determined your weak areas. Now plan to be successful by devising a plan to learn the concepts. The first step in preparing a personalized study plan is to analyze each day of the week to find the time to study.

SCHEDULE OUT YOUR ACTIVITIES

The definition of a plan is a detailed method by which a thing is done. You must divide up the overwhelming amount of technical material into bite-sized chunks and then prepare a plan that gives you study time to learn the concepts tested. Finding time to study is easier said than done. Begin to find study time by listing how you spend your time each day. Use a chart, like the one in Exhibit 1, to write down your daily activities. Prepare a different chart for every day of the week. Sample charts for a workday, say Monday, may look like Exhibit 1. A sample chart for a weekend day such as Sunday might look like Exhibit 2. Take note of the times when you can study. During the week, the most obvious study times will be early morning before work, during the lunch hour, and late evenings after work. Notice how much more study time is available on a weekend. The problem is forcing yourself to use the time to study. It's very tempting to waste time on a weekend, just because there seems to be so much extra time. This is why you prepare a plan. Establish the plan and stick to it.

Plot out your day, listing times beginning early in the morning to late at night. Allow for about 7 hours of sleep. You can't afford to be lazy. Optional activities such as playing on the softball team, watching television, and taking naps can be abandoned to make time to study. Even your volunteer work at the church or in the community could be postponed until you pass.

After you list your daily routine, you must stand back and examine how you use your time. Obviously, you cannot cancel work every day or you will be too poor to sit for the CPA exam. However, why can't you study during your lunch hour?

Exhibit 1: Sample Weekday of Activities

Day of the Week: *Monday*

Time	*Activity*
6:00 a.m.	Wake up at 6:15 a.m. *TIME TO STUDY*
7:00 a.m.	Shower, eat breakfast, get ready for work, housework, drive kids to school
8:00 a.m.	Leave to catch train to work; arrive at work at 8:30 a.m.*
9:00 a.m.	WORK
10:00 a.m.	WORK
11:00 a.m.	WORK
Noon	Lunch hour *TIME TO STUDY*
1:00 p.m.	WORK
2:00 p.m.	WORK
3:00 p.m.	WORK
4:00 p.m.	WORK
5:00 p.m.	WORK
6:00 p.m.	Leave work at 5:10 p.m. and travel home on train*
7:00 p.m.	Cook dinner, eat dinner, spend time with family
8:00 p.m.	*TIME TO STUDY*
9:00 p.m.	*TIME TO STUDY*
10:00 p.m.	*TIME TO STUDY*
11:00 p.m.	Get ready for the next day. Go to bed 11:15 p.m., to get 7 hours of sleep.

See Chapter 7, "Study Strategies to Improve Your Memory," for tips on how to study while you are doing household chores and commuting to work.

Use the above schedule to find time to study during the week. Perhaps on some evenings you will write down other activities such as bowling, exercise, school events, and church meetings. Prepare a separate schedule for every day of the week. Then examine your schedule and find times to study.

Exhibit 2: Sample Weekday of Activities

Day of the Week: *Sunday*

Time	*Activity*
6:00 a.m.	Wake up at 6:15 a.m. *TIME TO STUDY*
7:00 a.m.	Shower, eat breakfast, get ready for church, read the paper
8:00 a.m.	Church
9:00 a.m.	Church, travel back home, visit with family
10:00 a.m.	*TIME TO STUDY*
11:00 a.m.	*TIME TO STUDY*
Noon	Eat lunch
1:00 p.m.	*TIME TO STUDY*
2:00 p.m.	*TIME TO STUDY*
3:00 p.m.	Watch football game, wash clothes*
4:00 p.m.	Watch football game, run to the grocery store*
5:00 p.m.	Continue washing clothes and other household chores*
6:00 p.m.	Go out to dinner with family and friends
7:00 p.m.	Family dinner
8:00 p.m.	Pay bills, get mail ready for the week, e-mail friends
9:00 p.m.	*TIME TO STUDY*
10:00 p.m.	*TIME TO STUDY*
11:00 p.m.	Get ready for the next day. Go to bed 11:15 p.m., to get 7 hours of sleep.

See Chapter 7, "Study Strategies to Improve Your Memory," for tips on how to study while you are doing household chores and commuting to work.

Most accountants stick to a predictable schedule of activities. Notice that the schedules do not include much time for phone calls, watching television, surfing the Internet, or shopping at the mall. These activities are considered fun things that you can do after you pass the exam. For now, keep the extracurricular activities to a minimum.

FINDING TIME TO STUDY

Does a person need 60 minutes to eat lunch? No one ever said passing the exam was going to be easy, and certainly no one ever pretended that you could prepare without sacrificing something that you enjoy. Make the commitment to pass; find the time in your schedule to study. Where can you find time?

Try the morning. In Chapter 7, "Study Strategies to Improve Your Memory," it is suggested that you listen to recordings of lectures about law and audit topics. You must also find some time to sit down and work questions to test your retention and understanding of the material. Determine when you will study and make it a habit.

It takes about 3 weeks of constantly doing something to make it a habit. If you set your alarm to wake up 45 minutes earlier to study before you go to work, you could form a morning study habit in a very short time. Five 45-minute morning sessions each week gives you a total of almost 4 hours a week. A suggested study plan could be scheduled as follows:

Study Time	*Minutes of Study per Day*	*Total Study Time per Week*
In the morning, before you go to work or school	45 minutes per day, 5 days a week	3.75 hours
During your lunch hour	45 minutes per day, 4 days a week (go out to lunch with your friends on Friday)	3.00 hours
Evening time after work	2 hours, 4 nights per week	8.00 hours
Saturday morning	3 hours and 15 minutes	3.25 hours
Sunday evening	3 hours	3.00 hours
Total study time		21.00 hours per week

Organized people who deliberately make time to study can easily find 21 hours per week outside of work time to study. Notice that Friday is a light day, with no studying during lunch or in the evening. Adjust the plan to fit your life. For example, if you make the decision to continue bowling, you might give up a weeknight and study for 3 hours on 3 evenings instead of 2 hours for 4 nights. If you must attend a family event on Sunday, add 3 hours of study time to Saturday so as to free up the entire day on Sunday or exchange Sunday study time with Friday evening. Flexibility is required to stick to the plan. However, just spending time looking at the material while you tick off the minutes spent is not going to help you.

REAL STUDYING

Real studying means that you are using time to learn topics, not just wasting time by ticking off the minutes you spend sitting in a chair staring at your review manuals. Real studying means the candidate will spend about 25% of the study time reading, and about 75% of the study time doing. See Chapter 9, "Writing a Beautiful Essay Answer," for tips on how to study for essay questions. See Chapter 10, "Practice Makes Perfect," for tips on how to use multiple-choice and other objective answer formats to help you identify and comprehend the testable concepts. Whatever you do, don't confuse staring at the material with actively studying to learn the material.

It is easy to determine if you have wasted study time or used your time wisely to learn and retain information. Simply attempt to answer the sample questions in your review manuals. You learned if you can correctly answer the questions. You've wasted time if you are unable to correctly answer the questions.

HOW MUCH STUDY TIME

How much time should a candidate study? The answer depends upon the following factors:

- **How much time is there before the exam?** If there are 5 months, you don't need to study as much each day as you would if there were only 3 months left.
- **How much do you know?** If you recently graduated from college and took all of the courses discussed in Chapter 5, "Assessing Your Strengths and Weaknesses," you probably know a great deal. You are current and need to study less than the person who has been out of college for 5 years.
- **How quickly do you absorb technical material?**
- **How current are you in the particular area?**
- **What activities do you perform on your job that may help you learn an area?** If you prepare corporate tax returns, you will be well versed in this area and will require less study time. If you audit for a public accounting firm, your audit skills will help you absorb the audit examples more quickly than if you didn't audit.
- **How many exam sections must you take?** In some states, candidates may take the exam one or two sections at a time. Perhaps you have conditioned by passing some sections and only have one or two sections to pass.

It is almost impossible to establish the amount of time a person must study. The above schedule of 21 hours per week is about the average time it takes to prepare for all four exam sections the first time through. Keep in mind that if you attend a review course, the hours spent at the review course should count as study time. The basic rule is to study as much as you can to learn what you need to learn. Don't let time be the driving force. When preparing your study plan, let the number of topics you must learn and review be the driving force.

PREPARING A STUDY PLAN BY TOPICS

Examine your review materials. All materials should be divided up by exam area and then further divided into concepts tested within the exam section. The subtopics could be called chapters, modules, or units. For simplicity, we will call them modules. Count up the number of modules you should study and review. If your materials contain 36 modules and you have 12 weeks to go before the exam, you should study 3 modules per week to complete all 36 modules. Notice that the assumption is that you can and will complete 3 modules per week and this takes you right up to the exam date.

One can quickly see that 3 modules per week is a pretty tough schedule. Making the assumption that there will be no major interruptions is probably unrealistic. Don't set yourself up for failure. The plan for success allows for interruptions by periodically booking extra time to catch up. In other words, leave some holes in your personalized study plan to catch up. When you reach the catch-up time, if you are already caught up, reward yourself by taking some time out for fun. Once you determine how many modules you must study per week, take some time to consider the mix of subjects that you must learn.

SUBJECT MIX

If you have more than one exam section to study, mix up the exam sections and the subject matter. Schedule a tough subject with an easy one. Mix the fun topics with the dry and difficult areas. For example, if you plan to study three modules per week, don't select three difficult FARE topics for the same week. Help yourself stick to the plan by picking one difficult area, one medium difficult area, and one easy and fun area. An example of a mix of material might be

- **Difficult:** FARE--Pensions
- **Medium difficulty:** ARE--Subchapter S Corporations
- **Easy:** Law--Insurance

Take a pretest of the concepts to determine if the area appears to be difficult or easy. See Exhibit 3 for a sample study plan (to accompany the *CPA Examination Review* by Patrick R. Delaney). Once you determine the subject mix for the week, take a look at how you will accomplish the plan. Begin the week with the difficult area by further dividing the pension area into three topics such as

1. Pension definitions and terms
2. Pension calculations
3. Pension footnote disclosures and financial statement presentations

Early in the week, you may use time on the subway or train commuting to work to study the terms. During the lunch hour, you review the terms and begin learning the formulas for the computations. The wise candidate will study for a short time period, not to exceed 1 hour. Studying for a long stretch of time greatly decreases your retention rate and your efficiency. We absorb things more quickly and easily using short time periods and by dividing the material into bite-sized chunks of information.

BITE-SIZED CHUNKS

Research studies show that a person learns more quickly when the material is divided into small, manageable study areas. Not only is it easier to study, but it also gives the person a chance to gain confidence by noting that progress was made. Another advantage of studying small areas is that this method allows the candidate to utilize a building-block approach. We all know you can't divide until you master the areas of addition, subtraction, and multiplication. Accounting, like math, keeps building. New information is learned by using previously mastered techniques. For example, to understand how to account for liabilities, you must know how to compute the net present value. Once you know how to compute present value, you will find bond and lease accounting much easier since the areas begin with the computation of the net present value of the item. Prepare your study plan by blocking out several short time intervals throughout the day to study. Your careful planning will reap big rewards by not only giving you several breaks, but also improving your long-term memory. The retention rate is much higher when you study over short rather than long time periods.

TO THINE OWN SELF BE TRUE

"To thine own self be true." This is an old fashioned way of saying be honest and see things as they are. Be honest when you develop your study plan. If you must travel to see the in-laws for the weekend, you shouldn't schedule a difficult area for review, not unless the unusual situation occurs where your in-laws allow you to study during the day and then plan a relaxing evening for you. Look at the week as it is going to be. For a busy week, schedule for light study and vice versa.

Plan for sickness, family crises, and overtime at work. It's inevitable that problems will occur. Once every 5 to 6 weeks, schedule a week with no study. This is your catch-up week. It is best to take at least 2 to 3 days off work to catch up. Use your vacation time for study.

BOOK YOUR VACATION NOW

Plan to take the week before the examination off work. Book your vacation or unpaid leave of absence early. The last thing you need is an argument with your boss about getting the days off to take the exam. Whatever you do, don't plan to work the Monday and Tuesday before the exam. Your work will be worthless, as your mind will be on the studying that you wish you could do. If bosses would only realize that passing the CPA examination is a major professional hurdle for which most candidates need some help! Help yourself by arranging to take the time off work several months in advance of the actual date.

BUDGET TIME FOR REVIEW

Don't forget to budget time to review previously studied material. Schedule the entire week and the weekend before the exam for some review. Use purchased course software to create tests for yourself. Look for review manuals that contain sample exams. Review questions and index cards that you wrote as you discovered difficult areas. Skim your notes. For each area, work every fourth multiple-choice question. Scan essays, spending time reading the AICPA answer. Select some other objective questions to bring back multiple-choice topics. Meet with your study buddy and quiz each other out loud or by exchanging a list of your favorite CPA questions. Remain focused on the CPA exam. Be happy that by developing and sticking to a detailed course of action, you actually created time for review just before the exam.

APPRECIATE THE PLAN

Don't ever underestimate the value of planning. Audit planning is required by generally accepted auditing standards because it is crucial to the auditor's performance in accomplishing his goals. The time you spend planning for a big event will benefit you later by helping you meet your goal of passing the CPA exam.

Candidates often spend more time planning a New Year's Eve party than they do preparing a study plan to accomplish a lifetime goal that is as prestigious as passing the CPA exam. Look at your study plan as a road map to the end of the CPA journey. Each topic that you learn, study, and review means you are that much closer to reaching your destination. A detailed study plan lets you know just how much more you have left to accomplish. A plan serves as a reminder that you must study early and often. If you slack off 1 day, you must pay in the future by carving time out of an already jam-packed schedule.

PERSONALIZE THE STUDY PLAN

There is no magic amount of study time. Personalize your study plan by thinking about your weak areas and the time you have each day to study. Don't be overly ambitious. A person simply cannot study for 10 hours a day and be effective. Look for small bits of time to learn the bite-sized chunks of material. As the days get closer to the exam, you will be surprised at how much better prepared you will be if you personalized your plan to meet your goals. Don't forget an important rule: study what you don't know, not what you do know. Have some confidence in your ability to retain information. There is no time to waste. Use you time and your abilities wisely. Make the sacrifice.

GIVE UP ACTIVITIES

There is no doubt that during your CPA exam preparation you will have to give up some things that are fun to do. You may even have to sacrifice and give up helping with the lawn work or the cooking and cleaning chores. You just can't do what you were doing before. You can't squeeze time into an already-too-busy schedule. Take a careful inventory of all of the activities you are involved in and give up something to make room for study time. Who knows? After the exam is over, you might discover that your new streamlined plan allows you time to return to school to get another degree, spend more time with your family, or just plain spend time reading and relaxing.

DESIGN A PLAN TO SUCCEED

Designing a plan to succeed is so much more fun than designing a plan that on paper looks great, but after 1 to 2 weeks, you haven't accomplished a thing. If you are not a morning person, by all means, don't schedule early morning times. Plan to spend the late evening hours studying. Incorporate all of the topical areas into your plan. Mastering some areas and leaving other areas untouched could be dangerous. The AICPA board of examiners has a way of testing the areas that you didn't study. Spend some time on a subject area to do your best at learning something about everything. Believe that your plan will be a guide to success. Believe that you can pass the CPA exam.

DON'T WASTE TIME--COMPLETE THE JOB

Don't be lazy. You must perform and study every day. There is no slack time. Realize that the hypothetical schedule in Exhibit 3 requires you to begin studying 14 weeks before the exam, which is the first week in February for a May exam, and the first week of August for a November exam. If you want a less compacted schedule, begin earlier and study less each week. If it's been a long time since you took an exam or studied accounting material, you may need to begin a month earlier, to provide for extra time to learn and review the material. If you find yourself not completing the assignments on time, you should make extra time in your day to study or study Friday and/or Sunday to always stay on target. When you fall behind, you will find it very difficult to catch up. Make studying a habit by making studying one of your daily chores.

PERSONALLY SPEAKING

I can't tell you how much fun I gave up the summer that I wrote this book. At the beginning of the summer my golf game was improving because I had some time to golf almost every day. Then, when crunch time arrived, I had to give up even the simple things like meals with my family and Sunday drives. I had to work around the clock. I am a procrastinator who always works better under pressure. Don't think this works for the CPA exam. You will be assured of running out of time. The CPA exam waits for no one. No matter how much you would like to postpone the date, it arrives. This is why it is so critical to establish a detailed plan and stick to it. Make the sacrifice each day to meet the end goal. In the end, you will be able to say you really did do the best that you could.

I kept pushing to finish this book so that I could get some sleep, take some time to see my daughter's volleyball games, and take my son to visit some colleges. I can take time for the fun things only when I have accomplished my work goals. When it comes down to it, you have options. You can always give up the plan and not become a CPA. I could have given up on writing this book or on taking the CPA exam. In the end, I would never have accomplished a dream that I always had. I often dreamed of being a CPA or of authoring a book.

CPAs like to be organized. Preparing a study plan keeps you organized. Use a bright highlighter to ceremoniously check off what you have studied. Use incentives to reward yourself. When I was studying for the Certified Internal Auditor's (CIA) exam, I was in a position where I could afford to take a week off from work and fly to Florida to study on the beach. It was great. Each morning I would wake up early, study until noon, sit in the sun from noon to 3 p.m., shop until 5 p.m., and after dinner go back to studying. If I didn't accomplish the modules I wanted to, I wouldn't let myself go have fun. My reward for accomplishing my daily goals was to do something I enjoy.

Your incentive could be something simple like go to a movie, take a bubble bath, or hit golf balls at the driving range. Maybe you want to shoot some hoops or attend a play or opera. You can go only if you accomplish your goal. You must stay home if you don't. Allow time for fun, but not at the expense of achieving your goal.

Every 6 months I talk to successful and unsuccessful CPA candidates. With almost no exceptions, those who pass have made sacrifices to achieve their goal. A recent e-mail from an unsuccessful candidate summed it up simply by saying: "I failed the exam because I failed to give up anything." She went on to explain that during the 4 months she took the review class she didn't take time to study. She didn't take the time to study because she said she had no time. After the exam, she realized that passing would have been attainable if she had sacrificed a few activities to make time to study. Sacrifice for the important matter at hand, passing the exam. Successful candidates realize that they have no time to lose. Every minute of study makes a valuable contribution to the goal.

Let's say you use the example time allotment of studying 21 hours per week. What should you do when you use only 16 hours of study time and you have completed the necessary weekly modules? You're fully prepared for the three topics listed that week and you spent 5 hours less than you budgeted for. This is the fun part. You get to choose what you want to do. Here are four good options

1. Use the extra time to go back to a previous area and review it.
2. Use the extra time to move forward to get ahead in other areas.
3. Use your software to generate mock exams to test your time-management skills and your long-term memory.
4. Reward yourself--go have some fun!

You pick the option. You worked hard to stick to the plan and it paid off. What you do with the extra time is all up to you. Because you have a plan that details what you must to achieve success, you can pause along the way. It's all part of the plan. Trust your study plan. It will guide you to success. Believe that you can pass the exam by learning one concept at a time over the course of several days and months.

Exhibit 3: Sample study plan: 21 study hours per week

Schedule for 14 study weeks

NOTE: This study plan has been prepared using the modules as written in **CPA Examination Review** *by Patrick R. Delaney, published by John Wiley & Sons, Inc.*

Assumptions:

Friday and Sunday are free days--No study!
Saturday study 6 hours
Study weekday mornings, Monday-Thursday for 45 minutes
Study weekday lunch hours, Monday-Thursday for 45 minutes
Study Monday, Wednesday, and Thursday evenings for 2½ hours.
Study Tuesday evening for 1½ hours.

Your study week looks like this.

Study Time	Monday	Tuesday	Wednesday	Thursday	Saturday
Morning	45 minutes	45 minutes	45 minues	45 minutes	3 hours
Lunch Hour	45 minutes	45 minutes	45 minues	45 minutes	
Afternoon					3 hours
Evening	2 hours, 30 minutes	1 hour, 30 minutes	2 hours, 30 minutes	2 hours, 30 minutes	
TOTAL	4 hours	3 hours	4 hours	4 hours	6 hours

Your study topics look like this

Week	Monday	Tuesday	Wednesday	Thursday	Saturday
1	• 22A, Basic concepts • 22B, Error Correction	• 22C, Accounting Changes	• 22D, Financial Statements	• 7, Contracts	• 23, Inventory • 20, Insurance
2	• 24, Fixed Assets	• Begin 1, Engagement Planning	• Continue 1, Engagement Planing	• Complete 1, Engagement Planning	• 34, Costing Systems
3	• Begin 25, Monetary Current Assets & Current Liabilities	• Complete 25, Monetary Current Assets & Current Liabilities	• 8, Sales	• 13, Agency	• Begin 2, Internal Control
4	• Continue 2, Internal Control	• Complete 2, Internal Control	• Begin 9, Commercial Paper	• Complete 9, Commercial Paper	• Begin 26, Present Value and Bonds
5	• Continue 26, Debt Restructure and Pensions	• Continue 26, Leases	• Complete 26, Leases	• 10, Secured Transactions	• 3, Audit Evidence
6	• 27, Deferred Taxes	• Continue 27, Deferred Taxes	• Complete 27, Deferred Taxes	• 11, Bankruptcy	• 29, Investments
7	• Catch-Up Week	• Catch-Up Week	• Catch-Up Week	• Catch-Up Week	• Catch-Up Week
8	• Begin 28, Stockholders' Equity	• Complete 28, Stockholders' Equity	• 12, Debtor-Creditor Relationships	• Begin 31, Business Combinations & Consolidations	• Complete 31, Business Combinations & Consolidations • Begin 19, Property
9	• Complete 19, Property • Begin 4, Audit Reporting	• Continue 4, Audit Reporting	• Complete 4, Audit Reporting	• 14, Partnerships & Joint Ventures	• Begin 40, Individual Taxation
10	• Complete 40, Individual Taxation	• Begin 32, Derivative Instruments and Hedging Activities	• Complete 32, Derivative Instruments and Hedging Activities • Begin 33, Miscellaneous	• Complete 33, Miscellaneous • Begin 30, Statement of Cash Flows	• Complete 30, Statement of Cash Flows
11	• Begin 41, Transactions in Property	• Complete 41, Transactions in Property	• 35, Planning, Control, & Analysis	• 15, Corporations	• Begin 38, Governmental Accounting
12	• Complete 38, Governmental Accounting	• 36, Standards & Variances	• Begin 42, Partnership Taxation	• Complete 42, Partnership Taxation	• 43, Corporate Taxation
13	• 44, Gift & Estate Tax	• 37, Nonroutine Decisions	• Begin 39, Not-for-Profit Accounting	• Complete 39, Not-for-Profit Accounting	• 17, Professional Responsibilities
14	• 16, Federal Securities Acts	• 18, Regulation of Employment	• Begin 5, Statistical Sampling	• Complete 5, Statistical Sampling	• 6, Auditing With Technology • 21, Trusts and Estates
15	• Review and Work Sample Exams	• Review and Work Sample Exams	• CPA EXAM	• CPA EXAM	• FREEDOM

7 STUDY STRATEGIES TO IMPROVE YOUR MEMORY

Are you studying to remember the material or are you simply studying to pass the time away? Of course you want to remember the concepts when it comes time to use them. Most candidates don't really know how to study. As a college student you might have studied for the moment. The kind of person who studied for a day or all night and then dumped the material out on the exam the next day has far less retention than the person who learned the material over the course of time, and then reviewed the day before the exam. This chapter gives you proven study strategies that not only help you assimilate the material, but also help improve your long-term memory. Not all study techniques work for everyone. Review the techniques suggested below and select the study strategies that will help you.

PROVEN STUDY STRATEGIES

Study to learn and retain. Chapter 5, "Assessing Your Strengths and Weaknesses,'" demonstrates how to determine your strong and weak areas. Chapter 6, "Developing Your Personal Study Plan," helps you prepare a study plan to fit your life and to meet the deadline of the CPA exam. How do you go about studying the material that you have identified? Use a variety of study techniques, and practice, practice, and practice.

BREAK THE MATERIAL INTO SUBTOPICS (BITE-SIZED CHUNKS)

Divide the material into bite-sized chunks. Like the process of eating, a person who quickly gulps down a meal is subject to an upset stomach; whereas, the person who eats slowly, taking time to chew several times, has a much easier time digesting a meal. Subtopics are easy to study for a few minutes at a time. Research shows people absorb concepts quicker when they break the material into small themes. Before you can compute the amount of interest expense paid on a particular bond, you must first understand how to compute the amortization of the premium or discount. Take baby steps first, then start walking, and before you know it, you will be running. In other words, take the time to understand the foundation first.

Refer to your study plan. If you are taking a CPA review, the material should be broken up for you. If you are self-studying, break the material into chapters or modules as shown in your CPA review textbooks. Recall that your college accounting, auditing, and tax texts contain too much material, are probably out of date, and are class-focused instead of CPA exam-focused. Try not to study from your texts. Use CPA review-oriented manuals that are less than 1 year old.

People learn best when they divide up the material. A bite-sized chunk is a portion of the material, not the entire area. For example, bonds are tested on the financial and accounting (FARE) portion of the exam. The area of bonds is a very broad area. Are we talking about bond investments or bonds payable? Let's say bonds payable. Now, we can further subdivide bonds payable into nine concept areas.

1. Bond terminology and definitions
2. Determining the present value
3. Accounting for bond issue costs
4. Bonds issued between interest payment dates
5. Bonds issued with detachable warrants
6. Accounting for convertible bonds
7. Amortization of bond discounts and premiums using the straight-line method
8. Amortization of bond discounts and premiums using the effective interest methods
9. Retirement of bonds

Studying the concepts one area at a time will allow you to master topics in a short period of time.

STUDY OVER SHORT TIME INTERVALS

Do you really need a big block of time to learn something? Most candidates believe they do. Here's what typically happens. All week long you say you will postpone your studying until Saturday with the idea that you will have a big block of time. Saturday comes around and you wake up and say you will study as soon as you run errands. At the dry cleaners you run into a friend and go out for lunch. Then after lunch, on the way to the library, you decide your car is dirty. After you wait in line at the car wash, you decide it's almost time for dinner. Your day has been used up without you ever having cracked open a book. Wait a minute. Why didn't you study in your car while you were waiting in the line at the car wash? In less than 15 minutes you could have learned the terms that pertain to bonds. Why didn't you tell your friend you planned to study today, and you will lunch with him or her for 30 minutes as long as he or she spends another 30 minutes quizzing you? No sacrifice, little accomplished. Even if you spend the whole day studying, is it possible to really stay focused the entire time?

Most studies show that 15- to 30-minute study intervals are far more productive than large blocks of time.

The story above demonstrates that if you had divided the material into bite-sized chunks, you would not have wasted so much time. You could have studied between errands. In fact, your errands could have served as a study break. You don't need an entire block of time. Once you break the old habit of believing that you must have several hours to study, you will find you have more study time. You will be less likely to procrastinate and more likely to jump in and learn.

Should you worry about dividing the material? No. You really don't have the time to analyze the entire CPA exam content. By purchasing reputable CPA review materials, you will already have the material broken down into enough subheadings. Check your review manuals for topic subdivisions. The more subtopics you see, the better.

Where does one find short bits of time? The following list suggests how to carve short study intervals out of your normal day:

- In the morning, when you are drinking your morning beverage, try reading CPA materials instead of the newspaper.
- Throughout the day, whenever you sit down, read CPA materials instead of a book or those old magazines.
- Whenever you are in a line, use the time to study--lines at the school waiting for your children, lines at the subway, lines at the car wash, and any other line
- During your work commute why not study on the train or subway? You can even study in your car driving to and from work. Of course, this would be via recorded lectures. Be careful not to read and drive at the same time.
- In the evening, when you go to bed, study. Get used to putting yourself to sleep with your study materials. Not only will you go to sleep quicker, you will also retain the material longer, as your mind will be clear, ready to absorb the information.
- When performing routine workouts, such as stepping stairs, jogging, or bicycling, you can study. This time doesn't have to be used for practicing problems or reading. Use the time to listen to recordings of the material. Recordings are especially useful when studying Law and Auditing, the two exam sections that require words.
- During your lunch, study. Passing the CPA exam takes sacrifice. Give up 30 to 40 minutes of your lunch hour. Pretend you no longer have a lunch hour. Now, you have a quick brown bag lunch

that takes 10 minutes to eat, and the rest of the time is spent studying.

- When you are in the passenger's seat en route to the mall or to the relatives, study. If you happen to be driving, listen to recordings.

These are just some of the many ways you can find time to study. Take a moment and think about your typical work day by listing your normal routine. Once you write down your daily activities, you will see where you might find time to study. Break the habit of believing it must be a day off from work before you can study. Start new habits. It only takes about three weeks to form a habit. After three weeks, you will have a new habit of taking time out of your day to study every day. Your confidence level will increase each day as you learn more material. You can be proud that every day you are one step closer toward your goal of becoming a CPA.

WRITE IT DOWN

The age-old image of school children writing each spelling word 10 times is a good model to follow when you are struggling to absorb and remember a difficult technical concept. Let's say you have trouble remembering the formula for computing the amount of revenue from an installment sale contract. The formula is quite involved. Write it down. Use pen and paper or type it on the computer. It's the performance of the repetitive task that will help you. Take a break and write the formula down over and over again. Make an index card of the formula and put it in a pile that you will review once a week. Repeat it often.

Having trouble grasping a topic? Draw two columns. In one column write down what you know. In the other, write down the question areas, in other words, what you don't know. Ask your review instructor, your friend, or your accounting professor for tips on the question areas, but be sure the person you ask is technically competent and up to date on the topic.

SAY IT OUT LOUD

You learn by hearing. What better voice to hear than your own. Wouldn't it be wonderful if in the middle of the Law exam, you hear your voice reminding you about the elements of a contract? Talk to yourself. Repeat concepts out loud and repeat them often.

Prepare your own tape recordings. Record yourself listing the fraud risk factors for auditing. Later, listen to the recording on your way to work or to the mall. Sort the laundry, do the dishes, and listen to yourself repeating the concepts. After a while you will be able to fast-forward the tape over the sections that you could repeat in your sleep.

Give your index cards, book, or notes to someone else and let the person quiz you. Answer the questions out loud. Your long-term memory will improve greatly by repeating concepts out loud.

TAPE IT TO THE BATHROOM MIRROR

It's time to learn a particular audit report. You must know the elements of a classified balance sheet and a multiple-step income statement. Tape the model to your bathroom mirror. Every morning, when you brush your teeth, read the model. As you are putting away your toothbrush and toothpaste or combing your hair, look in the mirror and recite aloud what you have just read. One week of grooming with CPA exam concepts and you will have memorized many concepts. Time to replace the model. Tape another example up to study the next week.

PREPARE A SUMMARY

Some areas require the preparation of a summary. The four steps to considering internal control is a good example of several concepts that are important to learn for the Auditing exam. Spending time to summarize the process helps reinforce the main ideas. See Exhibit 1 for a summary example. Review your summary and make several copies of it. Place copies in strategic places like the bathroom, car glove compartment, work desk drawer, your briefcase, nightstand, or near your favorite chair. Whenever you have a free moment, review the summary sheets. You learn as you prepare the summary. You will recall the concepts when you review them and when you complete practice quizzes.

Exhibit 1: Summary--Four (4) step approach to internal control

1. **Obtain and document an understanding of internal control**

    Why is the auditor understanding the internal control process?

    - **To plan the audit** by determining the nature, timing, and extent of tests to be performed
    - **Required by GAAS**
    - Identify **potential misstatements**
    - Consider factors that affect the **risk** of material misstatement

    What is internal control?

    - A **process** established by the Board of Directors, management, and other personnel, designed to provide reasonable assurance that management achieves three (3) objectives:
        - Reliable financial reporting

- Effective and efficient operations
- Compliance with laws and regulations

*What must the auditor **understand**?*

- The five (5) internal control components (**MARIE**)

  - Control Environment (Also know the 7 factors--**HAMBOCI**)
  - Risk Assessment
  - Control Activities (performance reviews, information processing, physical controls, and segregation of duties)
  - Information and Communication
  - Monitoring of the Controls

- **Direct** relationship between the above **internal control components** and the three (3) **management objectives** listed above

*What is the auditor doing during the **understanding**?*

- Understanding the **design** and whether the controls have been **placed in operation**--is the client **using** controls?
- **Document** by flowcharts, narrative memos, questionnaires, and/or decision tables

*NOTE: When the auditor is **understanding** the controls, they are not evaluating the **control effectiveness**--evaluating control effectiveness is done by performing tests of controls*

2. **Assess Control Risk**

- Definition of control risk: The risk that the internal controls will not prevent or detect a material misstatement in the FS on a timely basis.

- Auditor hopes to keep control risk low and assess control risk **below maximum.**

- Definition of assessed level of control risk: The conclusion reached as a result of assessing control risk.

- Assessing control risk is the process of evaluating the effectiveness of an entity's internal control in preventing or detecting material misstatements in the FS. **Control risk should be assessed in terms of the FS assertions.**

- **Assessing control risk at below maximum** involves:

  - Identifying specific controls relevant to specific FS assertions that will be likely to prevent or detect material misstatements in those assertions **and**
  - Performing tests of controls to evaluate the control **effectiveness**

- Control risk can be assessed below maximum for all or some of the FS assertions.

- Controls can be either directly or indirectly related to a FS assertion. The more indirect the relationship, the less effective that control may be in reducing the control risk for that assertion.

- The auditor must assess control risk at **maximum** when three (3) conditions occur:

    - The client is not using any controls. Therefore, it would be **ineffective (road kill)** to perform tests of controls.
    - In the unusual case where performing tests of controls would be more expensive **(inefficient)** than performing substantive tests. Skip the tests of controls. Recall, tests of controls are optional.
    - The auditor cannot relate (link) the client's controls to one or more FS assertions.

- If the auditor must assess control risk at maximum, the control risk is high and detection risk must be kept low. As detection risk decreases, the auditor should:

    - Increase the amount of substantive testing
    - Perform the tests closer to the balance sheet date
    - Use more effective audit procedures (obtain more outside evidence)

3. **Perform Tests of Controls:**

- Definition of tests of controls: Tests directed toward testing the **design** or **operation** of the internal controls to determine if the controls are operating **effectively**.

- Four (4) techniques used to perform tests of controls:

    - Observation (best for segregation of duties)
    - Inspection
    - Inquiry
    - Reperformance

- Tests of controls must be related to one or more FS assertion

- Tests of controls are optional. However, if the auditor wants to assess control risk below maximum, the auditor is **required** to perform tests of controls. Why? The auditor must provide proof that the controls are operating effectively.

- **Control effectiveness** is tested using three (3) questions:

    - **How** were the control procedures applied? Were the control procedures applied in the proper manner?

- **By whom** were the controls performed?
- Were the necessary controls **consistently** applied?

- Tests of controls are usually performed at **interim**. Test again at year-end only if circumstances or personnel have significantly changed.

- Does the auditor test all internal controls?   No, the auditor will only test those controls that relate to items the auditor uses in performing audit procedures.

4. **Reassess control risk**

   - Based on the results of the tests of controls, the auditor makes a final assessment of control risk.

   - If controls are not operating effectively, the auditor assesses control risk at **maximum** and documents the following two (2) items:

     1. The **understanding** of the internal controls and
     2. The **conclusion** that control risk is assessed at **maximum**

   - If the tests of controls prove that one or more controls are operating effectively as related to one or more FS assertions, the auditor can assess control risk at **below maximum** for that assertion and must document the following three (3) items:

     1. The **understanding** of the internal controls
     2. The **conclusion** that control risk assessed **below** maximum **and**
     3. The **basis** for the conclusion (the fact that the controls are operating effectively

   - **Recall:** The auditor may assess control risk at **maximum** for some FS assertions, and **below maximum** for other FS assertions.

   - Auditor does not rely entirely on internal controls because even the very best controls may break down due to the following **inherent limitations**:

     - Misunderstandings
     - Mistake in human judgments
     - Carelessness
     - Mistake due to human failure such as simple error
     - Collusion
     - Management override

PREPARE LAST-MINUTE STUDY PACKETS

You are fearful you will forget some very important concepts. Fear greatly decreases your ability to perform. To alleviate fear, prepare a last-minute study packet. Purchase four pocket folders, one for each exam section, as your "last-minute study packet." Place summary pages, last-minute lists, and troublesome formulas in the folder. Review your packets the night before the exams. Review the packets one more time, using the mornings to review the Law and ARE packets and the lunch period to review Audit and FARE.

PREPARE YOUR OWN FLASH CARDS

Purchased flash cards are convenient and easy to use. However, there is no substitute for preparing your own. Purchase four colors of index cards. Pick a different color for each exam section. Pick the size you want to use. Begin each index card with a heading so it is clear what you are talking about. For example, an index card acquainting the CPA candidate with the different funds used in accounting for governmental entities would say: "Eight Governmental Funds." Be specific to help you remember. If you just wrote "governmental funds" you would not be helping your mind to recall that there are eight funds. Then number the funds on your card. You have learned because you wrote it down. You will be reminded every time you study the card and every time you repeat the concepts out loud.

The color coding of the cards is important. You can shuffle them, drop them, or combine them, but if they are color-coded you will never forget what they pertain to. The color association also helps on the exam.

Make index cards only of things you **do not know**. It is a waste of time to write out a concept that you can recall. Too many cards can overwhelm you and cause loss of valuable study time. Believe in yourself. If you know the concept today, chances are you will remember the same concept 4 months from now. Periodically take practice quizzes to test your long-term memory.

Prepare the index cards from the questions. If you answer a homework question incorrectly, ask yourself if you have learned the concept and will retain the concept for later use. If the answer is yes, you will remember, do not prepare a card. If the answer is no, you won't remember, make the index card by using the information in the question. See Exhibit 2 for a sample law index card and its application.

Exhibit 2: Sample index card and its application

Assume you were answering the following law question about coinsurance.

Clark Corporation owns a warehouse purchased for $150,000 in 1999. The current market value is $200,000. Clark has the ware-house insured for fire loss with Fair Insurance Corporation and Zone Insurance Company. Fair's policy is for $150,000 and Zone's policy is for $75,000. Both policies contain standard 80%

coinsurance clauses. If a fire totally destroyed the warehouse, what total dollar amount would Clark receive from Fair and Zone?

a. $225,000
b. $200,000
c. $135,000
d. $150,000

You are totally clueless about the formula. You go to your review materials and see how they explain the answer. To make an index card from the question, you would do the following:

- Define what a coinsurance clause is
- List the formula to compute the dollar amount to be received by the insured
- List any special comments that you need to recall in this situation

Your index card should look like this:

HEADING:
Amount to be paid when coinsured

DEFINITION:
Insured party agrees to maintain insurance equal to a specified % of property value. If insured does not carry specified %, insurance company pays a proportionate amount.

FORMULA to determine proportionate amount:

$$\$\$ \text{ Recovered} = \text{Actual loss} \times \frac{\text{Amount of insurance}}{\text{Coinsurance \% x FMV property at time of loss}}$$

SPECIAL NOTES:
Formula does not apply when property is completely destroyed.
$$ Recovered when property is 100% destroyed is the lower of the market value of the property on the day of loss or total insurance carried.

QUESTION(S):
Page 67, # 4
Page 33, #16

Test the note card by working the above question:

The fire **totally destroyed** the warehouse so the above **coinsurance clause does not apply**. The insurance companies will each pay their proportionate share of the market value of the property on the day of the loss. Don't apply the coinsurance formula. Use a simple apportionment formula. Total insurance carried was $225,000 ($150,000 by Fair plus $75,000 by Zone). Current loss on the day of the fire was $200,000. The answer is "b" or $200,000. No need to apportion because the question asked what amount would the insurance companies pay in total. Let's keep it simple-- the total insurance was $225,000. No insurance company is going to pay you more than the property was worth ($200,000). Don't waste your time-- compare the value of the property on the day of the loss with the insurance. If there is enough insurance to cover the total loss (yes, there was $225,000 of insurance), the maximum the insured (Clark) can receive will be the market value of the property on the day of the loss.

See the reasoning used in the above question. Learn to talk to yourself to reason out answers. Use your common sense to understand the concepts, not just memorize the concepts. Clark shouldn't be making money on a fire. Clark should not receive more than the property is worth.

Your review materials should also contain an example question where you would apply the loss. Try this CPA law question:

In 1994, Pod bought a building for $200,000. At that time, Pod purchased a $150,000 fire insurance policy with Owners Insurance Company and a $50,000 fire insurance policy with Group Insurance Corporation. Each policy contained a standard 80% coinsurance clause. In 1998, when the building had a fair market value of $250,000, it was damaged in a fire. How much would Pod recover from Owners if the fire caused $180,000 in damage?

a. $90,000
b. $120,000
c. $135,000
d. $150,000

Time to apply the coinsurance formula. Apply the formula because the damage of $180,000 was less than the fair market value of $250,000. Plug your numbers in as follows:

$$\$\$ \text{ Recovered} = \text{Actual loss} \ \times \ \frac{\text{Amount of insurance}}{\text{Coinsurance \% x FMV property at time of loss}}$$

Actual loss $180,000
Amount of insurance from Owners $150,000
Coinsurance % Owners 80%
FMV at time of loss $250,000

$$\$\$ \text{ Recovered} = \$180,000 \ \times \ \frac{\$150,000}{80\% \text{ x } \$250,000} \qquad \text{Answer is: c. } \$135,000$$

The portion does not require many computations. However, the co-insurance formula is almost always tested. Don't leave home without knowing the concepts. Now you know your index card worked. At the bottom of the card, make notations of questions to use to test and review your knowledge. Two weeks from now, go to your review manual page and work the question number listed. Hopefully, you will still remember how to apply the concepts.

LINK THE CONCEPTS TO REAL-LIFE SITUATIONS

Build upon what you know. Link what you are learning to your real-life experiences. Once a year you file your individual tax return. Look at the tax form when you study the tax area. Think about the schedules you prepare for the external auditors. These schedules are what the auditors audit and what they include in their workpapers as audit evidence. You are a professional, so think professionally. Just because you are now studying for the CPA exam doesn't mean you should forget about what you have learned. CPA candidates tend to regress to the old college model where they study massive amounts of information over a short time period, using only the information from class notes and textbooks. Now you are a professional. The CPA exam is a professional exam. Use what you have learned from real-world experience to help you visualize and recall information. Linkage allows you to digest the information in bite-sized chunks. Build examples using your real-life experience.

USING MNEMONICS WITH CAUTION

Mnemonics is the use of letters to form a word that you will later use to recall concepts. For example, a common mnemonic to remember the five components of the internal control process is "MARIE." The memory device works like this:

M – **M**onitoring the internal control process
A – Control **A**ctivities
R – The entity's **R**isk assessment
I – **I**nformation and Communication system
E – Control **E**nvironment

One letter corresponds to one of the five internal control components. Mnemonics is helpful when you are first learning information. Realize the limitations. All you have learned is the list. The CPA exam of today no longer asks candidates to prepare a list. Today's CPA exam expects a candidate to be able to analyze and react to information. It would be terrible if all you could remember was "MARIE" and you couldn't recall what the mnemonic meant or how it was used. Employ mnemonics with caution.

DRAW AN EXAMPLE

Graphs, pictures, diagrams, and charts assist you in analyzing the information. Timelines are useful visuals to map out what is happening when. Graph what happens to the carrying value of the asset over time or what happens to the depreciation in the early years. Pictures help you remember;

a complicated audit topic such as control and detection risk can be dia-
grammed and easily analyzed for effects. A diagram of the audit risk model
is shown in Exhibit 3.

Exhibit 3: Example of an audit risk diagram

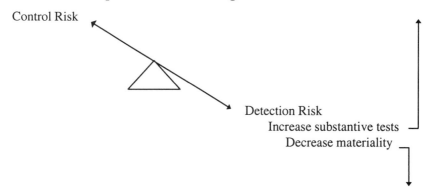

The above diagram reminds you that whenever control risk increases, detection
risk decreases. When detection risk decreases, substantive tests must increase
and materiality must decrease. A picture is easier to remember. The opposite is
true when control risk decreases. See the triangle in the middle. It represents a
teeter totter--when one end goes up the other must go down. If control risk goes
down (decreases), then detection risk would go up (increase). Now, substantive
testing would be decreased and materiality would be increased. All items are
now opposite. It takes many words to remember all of this, while one small
diagram shows it all.

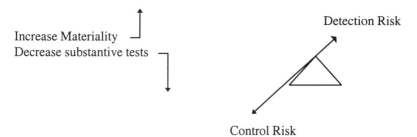

BOND WITH A STUDY BUDDY

Try studying with a coworker, college friend, or review course ac-
quaintance. A study buddy can help you stick to your study plan. A study
buddy works only if you study. When you meet your buddy at the library
only to spend the evening gabbing about the latest office gossip, the strategy
is not working for you. Here's how a study buddy situation works.

- Meet at a quiet place where you can each study on your own and later convene to discuss topics out loud. Library meeting rooms, your office at night or weekends, or a bookstore café are good places.
- Make a pledge to each other to be on time for the arranged study sessions. This gives you an excuse to leave your home and go study.
- Decide on a subtopic to study. If tonight's session is managerial accounting, bring the relevant materials with you.
- Determine the subtopics to study. Divide the topics into 30-minute time chunks.
- Go off and individually study the assigned topics.
- Reconvene at the established time. Work questions in your review materials one at a time. Go over the answers together. Assist each other to figure out and research answers to tough questions.
- Periodically test each other by selecting an essay or problem question for your buddy to complete. Exchange questions, go off to a quiet corner, and spend the correct amount of time preparing an answer. Grade each others' answers. Discuss the AICPA unofficial answer compared to your buddy's answer.
- Take a few minutes to complain about how difficult this exam is. Moan and groan about the breadth, depth, and timing of the exam. Go ahead, get it off your chest. It is far better to complain to your study buddy than it is to complain to your family, friends, and co-workers. Your study buddy really knows how you feel.
- Before you leave, agree upon the meeting time, place, and subject matter of the next study session. Tell your study buddy that you believe in him or her. Reinforce the idea that this exam is passable.

Study partners help to keep you on schedule, motivated, and encouraged. Two heads can solve a problem quicker than one. Dump your study buddy if he or she doesn't keep the schedule, isn't supportive, isn't serious, or won't share information that helps you. Don't keep a relationship going with a lazy person. The exchange of information should be rich and equal. Limit the number of people in your study group to three. Any more and you will need schedules just to keep track of the study group. Keep your study process simple.

REVIEW OF STUDY STRATEGIES

What do all of the above study techniques have in common? They give you the opportunity to study at a minute's notice. Your study materials are handy. They encourage you to study using small amounts of time to improve your long-term memory. They eliminate the guilt of not studying by allowing you to use every free moment to get something done. Consider using all of the above strategies. The variety will help keep you interested in the study process. Too many candidates think of studying as something to do when they want to punish themselves. Tell yourself that studying is fun; it can be if you frequently change the methods used. Studying is also rewarding. When you find you actually know answers, you will be so excited. Understand that all of the sacrifices and the time spent studying pay off. To give this exam your best, you must utilize every spare moment of time. There is much to learn--get excited about it!

TAKE THE TIME TO SLEEP

You can't study, read, write, or retain information when you are tired. Sleep is important throughout the study and exam process. If you find yourself waking up in the middle of the night with exam anxiety, simply switch on your night light, grab the study sheets that are conveniently sitting on your nightstand, and study yourself to sleep. The best cure for insomnia is reading CPA materials. They will put you to sleep quicker than anything sold on the market today.

TRY KEEPING IT QUIET

You like noise. You study in the middle of the family room while the television is blaring, your teenagers or roommates are talking on the phone, and the dog is barking. Try studying in a quiet place. Studies show you will learn the information more quickly and retain it longer. There won't be much background noise at the real exam. It's a good idea to get used to a similar environment now. Try to simulate the actual test atmosphere.

JUST KEEP GOING

Don't give up. Expect ups and downs in the study process. You may think the road to the CPA exam is linear. In actuality, it is full of bumps, hurdles, and ups and downs. The quickest method to dig yourself out of a rut is to sit down and study. Stop feeling sorry for yourself. Don't tackle the difficult areas if you are down. Select an area that you enjoyed studying while in college. Begin with an easy, fun area. The minute you get back to your original plan, you will feel the guilt and fear going away. Squelch your fears with action. Hard work and determination will help you feel better. Look at Exhibit 4 and admit that this is the way it's going to be. See that after every downturn there can also be an upswing.

Exhibit 4: The journey to prepare to pass the CPA Exam

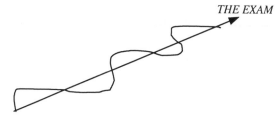

THE EXAM

THE START OF STUDY PROCESS

In Exhibit 4, the up and down line represents your performance. The straight-line shows how the ideal world would prepare for the exam. Exam preparation just isn't a linear process. Exam preparation is like a golf game. You see the hole and you attempt to drive the ball. The best plan would be to drive the ball straight to the hole, yet your game plan seldom turns out like that. Eventually you get to the green and putt in for the finish. Your journey was anything but straight. The ups and downs you experience are part of the game. Accept the hooks, sand traps, water holes, hurdles, and the rough, but never give up the game or the plan. Keep on trying. Your hard work will be rewarded at the finish line.

PERSONALLY SPEAKING

My biggest challenge is to motivate CPA candidates to never give up. Accountants are a unique group of people. We are dynamic, fun-loving, and extremely detailed. We can absorb great amounts of technical information, and numbers have never bothered us. We are anything but "bean counters." We are often overly critical of ourselves. It's time to give yourself a break. Understand the problems you might encounter. Accept the ups and downs. Talk to yourself. Listen to the CD recording. Perfection is not your goal. You only want to learn enough to pass. A score of 75% allows some room for mistakes, misunderstandings, and misapplication of concepts. Your choices are few. You can give up now and you will never be a CPA. You can continue to work toward the dream of accomplishing your goal. The choice is yours. Keep the dream alive--continue to study.

8 TIME MANAGEMENT

This chapter deals with time management at the actual CPA exam. See Chapter 6, "Developing Your Personal Study Plan," for tips on how to manage your time while studying. Time management is crucial. Suggested time allotments are no longer provided on the exam. Be prepared to allocate your time. Take control of the exam by apportioning the total exam time among the questions at the beginning of each exam section. Traditionally you will be pushed for time on the Law section. Time pressure may be a factor in FARE, because you are tired and eager to complete the exam process. The total time for Audit is comfortable as long as the candidate sticks to the time management plan and doesn't spend too much time on one particular area. The total time allocated to the ARE section is very generous; candidates usually finish early with as much as 50 to 90 minutes to spare. Don't take time for granted--time can be your greatest enemy. Plan and apportion your time and apply the appropriate techniques to each question type.

MULTIPLE-CHOICE TIME MANAGEMENT

Examine the suggested time management plans shown in Exhibits 1-4 at the end of this chapter. Apply a per question time factor to the multiple-choice. For example, Law requires 1½ minutes per each multiple-choice question. In other words, you want to complete 20 multiple-choice questions every 30 minutes. Take control of the exam by sectioning off the questions. As soon as the proctors announce, "You may begin," open your question booklet and write 9:30 by multiple-choice question number 20. Write 10:00 by multiple-choice number 40 and 10:30 by question number 60. Use the times as your guideline. If you get to question number 20 and it is 9:20, slow down! There is no need to rush. Read each question carefully so as not to miss clues, dates, and terms. If you reach question number 20 and it's 9:45, you are working too slowly. Stay calm but be aware that you are now running behind. Perhaps you will make the time up on the next 20 questions. Try skipping questions you cannot figure out. If you have time you can come back to them.

Should you practice time management when you study? Yes, occasionally take a practice quiz by selecting 20 multiple-choice quesitons to see if you can complete them within 30 minutes for the Law and ARE sections. Please note that Law and ARE questions require 1½ minutes per multiple-choice, Audit takes 2 minutes per question, and FARE requires about 2½ minutes per question. A quick reference for how many multiple-choice questions to complete in 30 minutes is as follows:

- Complete 20 multiple-choice questions every 30 minutes for Law and ARE
- Complete 15 multiple-choice questions every 30 minutes for Audit
- Complete 12 multiple-choice questions every 30 minutes for FARE

Don't worry about time management when you are trying to learn a topic. The important factor during the study process is to learn the concept. A hurry-up attitude is not conducive to learning. However, you have no choice but to budget your time on the real exam. A well-trained candidate will see questions he or she studied. This is wonderful, as you will gain confidence from the fact you have seen the concept before and remember it. You know you have answered at least one question correctly. Remain confident and continue to believe that you really do know something.

Count on seeing questions that you know nothing about. Sometimes you must guess. Always attempt an educated guess rather than an outright guess. An educated guess means you have eliminated answers you know are incorrect and have narrowed your choices. For all outright guesses, pick a letter and use it consistently. The letter "b" is a good choice. Whenever you truly know nothing about the topic, answer "b." Don't waste valuable time deciding which letter to pick. The answer "b" is bound to be correct for at least some of your guesses.

The time management process must also include time to transfer the answer to the Scantron™ sheet. The best method is to select your answer, circle it in your exam booklet, and immediately transfer the answer to the scan sheet. Take the time as you go along to blacken in the ovals. Carefully match the question number with the number on the answer sheet. Be aware that multiple-choice question answer sheets may vary. Law Scantron numbers could go across the answer sheet. Audit answers may run down the sheet. ARE answers may go diagonally. There can be as many as four different answer forms. Be deliberate and carefully match the question number to the answer sheet.

CHANGING MULTIPLE-CHOICE ANSWERS

Why should you take the time to circle the answer in your question booklet when you know the question booklet will be shredded and the graders will not look at it? You are circling the answers for your edit and review process. Complete the entire exam first. Proofread the essays and problems. If you still have time, go back and review your multiple-choice and other objective formats. Change answers only when it is clearly evident that you made a mistake. If you are unsure, leave your answer as is. Changing your first answer is dangerous. Your first selection is probably the best one. Change answers with caution and only when you are absolutely certain that your first selection was incorrect.

ESSAY, PROBLEM, AND OTHER OBJECTIVE ANSWER FORMAT TIME MANAGEMENT

Essays, problems, and other objective answer format questions utilize a formula of minutes to points. For example, if an essay is worth 10 points, you should allocate 20 minutes, or 2 minutes per point. How do you know how many points a question is worth? Look at the front of your exam question booklet. Here you will see how many points each question is worth. Don't worry about the multiple-choice points, as you are applying a time factor per question, not per point. (See Chapter 10 for special tips about writing essays.) Control your time from the start. Before you begin an essay question, determine the time to be spent (e.g., 15 point essay, 30 minutes) and write the time you should complete the essay at the top of your paper. Don't write the time you began the essay because every time you check your watch, you would have to spend extra time recalculating how much time you have left. By writing the time you should complete the essay by, you can quickly glance at your watch and see how many minutes you have left.

TIME IS TIGHT ON LAW

Expect the time on Law to be tight. (See Chapter 17 for special techniques to increase your speed on Law.) Expecting a tight timetable and reacting to a tight timetable are two different things. Relax and follow the guidelines. Think about the untrained CPA candidate who doesn't even know they must control and manage their time. You have a great advantage. You know what you must do and you know how to do it. You won't be surprised at the end of the Law exam, as you are monitoring your time throughout the exam. On the first set of 20 multiple-choice questions you will know whether you are working too slowly, too quickly, or just right. You can lose time by reading the question too slowly, reading questions without focus and not remembering what you just read, or spending too much time trying to guess. Read carefully but quickly, always concentrating on the question and not on what is going on around you. Don't think beyond the question you are working on. Focus on the task at hand by highlighting key points, diagramming the situation, and reading the requirements before you answer the question. Read the question part first, then up to the data. Now when you read the data, you will be able to label what is important and cross out the information that is not needed. Expect time pressure on Law and budget and monitor your time carefully.

Your Time Is Up--It's Serious Business

Fifteen minutes before each exam section ends, the proctors will make an announcement. The sound of the proctor's voice will probably make you jump because you are concentrating so hard. The proctors are very serious about time. The Law exam will end at noon, whether you are ready or not. When you hear the 15-minute announcement, stop and make sure you have blackened in your ovals on the Scantron sheet. Don't risk the chance that you will not have time to complete the answer sheet. The proctors do not allow extra time to complete an answer sheet. Keep the end times in mind. Law and ARE end at noon. Audit and FARE end at 6:00 p.m. Time is serious business. Watch it!

A Good Watch Is a Must

Use a familiar watch. If you buy a new watch for the CPA exam, be sure you have used and practiced with it for 1 to 2 weeks before the exam. Be assured that you can easily read the time and that the watch keeps accurate time. Don't count on a clock being visible from your seat. Setting beepers or alarms to go off during the exam is forbidden. The proctors could confiscate your watch. Learn to gauge your time without an alarm going off. Change the watch battery so it does not run out at the exam.

TIME MANAGEMENT GUIDELINES

Make several copies of the time management guidelines shown in the following exhibits. Put one copy in your last-minute study packet folder. Review the guidelines before each exam section, as they vary from section to section. Put the other copies in the places where you occasionally rest. Review them frequently. Have a family member or friend quiz you on the applicable times per question type and per exam section.

Don't Assume You Will Have Extra Time

People say not to worry about time pressure on ARE. You never know. You never know when the examiners may write a difficult exam that requires many computations and the use of every minute. Always arrive on time for each exam section, about 15 minutes before the scheduled start time. Take control and budget your time. Monitor your time as you progress. Don't take any chances. You want to show the graders what you know by having the time to at least attempt each and every question. The general guidelines are easy to remember.

- Essay, problem, and other objective answer format questions: allow 2 minutes per point for all exam sections
- Law and ARE multiple-choice questions: allow 1½ minutes per question; complete 20 multiple-choice questions every 30 minutes
- Audit multiple-choice questions: allow 2 minutes per question; complete 15 multiple-choice questions every 30 minutes
- FARE multiple-choice questions: allow 2½ minutes per question; complete 12 multiple-choice questions every 30 minutes.

Follow the time guidelines and always take time seriously.

PERSONALLY SPEAKING

Take time management seriously. Firsthand evidence of how misapplication of time can really hurt was painfully apparent in the situation where one candidate overlooked time management. She had had no time issues until she reached the FARE exam. Feeling confident that she had performed well and knowing that the exam was soon going to be over, she did not take the time to allocate or even worry about applying her time management techniques. After all, her friends had told her she would have no problems with time since she always completed tests quickly in college. She, like the other candidates, was very tired but looked forward to the end. She was sitting in the back of the room and did not hear the 15-minute announcement. In fact, she didn't hear any of the closing announcements. It wasn't until a proctor came over and told her to put her pencil down (the exam was over) that she realized she had made a terrible mistake. She was in the process of reviewing her multiple-choice answers. She told the proctor that she would put her pencil down after she had blackened in the ovals on her Scantron sheet. The proctor calmly and politely informed her that she was not allowed to do so. Time was up. She was not permitted to complete the scantron sheet. She cried and begged to be allowed to complete the Scantron. Her appeal was denied. It was turned in blank, no marks, resulting in zero points on the multiple-choice and other objective portion.

The above mistake cost her dearly. Her scores were as follows:

- Law   92
- Audit   98
- ARE   97
- FARE   37

Do you see the problem? She not only failed FARE, but she did not even obtain a condition, as she did not receive at least a 50 on the FARE, a requirement in the state of Illinois where she sat for the exam. She had to repeat the entire exam. If she had been allowed to enter her other objective and multiple-choice answers on the Scantron, she would have passed. Her question booklet was shredded. The grades are taken off the answer sheets. Let this be an important lesson. Complete the answer sheets as you progress through the exam. The AICPA makes it very clear that you will not be given extra time to complete the exam. The candidate was devastated; she was on target to pass the exam and to probably receive an award for her high scores. The only comfort I could offer was to tell her she really knows the material and that I would give her a free CPA review for the next exam.

She did not repeat the review. She took the next exam, which cost her time and money, and 6 months later, did pass with scores in the upper 70s. Learn from her story and watch your time carefully. Know that you will not receive additional time. Take the time to learn, practice, and apply time management techniques.

Exhibit 1

LAW
(Business Law and Professional Responsibilities)

TIME MANAGEMENT

➤   Budget your time--take control of the exam

➤   Wednesday, Law 9:00 – Noon

CAUTION: Watch your time! Candidates have experienced time pressure on Law.

- **Multiple-choice questions:**   1½ minutes per **question** (Complete 20 multiple-choice questions every 30 minutes)
  - Usually worth 60 points
  - Usually 66 multiple-choice questions, with 60 used to score at 1 point each

- **Essays and other objective answer format questions:**   2 minutes per point
  - Points are listed by question on the front of the exam question booklet
  - Essays can be one 20-point essay or two 10-point essays

SUGGESTED TIME ALLOTMENT FOR LAW

Question type	Estimated percentage	Time per	Estimated total time
Multiple-choice	**60 points**--66 questions with 6 thrown out--grade based upon 60 questions at 1 point each	1½ minutes per question HINT: 20 multiple-choice questions every 30 minutes	100 minutes
Other objective answer format	**20 points**--could be two at 10 points each, or one at 20 points, or one 15 point and one 5-point (please remain flexible)	2 minutes per point	40 minutes
Essays	**20 points**--could be one large essay worth 20 points or two 10-point essays	2 minutes per point	40 minutes
			180 minutes (3 hours)

Exhibit 2

AUDIT

TIME MANAGEMENT

> ➤ Budget your time--take control of the exam

> ➤ Wednesday, Audit 1:30 – 6:00 p.m.

RELAX! Watch your time! However, candidates usually complete exam about 5:30 p.m. Use extra time to read and understand the other objective answer format questions. Remember to work from the charts and label items in the other objective answer format questions BEFORE you begin answering the questions. Proofread your essay(s).

- **Multiple-choice questions:** 2 minutes per **question** (Complete 20 multiple-choice questions every 40 minutes)
    - Usually worth 50 points
    - Usually 85 multiple-choice questions, with 75 used to score at 2/3 point each

- **Other objective answer format:** 2 minutes per **point**
  - Points are listed by question on the front of the exam question booklet
  - Usually 30 points

- **Essay(s):** 2 minutes per **point**
  - Usually 20 points

SUGGESTED TIME ALLOTMENT FOR AUDIT

Question type	Estimated percentage	Time per	Estimated total time
Multiple-choice	**50 points**--Eighty-five questions with 8 thrown out-- grade based upon 75 questions at 2/3 point each.	2 minutes per question HINT: 20 multiple-choice questions every 40 minutes	170 minutes
Other objective answer format	**30 points**--could be three at 10 points each, or one at 30 points, or two 15-point questions (please remain flexible)	2 minutes per point	60 minutes
Essays	**20 points**--could be one multiple-part essay worth 20 points or two 10-point essays	2 minutes per point	40 minutes
			270 minutes (4½ hours)

Exhibit 3

ARE
(Accounting and Reporting)

TIME MANAGEMENT

➢ Budget your time--take control of the exam

➢ Thursday, ARE 8:30 – Noon

RELAX! Watch your time! However, candidates usually complete exam about 11:00 a.m. Use extra time to read and understand the other objective answer format questions. Remember to work from the charts and label items in the other objective answer format questions BEFORE you begin answering the questions.

- **Multiple-choice questions:** 1.5 minutes per **question** (Complete 20 multiple-choice questions every 30 minutes)
  - Usually worth 60 points
  - Usually 83 multiple-choice questions, with 75 used to score at 8/10 (.8) point each

- **Other objective answer format:** 2 minutes per **point**
  - Points are listed by question on the front of the exam question booklet
  - Usually 40 points

SUGGESTED TIME ALLOTMENT FOR ARE

Question type	Estimated percentage	Time per	Estimated total time
Multiple-choice question	**60 points**--Eighty-three questions with 8 thrown out--grade based upon 75 questions at 8/10 (.8) point each.	1.5 minutes per question HINT: 20 multiple-choice questions every 30 minutes	125 minutes
Other objective answer format	**40 points**--could be four at 10 points each, or one at 40 points, or two 15-point and two 5-point questions (please remain flexible)	2 minutes per point	80 minutes
	CUSHION: Use extra 5 minutes to test calcula-tor. Follow instructions on the calculator box. Report calculator failure to proctor and request a new one.		5 minutes
			210 minutes (3½ hours)

Exhibit 4

FARE
(Financial Accounting and Reporting)

TIME MANAGEMENT

➢ Budget your time--take control of the exam

➢ Thursday, FARE 1:30 – 6:00 p.m.

> CAUTION: Watch your time! Candidates have experienced time pressure on FARE.

- **Multiple-choice questions:** 2½ minutes per **question** (Complete 20 multiple-choice questions every 50 minutes)
  - Usually worth 60 points
  - Usually 66 multiple-choice with 60 used to score at 1 point each
- **Other objective answer format:** 2 minutes per **point**
  - Points are listed by question on the front of the exam question booklet
  - Question could be part essay/problem and part other objective

SUGGESTED TIME ALLOTMENT FOR FARE

Question type	Estimated percentage	Time per	Estimated total time
Multiple-choice	**60 points**--66 questions with 6 thrown out-- grade based upon 60 questions at 1 point each	2½ minutes per question HINT: 20 multiple-choice questions every 50 minutes	165 minutes
Other objective answer format	**20 points**--could be two at 10 points each, or one at 20 points, or one 15-point and one 5-point (please remain flexible)	2 minutes per point	40 minutes
Essay(s) and problem(s)	**20 points**--could be one essay and one problem.	3 minutes per point	60 minutes
	CUSHION: Use to test calculator if FARE is first section you are taking. Report calculator failure to proctor and obtain a new one.		5 minutes
			270 minutes (4½ hours)

9 WRITING A BEAUTIFUL ESSAY ANSWER

Essay questions are utilized in three of the four exam sections: Law, Audit, and FARE. Answers to the essay questions must be written on the paper provided in the *Essay Paper* portion of the candidate examination booklet. Selected essay answers will be used to assess candidates' writing skills. Five percent of the total points available on each of the three examinations will be graded for adequate writing skills. It is very important for the candidate to understand how the graders award writing points. This chapter educates the reader about the proper techniques to use to earn concept points and writing skill points. The discussion begins with the evaluation of writing skills.

EVALUATION OF WRITING SKILLS

Five percent of the 100-point Law, Audit, and FARE examinations are graded for writing skills. The candidate does not have to be an expert in English and grammar. The AICPA has developed a list of six elements that they believe characterize effective writing as follows:

1. Coherent organization
2. Conciseness
3. Clarity
4. Use of standard English
5. Responsiveness to the requirements of the question
6. Appropriateness for the reader

Coherent organization refers to writing that flows in a logical manner. The reader easily follows the train of thought. Each main idea is presented in a well-developed separate paragraph. The main idea of the paragraph is discussed in the first sentence, and supporting sentences within the paragraph elaborate upon the main points. Each paragraph makes a smooth transition to the next paragraph.

Conciseness requires that the writer gets to the point without added detail. Ideas are fully supported without additional embellishment. Leave out the extra adjectives and flowing descriptions. Use lists to present ideas. Short sentences are preferred.

Clarity refers to a clear, well-constructed presentation. The writer's meaning and reasoning are clearly presented. Relevant and proper technical terms are used.

Standard English as defined in *The Business Writer's Handbook,* 4th Edition, New York, St. Martin's Press, 1993, refers to the language used to carry on the daily business of the nation. On the CPA exam, this means the writer should use the language most accountants use. Characteristics of standard English include proper punctuation and capitalization. Accurate spelling is necessary.

Responsiveness to the requirements of the question requires that the writer address the question requirement by responding in detailed specific terms rather than a broad exposition of general areas. The answer should focus on the specific elements presented in the question.

Writing that is appropriate for the reader takes the reader's background into account. For example, a different type of response is required for an eight-year-old child versus an adult. On the CPA exam, the candidate should assume the reader is a knowledgeable CPA unless told otherwise.

Most candidates believe that the graders award at least one point for each of the elements until the total writing points add up to five points. This is not how the essay grading process works.

ESSAY GRADING PROCESS

The selected essays are graded for writing skills using a "holistic" grading approach. Holism is defined as a theory that believes the whole is greater than the sum of the parts. By using a holistic grading approach, the graders read the essay and assign a score based on the incorporation of all six elements rather than awarding one point per element. The graders receive extensive training in applying the holistic grading method. Writing skills are assessed at levels ranging from weak to very good. A hypothetical grading scale developed by the author could be presented as follows:

Writing Skills Evaluation	*Number points earned*
Paper blank or almost blank	0
Writing **very** weak	1
Writing weak	2
Writing average	3
Writing good	4
Writing **very** good	5

See Exhibit 1 (page 225) in Chapter 21, "The Waiting Game," for a demonstration of how the essay writing score might be incorporated into the overall final essay grade. The AICPA *Information for Uniform CPA Examination Candidates* booklet contains an example of weak writing and an example of very good writing.   The weak writing sample includes the following problems:

- The writer did not specifically address the question requirements. The candidate talked about the question instead of directly answering the question.
- The writer jumped from one thought to another without providing a connecting link.
- Numerous grammar, punctuation, capitalization, and spelling errors were noted.
- The writer discussed irrelevant topics.
- Not all sentences were complete; several fragments were noted.

The assessment of very good writing cited the following strengths:

- No irrelevant information was given. The essay spoke to the question and provided a concise, clear answer.
- The essay was coherent with principal ideas presented in the first sentence of each paragraph. The remaining sentences developed and explained the ideas.
- The passage did not contain any ambiguous or misused words.
- The vocabulary was above average.
- The essay was relatively free of spelling, grammar, punctuation, and capitalization errors.

The best essay answers are simple, short, and address the question. Even the very good writing samples may contain some mistakes. The graders are not looking for perfection, as they understand that the typical CPA candidate is under considerable time pressure to complete the exam. Mistakes will be tolerated. However, the candidate should attempt to make it as easy as possible for the grader to award points.

MAKE IT EASY TO GRADE

Why make the graders work to find points? The graders are comparing the candidate's answers against a standardized grading guide. The more concepts the graders locate, the higher the score. Ideas to make the grader's job easier include

- Avoid the use of abbreviations
- Write legibly so the answer can be read
- Label all essay sections
- Begin every essay section with a lead-in sentence

- Use short, simple sentences
- Present a neat, clean paper

Avoid the use of abbreviations.   Jargon is commonplace in today's business world. Abbreviations and jargon have no place on the CPA exam. Written responses are not subject to interpretation. The exam graders are trained to limit their personal interpretations of the subject matter. For example, you may always use the abbreviation "IC" for internal control. If you use "IC" in your essay answer, the graders may not interpret the "IC" to mean internal control. Who knows, if the graders are hungry when they read your essay, they may think the "IC" stands for ice cream and become distracted thinking about the best flavor of ice cream to eat on the next break. Leave no room for interpretation. Take the time to fully write out all terms so there can be no misinterpretation of what you meant. Clearly state the facts.

Write legibly so the grader can read it. The average time spent on the initial production grading is 60 to 120 seconds per essay. The graders quickly read the response, looking for key words. If you write sloppily, your key words may not be noted. If you have poor handwriting, try printing the essay answer.

Label all essay sections. If there are five parts to the essay, label each part using the same notation as was used in the question. For example, if the essay parts were shown as a, b, c, d, and e, the candidate should label using the a-e notations. See Exhibit 2 (page 178) in Chapter 17, "Law-- You've Only Just Begun," for an example of an essay answer that is clearly labeled.

Begin each essay section with a lead-in sentence. A lead-in sentence simply repeats the question in sentence form. For example, if the question asks the candidate to identify the five components of internal control, the response would begin as follows:

The five components of internal control are control environment, control activities, business risk assessment, information and communication, and monitoring.

An alternative answer could be written using a numbered list. Numbered lists are quick for the grader to grade and look like this:

The five components of internal control are as follows:

- Control environment
- Control activities
- Business risk assessment
- Information and communication

• Monitoring

Note how the above list uses a complete sentence structure but makes it easier for the grader to quickly read the answer. Maximize points by using lists whenever possible.

Use short, simple sentences. Long sentences that continue on for lines and lines are very difficult to read. The graders don't have time to follow your thought process. A simple sentence structure helps the writer state the facts more concisely.

Present a neat clean paper. Write with a pencil instead of a pen. A pencil can be erased. Candidates are nervous and make mistakes. If the mistake is minor, take the time to erase. If you realize that you have used two pages of essay paper writing an answer that did not address the question requirement, simply cross out the entire two pages. Don't take the time to erase major mistakes. The graders understand the pressure that you are under. False starts are to be expected. If you run out of paper, ask the proctors for more.

HOW TO GET MORE ESSAY PAPER

Additional paper can be obtained from the proctors. When you see that you are on the last sheet of essay paper, raise your hand. Keep your hand in the air as you are writing. Show the proctor that you are on the last sheet of paper and need more. Obtaining additional paper should not create a problem. However, if the proctor refuses your request, get up and go to the front of the room and ask a proctor there. Usually the head proctors monitor the front of the exam room.

When you write your essay, use every line. Do not skip lines by using every other line. Read the instructions carefully. Sometimes candidates are asked to begin a new essay section on the next page. The rules will always require the candidate to begin an answer to a new question on the top of a new page. Use both the front and the back of the pages. See Exhibit 1 for a sample of official AICPA essay paper.

Insert the additional paper behind the other paper in the answer booklet. Insert both used and unused paper in the booklet. Recall that with a closed examination, it is considered cheating to remove examination paper from the exam room. Be sure to turn in all paper to the proctor at the end of the exam.

All papers turned in with the answer booklet will be graded. If you do not want the graders to grade something, such as your keywords, cross out the notations. Keywording essays is one of the six steps the candidate should follow.

SIX STEPS TO COMPLETE ESSAY ANSWERS

The preceding discussion deals with the form of the essay answer. While earning the five writing points is important, the candidate must not overlook the technical aspects of an essay question. The candidate must present both the correct form and the correct technical substance. There are six steps for completing an essay answer as follows:

- Calculate the time budget and write down the time you will **complete** the essay
- Read the essay requirements first
- Keyword each requirement
- Go back and read the question information, adding to the keyword list
- Write the essay answer in the answer booklet, using proper writing techniques
- Proofread the answer

Complete the steps in the order shown above. Exhibit 2, a sample Audit essay given on the May 1998 Audit exam, is used to demonstrate how the six steps are to be performed. Exhibit 2 presents a keyword outline. Note that the outline is not to be graded. The candidate lists the keywords in the **question** booklet, not the **answer** booklet. The written essay serves as a model of a well-written response with all sections clearly labeled. The first step to any essay is to calculate the budgeted time.

Step One--Budget: The Completion Time

For all essays on all sections, Law, Audit, and FARE, allow 2 minutes per point. If it's a five-point essay, allow 10 minutes to complete. The sample essay in Exhibit 2 was a ten-point essay, so a candidate should budget 20 minutes to complete. Look at your watch and note the time. Add 20 minutes to the time shown on your watch and write that time down at the top of the essay. For example, if it's 3:00 p.m., the candidate should write 3:20 at the top of the essay. By writing down the completion time, you will always know at a quick glance how much more time you have to finish writing the answer.

Step Two--Read the Requirements and Step Three--"Keyword" the Requirements

The sample essay in Exhibit 2 has three question requirements. Deal with one at a time. Requirement a. asks the candidate to describe the fraud risk factors that are indicated in the dialogue above. Stop and list (keyword) all of the fraud risk factors that you can remember. Note how we began the essay with the requirements. We did not start by reading the discussion between Kent, the engagement partner, and Smith, the senior auditor. Candidates who start at the beginning are likely to get too involved with the discussion and therefore become distracted by the words. Go directly to the requirements and list what you can. You don't need the discussion to guide you.

Continue to read each requirement and keyword them individually as you proceed. Don't read the data until you have finished outlining all of the requirements. There should be room in the margins of the question for the outline of keywords. Obviously you will have trouble outlining your answer to requirement b. before you read the discussion. It's important to see that in requirement b., the candidate is required to describe each misconception and to explain why each point is a misconception. When you encounter this type of requirement, stop and draw a chart to serve as a reminder that you must list and explain the misconceptions. The chart might look like this.

Describe the misconception	*Explain why* each point is a misconception

Step Four--Read the Question Information

Now it's time to go to the beginning of the essay and read all of the information. The candidate has not wasted time. Now as the person reads the question they know that they are looking for misconceptions regarding the consideration of fraud in the financial statement audit. As you read the discussion, highlight or underline everything you think might be a misconception. Add to your chart and the keyword outline as you go along. Take some time to reflect about each of the commentaries. Read slowly so as to comprehend what Smith and Kent are saying. You are using an organized essay approach that helps the candidate keep within the budgeted time frame. Reread some of the discussions. Then reread your keyword outline. Add anything that you think might be relevant.

Step Five--Write the Answer in the Answer Booklet

Spend most of the time formulating the answer. A well-planned outline makes the actual writing of the essay an easy task. Begin by labeling each requirement. Use a lead-in sentence for each requirement. Whenever possible, use lists. Keep the writing elements in mind and write so the grader can read your answer. Short, simple sentences are the best. Write on every line, skipping two to three lines in between the requirements. Then, when you proofread, you will have room to add additional information.

Step Six--Proofread the Answer

Most people think proofreading means just reading over your answer. That's only half the task. To make proofreading a meaningful exercise, the candidate should first reread each requirement and then go back and read over the answer. By rereading the requirement first, the candidate is verifying that he or she has answered what was asked.

Proofread slowly, looking for misspellings, incorrect verb tenses, and missing or incorrect punctuation. Look for missing words. It would be a terrible mistake to leave out a little word like "not," as this omission could change the whole meaning of your answer. It's no fun to proofread, yet it is a very important step that can make a huge difference in the total grade. If you have any time left after completing the proofreading step, think about your answer. Did you say enough?

SAY EVERYTHING YOU KNOW

While the sample Audit essay question was pretty straightforward, many exam essays are vague. Follow the simple essay rule of "if you think it is relevant, then say it." Demonstrate your knowledge by writing it down. The graders can't read your mind. There is no benefit to keeping the concepts in your head. Put all relevant information in your answer. After all, the exam is positively graded. Points will not be deducted from your grade for wrong statements. You must try. You'll earn points by stating the necessary concepts. Don't be timid--say it or you will be sorry. Be confident that you know what you are doing. Fight for those points.

Personally Speaking

The biggest mistake you can make on an essay it to leave the knowledge in your head. What do you plan to do with all of this concept knowledge after the exam? Yes, you will use much of what you have learned and reviewed in your daily work. However, I say give your brain a break by lightening up the load. Write the information down. Let the graders tell you whether or not your statement is important. List much more information than you think the graders might want.

In the days of the open exam, candidates used to share their individual essay answers and scores with me. We could purchase a copy of the actual essay response they wrote. By comparing the written response with the AICPA grade, we could get a pretty good idea of what the graders were looking for. This useful exercise taught me that a candidate must list as much as they can possibly think of for every essay answer. Sometimes a candidate would list 23 concepts just to obtain a score of seven points. You must not stop short of trying. You must keep on fighting, scratching, and crawling for points by listing every concept you can think of. I am always most proud of the candidate who tells me that his or her hand is about ready to fall off because he or she wrote so much. I know that you also want to earn the five writing points. You can earn those too by writing clearly. Don't stop short of a good answer. If in doubt, say it. You won't be disappointed.

Exhibit 1: Sample of AICPA official essay paper

E S S A Y   R U L E D   P A P E R

UNIFORM CERTIFIED PUBLIC ACCOUNTANT EXAMINATION
Business Law & Professional Responsibilities

CANDIDATE NUMBER
Record your 7-digit candidate number in the boxes.

QUESTION NUMBER
Write the question number in the box,
then completely blacken the oval.   ④✕⑤

Print your **STATE**
name here.

Question Number _____ Continues on Page _____ *OR* Question Number _____ Ends on this Page.

Exhibit 2: Sample audit essay

Kent, CPA, is the engagement partner on the financial statement audit of Super Computer Services Co. (SCS) for the year ended April 30, 1998. On May 6, 1998, Smith, the senior auditor assigned to the engagement, had the following conversation with Kent concerning the planing phase of the audit:

Kent: Do you have all the audit programs updated yet for the SCS engagement?

Smith: Mostly. I still have work to do on the fraud risk assessment.

Kent: Why? Our "errors and irregularities" program from last year is still OK. It's passed peer review several times. Besides, we don't have specific duties regarding fraud. If we find it, we'll deal with it then.

Smith: I don't think so. That new CEO, Mint, has almost no salary, mostly bonuses and stock options. Doesn't that concern you?

Kent: No, Mint's employment contract was approved by the Board of Directors just 3 months ago. It was passed unanimously.

Smith: I guess so, but Mint told those stock analysts that SCS's earnings would increase 30% next year. Can Mint deliver numbers like that?

Kent: Who knows? We're auditing the '98 financial statements, not '99. Mint will probably amend that forecast every month between now and next May.

Smith: Sure, but all this may change our other audit programs.

Kent: No, it won't. The programs are fine as is. If you find fraud in any of your tests, just let me know. Maybe we'll have to extend the tests. Or maybe we'll just report it to the audit committee.

Smith: What would they do? Green is the audit committee's chair, and remember, Green hired Mint. They've been best friends for years. Besides, Mint is calling all the shots now. Brown, the old CEO, is still on the Board, but Brown's never around. Brown's even been skipping the Board meetings. Nobody in management or on the Board will stand up to Mint.

Kent: That's nothing new. Brown was like that years ago. Brown caused frequent disputes with Jones, CPA, the predecessor auditor. Three years ago, Jones told Brown how ineffective the internal audit department was then. Next thing you know, Jones is out and I'm in. Why bother? I'm just as happy that those understaffed internal auditors don't get in our way. Just remember the bottom line is ... are the financial statements fairly presented? And they always have been. We don't provide any assurances about fraud. That's management's job.

Smith: But what about the lack of segregation of duties in the cash disbursements department? That clerk could write a check for anything.

Kent: Sure. That's a reportable condition every year and probably will be again this year. But we're talking cost effectiveness here, not fraud. We just have to do lots of testing on cash disbursements and report it again.

Smith: What about the big layoffs coming up next month? It's more than a rumor. Even the employees know it's going to happen, and they're real uptight about it.

Kent: I know it's the worst-kept secret at SCS, but we don't have to consider that now. Even if it happens, it will only improve next year's financial results. Brown should have let these people go years ago. Let's face it, how else can Mint even come close to the 30% earnings increase next year?

Required:

a.   Describe the fraud risk factors that are indicated in the dialogue above.

b.   Describe Kent's misconceptions regarding the consideration of fraud in the audit of SCS's financial statements that are contained in the dialogue above and explain why each is a misconception.

c.   Describe an auditor's working paper documentation requirements regarding the assessment of the risk of material misstatement due to fraud.

ANSWER OUTLINE

a.   Risk factors

- Mint's compensation based largely on bonuses and stock options
- Aggressive and unrealistic forecast
- Weak audit committee
- Mint dominates management
- Disputes with Board of Directors and predecessor auditor
- Understaffed and ineffective internal audit department
- Lack of correction of inadequate segregation of cash disbursements duties
- Future layoffs

b.   Kent's misconceptions

- Overall responsibilities for fraud
- Lack of concern over Mint's contract
- Lack of concern over forecast
- Programs are not adequate; they must consider risk factors
- Lack of concern over internal audit department
- Unaware that assurances with respect to fraud are included in an audit
- Lack of concern over uncorrected reportable conditions
- Lack of concern over layoffs

c.   Documentation requirements (both in planning and performance)

- Performance of assessment of risk of material misstatement due to fraud
- Risk factors identified and response

Unofficial Answer

a.   There are many fraud risk factors that are indicated in the dialogue. Among the fraud risk factors are the following:

- Significant portion of Mint's compensation is represented by bonuses and stock options. Although this arrangement has been approved by SCS's Board of Directors, this may be a motivation for Mint, the new CEO, to engage in fraudulent financial reporting.
- Mint's statement to the stock analysts that SCS's earnings would increase 30% next year may be both an unduly aggressive and unrealistic forecast. That forecast may tempt Mint to intentionally misstate certain ending balances this year that would increase profitability of the next year.
- SCS's audit committee may not be sufficiently objective because Green, the chair of the audit committee, hired Mint, the new CEO, and they have been best friends for years.
- One individual, Mint, appears to dominate management without any compensating controls. Mint seems to be making all the important decisions without any apparent input from other members of management or resistance from the Board of Directors.
- There were frequent disputes between Brown, the prior CEO, who like Mint apparently dominated management and the Board of Directors, and Jones, the predecessor auditor. This fact may indicate that an environment exists in which management will be reluctant to make any changes that Kent suggests.
- Management seems to be satisfied with an understaffed and ineffective internal audit department. This situation displays an inappropriate attitude regarding the internal control environment.
- Management has failed to properly monitor and correct a significant deficiency in its internal control--the lack of segregation of duties in cash disbursements. This disregard for the control environment is also a risk factor.
- Information about anticipated future layoffs has spread among the employees. This information may cause an increase in the risk of material misstatement arising from the misappropriation of assets by dissatisfied employees.

b.   Kent has many misconceptions regarding the consideration of fraud in the audit of SCS's financial statements that are contained in the dialogue. Among Kent's misconceptions are the following:

- Kent states that an auditor does not have specific duties regarding fraud. In fact, an auditor has a responsibility to specifically assess the risk of material misstatements due to fraud and to consider that assessment in designing the audit procedures to be performed.
- Kent is not concerned about Mint's employment contract. Kent should be concerned about a CEO's contract that is based primarily on bonuses and stock options because such an arrangement may indicate a motivation for management to engage in fraudulent financial reporting.

- Kent does not think that Mint's forecast for 1999 has an effect on the financial statement audit for 1998. However, Kent should consider the possibility that Mint may intentionally misstate the 1998 ending balances to increase the reported profit in 1999.
- Kent believes that the audit programs are fine as is. Actually, Kent should modify the audit programs because of the many risk factors that are present in the SCS audit.
- Kent is not concerned that the internal audit department is ineffective and understaffed. In fact, Kent should be concerned that SCS has permitted this situation to continue, because it represents a risk factor relating to misstatement arising from fraudulent financial reporting and/or the misappropriation of assets.
- Kent states that an auditor provides no assurances about fraud because that's management's job. In fact, an auditor has a responsibility to plan and perform an audit to obtain reasonable assurance about whether the financial statements are free of material misstatement, whether caused by error or fraud.
- Kent is not concerned that the prior year's reportable condition has not been corrected. However, Kent should be concerned that the lack of segregation of duties in the cash disbursements department represents a risk factor relating to misstatements arising from the misappropriation of assets.
- Kent does not believe that the rumors about big layoffs in the next month have an effect on audit planning. In planning the audit, Kent should consider this risk factor because it may cause an increase in the risk of material misstatement arising from this misappropriation of assets by dissatisfied employees.

c.   In planning a financial statement audit the auditor should document in the working papers evidence of the performance of the assessment of the risk of material misstatement due to fraud. Where risk factors are identified, the documentation should include those risk factors identified and the auditor's response to those risk factors, individually or in combination. In addition, during the performance of the audit the auditor may identify fraud risk factors or other conditions that cause the auditor to believe that an additional response is required. The auditor should document such risk factors or other conditions, and any further response that the auditor concludes is appropriate.

10 PRACTICE MAKES PERFECT

All four exam sections assess candidate knowledge using multiple-choice and other objective answer format questions. This chapter shows the candidate how to answer and prepare for various question formats. Sample answer sheets are shown to give the candidate an idea of how they might look at the real exam. Both types of questions are machine graded. The chapter begins with a discussion of the percentages of questions in each format.

The percentages of exam questions in each format in each section are as follows in Exhibit 1:

Exhibit 1: Percentages of examination questions

Section	Multiple-choice	Other objective answer format	Essays or problems
Business Law & Professional Responsibilities (LAW)	50 – 60%	20 – 30%	20 – 30%
Auditing (AUDIT)	50 – 60%	20 – 30%	20 – 30%
Accounting & Reporting-- Taxation, Managerial, and Governmental and Not-for-Profit Organizations (ARE)	50 – 60%	40 – 50%	NONE
Financial Accounting & Reporting (FARE)	50 – 60%	20 – 30%	20 – 30%

As can be seen from the above chart, the ARE exam has no essays or problems. All exam sections use other objective answer format questions. Law and Audit will utilize the essay format, but not the problem format. FARE is the only section where the candidate can expect a problem format. See Chapter 20, "FARE--The Long Haul," for examples of problems types. All sections have 50-60% multiple-choice questions.

THE MULTIPLE-CHOICE FORMAT

The uniform CPA exam uses a four-option multiple-choice format. This means the answer choices will always be a choice of answer a, b, c, or d. The instructions clearly say the candidate should select the "one best answer." This statement implies that the answer choices could present more than one correct answer. However, it is up to the candidate to differentiate between two correct answers and select the best answer for the particular situation. Typical numbers of multiple-choice questions per exam section are as follows in Exhibit 2:

Exhibit 2: Breakdown of multiple-choice questions per exam section

Exam section	*Possible number of multiple-choice questions*
Law	60 – 70 multiple-choice questions
Audit	85 – 100 multiple-choice questions
ARE	75 – 90 multiple-choice questions
FARE	60 – 70 multiple-choice questions

When one examines the above chart, it can be assumed that not all multiple-choice questions are worth one point each. Law and FARE might be worth one point, but Audit questions are probably worth 1/2 to 2/3 of a point each. ARE multiple-choice questions are usually worth 2/3 of a point each. Why is there a possibility of such a high number of multiple-choice questions? Beginning with the closed exam in May 1996, the Board of Examiners began "pretesting" various questions.

PRETESTING MULTIPLE-CHOICE QUESTIONS

Pretesting is defined by the AICPA as questions that are embedded in an examination and are not used in computing a candidate's final grade. In others words, not all questions count in the candidate's final grade. From May 1996 through May 1999, the AICPA used only multiple-choice questions for pretesting. Beginning November 1999, the AICPA is not specifying what question type will be used for pretesting. This leads one to believe that all question formats could be used for pretesting in future exams. Why is the AICPA pretesting questions?

Pretested questions are used to assist the AICPA in developing a bank of questions that meet a high standard of quality and can be used in the future. Beginning in 2003, when the CPA examination becomes computerized, a large question bank will be needed. Pretested questions improve the quality of future examinations by ensuring that only high-quality questions are used. Candidates should be aware that the same exam section could include different pretest questions. For example, take a Law exam that uses 10 extra multiple-choice questions and one extra five-point other objective answer format questions for pretesting. One candidate's other objective answer format question may test contract issues, while another candidate's other objective answer format question may test uniform commercial code transactions. Understand that all final candidate reported scores have been determined using the exact same set of questions. The pretest questions do not count in the final score.

The AICPA claims that pretesting allows the organization to improve the quality of future exams. Pretested questions that meet high standards will be used in future examinations. Those questions that are not considered to be of a high quality are discarded. Pretesting contributes to a more consistent level of examination difficulty.

Don't let the pretest questions scare you. Since you won't know which questions they are, you can tell yourself that they are the questions you have trouble answering. Use the pretest questions to boost your spirits and keep your hope going. Examine the front of the question answer booklet to determine the points allocated to each question type.

POINT ALLOCATION PER QUESTION TYPE

The point values per question can usually be found in the *Examination Questions* portion of the *Examination Question and Answer Booklet* (booklet). A typical format might appear as follows:

Question number	Point value
No. 1	60
No. 2	10
No. 3	10
No. 4	10
No. 5	10
TOTAL	100

The usual question order presents the multiple-choice first, the other objective answer format questions second, and the essays and problems last. Let's say the above example is from a Law exam, where question number 1 represented 60 multiple-choice questions, questions numbers 2 and 3 were other objective answer formats, and questions numbers 4 and 5 utilized essay formats; candidates should always check the question type and the point allocation at the beginning of each exam section. The information will be used to manage time. See Chapter 8, "Time Management," for suggestions to budget examination time.

TECHNIQUES FOR MACHINE-GRADEABLE QUESTION FORMATS

Why do most candidates think multiple-choice questions are easier to answer than an essay question? The obvious reason is that the candidate can guess on a multiple-choice. Essay questions require the candidate to know something. This type of reasoning is very poor. The test preparation techniques should be the same for all question types. To learn concepts, the candidate must study. To answer the question correctly, the candidate must know how to use the concepts. It doesn't matter what the question format looks like. For example, if you know how to compute the alternative minimum tax, you can compute it for an other objective answer format question or for a multiple-choice question. If you know how to compute the net present value of a capital lease, you can compute it for a multiple-choice or other objective answer format question, or explain how you computed the net present value using words and examples in an essay answer. Candidates should not study differently for each question type. Study to learn the concepts and to learn how to apply them. There is no need to vary your study techniques for question types. In fact, many candidates think they are studying for multiple-choice questions, when all they really are doing is memorizing the question.

DON'T WASTE TIME MEMORIZING QUESTIONS

The CPA candidate's job is to answer the question, not to write the question. A highly trained person working for the AICPA board of examiners carefully prepares test questions. Don't learn the question; learn the concepts. Your job is to provide the answers, not the questions. It is very dangerous to just learn a particular question. For example, take a simple Audit multiple-choice question as follows:

To exercise due professional care an auditor should

a.   Critically review the judgment exercised by those assisting in the audit.
b.   Examine all available corroborating evidence supporting management's assertions.
c.   Design the audit to detect all instances of illegal acts.
d.   Attain the proper balance of professional experience and formal education.

The answer is a., critically review the judgment exercised by those assisting in the audit. If a candidate were to memorize the question, he or she may be sadly disappointed when the same question is repeated, but the answer "critically review the judgment exercised" is not there. The problem arises from the fact that there are actually four factors to professional due care, as follows:

1.   Possess the skills commonly possessed by others in the field and exercise reasonable care and diligence
2.   Critically review the judgments exercised by those performing the audit
3.   Critically review the work done at every level of supervision

4. Observe the Generally Accepted Auditing Standards of fieldwork and reporting, as well as the general standards

All of the above answers could be an excellent answer to the statement of: "The exercise of professional due care requires that an auditor..." Don't spend time learning the questions. Spend your valuable study time learning all of the possible concepts that apply. Chances are rare that questions will be repeated.

REPEAT QUESTIONS

Yes, it is rare that any type of question format is repeated word for word. Repeat questions seem to occur more frequently in the FARE and ARE tax area. Most other areas (law, audit, governmental, and managerial accounting) utilize different questions. Pretesting has allowed the AICPA to increase the number of questions in the test bank. Don't count on a question being totally repeated. Dates, names, and amounts are often changed. It is safer not to count on repeats, but when they do occur it is a real benefit.

The average candidate receives a big boost of confidence when a question is repeated and the candidate recognizes it. It is an extra bonus when the candidate not only recognizes the former question but also remembers how to complete the problem or essay. Be careful though. When a candidate works so many questions, dates, facts, names, and figures can become jumbled. To play it safe, assume the question has completely changed. Force yourself to work every component of the question again. Check your logic and formulas. Read the dates carefully. Something as simple as a change of date can entirely change the answer. Exercise caution and take the time to work the question again. This is the real exam, and there is no forgiveness for a wrong answer. How is it that candidates tend to remember questions that contain such detailed data?

PRACTICE AND YOU WILL REMEMBER

Michael Jordan, one of the greatest basketball players ever, practiced his game until the day he retired. Why is it that a pro like Michael found it necessary to practice his skills? If you were to ask him, he would tell you he didn't want to forget. He would talk about the time when he retired, and how after just a few months, he experienced a decline in his skill level. He would also tell you that he wanted to do his very best. He saw basketball as his job, even if it was an enjoyable job; he still found it necessary to practice to remain at the top of his profession. He wanted his moves to be second nature and just happen. Without practice, his body would not know how to move to respond to a situation. Take a hint from someone who understands the value of practice. Practice your test skills so that you will respond naturally to the questions. Your brain will just do what it needs to. Think about how you have learned important skills in your life. How did you learn to ride a bicycle? You didn't spend time reading about it in a book. No, you got on the bicycle and practiced. At first you started out slowly, maybe with special devices to help you such as training wheels. It wasn't easy. You wobbled, you fell, and you hurt yourself. Wasn't it worth it? In the end, you learned an important skill that gave you freedom as a child. Today, even if you haven't ridden a bicycle in years, you can still get on one and ride. Don't waste time reading about accounting. Spend your time working the problems and practicing.

READING VERSUS PRACTICING

Many candidates spend too much time reading about CPA exam topics and too little time working the questions. Be aware of this problem and limit the reading time to no more than 25% of your total study time. If you are taking a CPA review, your reading time may even be cut to 10–15% because you're spending time in a class hearing and learning the testable concepts. As a result, less time should be spent reading. Studies have shown that reading is one of the least effective techniques for learning. The most effective study technique is that of working the problems. Do the work and you will remember. Spend time reading and you might remember the concepts, but chances are great that you will forget what you read quite quickly. With so much to study and so little time, use the most effective study technique. Be a Michael Jordan; be a professional and practice, practice, and practice some more.

HOW MUCH PRACTICE

The title of this chapter, "Practice Makes Perfect," is a tease. CPA candidates don't need to obtain a state of perfection. CPA candidates know they can be less than perfect and still pass the exam. How much time a candidate should practice depends upon many factors, such as how much time the candidate has, what the candidate does for work, how long ago the candidate graduated from college, and what the candidate recalls from college learning experiences. There is no set time. Practice every spare moment that you have. Practice using bite-sized chunks of time. Work questions to assess your ability, then continue to work questions until you correct as many of your weaknesses as you can. When you arrive at the actual examination, don't rush into things. Take a deep breath, manage your time, and control your mind. Avoid making the silly mistake of misreading your objective answer sheets. Study Exhibit 3 for an example of a Law multiple-choice answer sheet. See how the examiners ask the candidate to verify that all booklets and answer sheets match. The answer sheet says: "In order to grade your objective answer sheet and essay answers, the booklet number below must be the same as the booklet number on page 3." Always verify the match of the booklet numbers before you begin answering questions. Report any discrepancies to an exam proctor.

See Exhibit 4 for a sample of an ARE other objective answer sheet. Notice how the Law multiple-choice questions ran across, while the ARE answer sheet runs five questions down and then back up to the top of the column. There are as many as four versions of answer sheets. Usually a candidate receives at least two to three different versions over the course of the two-day examination. Stay awake and match the question number to the answer number as you blacken in the oval.

At the bottom of Exhibit 4, question number 2, items 76–79 shows a sample answer sheet for completing dollar amounts. Note that the cents column is blocked out. This is quite typical as most answers are to be rounded to the nearest dollar. Items 80–81 show a sample true or false objective sheet. Other objective answer format questions use a variety of formats. Don't let the other objective answer format questions scare you, as they simply utilize a different format to test topics that most candidates should know.

Exhibits 5 and 6 show sample FARE answer papers for multiple-choice and a problem. Take time to study the problem answer paper before you begin answering the question. Study the format that is required. Since scratch paper is not distributed at the CPA exam, use your question booklet margins to sketch out the answer. Experiment with different answers before you begin writing on the answer paper. The proctors will not distribute extra objective or problem format paper. Respect the exam by using your question booklet for your notations. Use the answer paper for your final presentation. Use the additional paper included behind the answer format paper to show your supporting schedules. Take your time and you will prepare a great answer. Patience is very helpful. Think, reflect, and reread before you begin. Continue to believe that you can pass this exam by trying to do your very best.

PERSONALLY SPEAKING

Don't underestimate the value of learning by practicing. So what if you attempt a question during your studies that you cannot answer? By going to the answer explanation in your study materials, you can learn just what you did wrong. Over the years I have seen the exam change from an exam of memorization to a critical thinking, analytical type exam. Memorizing old CPA questions will no longer help you. You must know the concepts and understand them well enough to apply them.

Practicing will crystallize the concept in your brain. It's almost like brain-washing yourself. Actually, what you are doing is washing your brain and cleaning up the concept application by practice. When you practice you will find out for sure if you really know how to use what you have learned. When in doubt--find out. Go work the questions and find out what you don't know. Then work to correct your weaknesses.

Don't let the pretest idea scare you. Since these questions are thrown out, they aren't going to affect your score. Your paper is fairly graded using the same questions as everyone else. Let the pretest questions give you hope. When you come across a question that you're having difficulty answering, just tell yourself it's a pretest question and it won't matter in the end. Now of course, you can't instill hope when all of the questions appear to be pretest questions. Just joking--of course this won't be the case!

The more you practice, the better able you are to handle diverse situations. From your practice, you will be used to some of the other objective answer format questions. This will save time and should boost your confidence. You know how to handle this situation. Keep the hope alive. Practice until you become almost perfect.

Exhibit 3: Sample Law multiple-choice answer sheet

OBJECTIVE   ANSWER   SHEET

- Record your 7-digit candidate number in the boxes on the right, then blacken completely the oval for each digit you have recorded.
- Use a Number 2 pencil.
- Erase clearly any marks you wish to change. **Make no stray marks on this sheet.**
- INCORRECT MARKS   CORRECT MARK

CANDIDATE NUMBER

UNIFORM CERTIFIED PUBLIC ACCOUNTANT EXAMINATION
Business Law & Professional Responsibilities

For Proctor Use Only

LPR

November 1, 1995; 9:00 A.M. to 12:00 NOON   **VERSION 3**   Print your **STATE** name here.

Objective Answer Sheets may vary from examination to examination. Be certain that your answer corresponds directly in number with the examination item.

1 Ⓐ Ⓑ Ⓒ Ⓓ	6 Ⓐ Ⓑ Ⓒ Ⓓ	11 Ⓐ Ⓑ Ⓒ Ⓓ	16 Ⓐ Ⓑ Ⓒ Ⓓ	
2 Ⓐ Ⓑ Ⓒ Ⓓ	7 Ⓐ Ⓑ Ⓒ Ⓓ	12 Ⓐ Ⓑ Ⓒ Ⓓ	17 Ⓐ Ⓑ Ⓒ Ⓓ	
3 Ⓐ Ⓑ Ⓒ Ⓓ	8 Ⓐ Ⓑ Ⓒ Ⓓ	13 Ⓐ Ⓑ Ⓒ Ⓓ	18 Ⓐ Ⓑ Ⓒ Ⓓ	
4 Ⓐ Ⓑ Ⓒ Ⓓ	9 Ⓐ Ⓑ Ⓒ Ⓓ	14 Ⓐ Ⓑ Ⓒ Ⓓ	19 Ⓐ Ⓑ Ⓒ Ⓓ	
5 Ⓐ Ⓑ Ⓒ Ⓓ	10 Ⓐ Ⓑ Ⓒ Ⓓ	15 Ⓐ Ⓑ Ⓒ Ⓓ	20 Ⓐ Ⓑ Ⓒ Ⓓ	
21 Ⓐ Ⓑ Ⓒ Ⓓ	26 Ⓐ Ⓑ Ⓒ Ⓓ	31 Ⓐ Ⓑ Ⓒ Ⓓ	36 Ⓐ Ⓑ Ⓒ Ⓓ	
22 Ⓐ Ⓑ Ⓒ Ⓓ	27 Ⓐ Ⓑ Ⓒ Ⓓ	32 Ⓐ Ⓑ Ⓒ Ⓓ	37 Ⓐ Ⓑ Ⓒ Ⓓ	
23 Ⓐ Ⓑ Ⓒ Ⓓ	28 Ⓐ Ⓑ Ⓒ Ⓓ	33 Ⓐ Ⓑ Ⓒ Ⓓ	38 Ⓐ Ⓑ Ⓒ Ⓓ	
24 Ⓐ Ⓑ Ⓒ Ⓓ	29 Ⓐ Ⓑ Ⓒ Ⓓ	34 Ⓐ Ⓑ Ⓒ Ⓓ	39 Ⓐ Ⓑ Ⓒ Ⓓ	
25 Ⓐ Ⓑ Ⓒ Ⓓ	30 Ⓐ Ⓑ Ⓒ Ⓓ	35 Ⓐ Ⓑ Ⓒ Ⓓ	40 Ⓐ Ⓑ Ⓒ Ⓓ	
41 Ⓐ Ⓑ Ⓒ Ⓓ	46 Ⓐ Ⓑ Ⓒ Ⓓ	51 Ⓐ Ⓑ Ⓒ Ⓓ	56 Ⓐ Ⓑ Ⓒ Ⓓ	
42 Ⓐ Ⓑ Ⓒ Ⓓ	47 Ⓐ Ⓑ Ⓒ Ⓓ	52 Ⓐ Ⓑ Ⓒ Ⓓ	57 Ⓐ Ⓑ Ⓒ Ⓓ	
43 Ⓐ Ⓑ Ⓒ Ⓓ	48 Ⓐ Ⓑ Ⓒ Ⓓ	53 Ⓐ Ⓑ Ⓒ Ⓓ	58 Ⓐ Ⓑ Ⓒ Ⓓ	
44 Ⓐ Ⓑ Ⓒ Ⓓ	49 Ⓐ Ⓑ Ⓒ Ⓓ	54 Ⓐ Ⓑ Ⓒ Ⓓ	59 Ⓐ Ⓑ Ⓒ Ⓓ	
45 Ⓐ Ⓑ Ⓒ Ⓓ	50 Ⓐ Ⓑ Ⓒ Ⓓ	55 Ⓐ Ⓑ Ⓒ Ⓓ	60 Ⓐ Ⓑ Ⓒ Ⓓ	

QUESTION 1

Detach the Page at the Perforation

203912 S

QUESTION NUMBERS 2 AND 3 ARE ON PAGE 27

end

Objective Answer Sheet Booklet No.

DesignExpert™ by NCS Printed in U.S.A. Mark Reflex® EM-159582-2:654321   28

Exhibit 4: Sample ARE multiple-choice and objective answer sheet

OBJECTIVE ANSWER SHEET

- Record your 7-digit candidate number in the boxes on the right, then blacken completely the oval for each digit you have recorded.
- Use a Number 2 pencil.
- Erase clearly any marks you wish to change. **Make no stray marks on this sheet.**
- INCORRECT MARKS   CORRECT MARK

CANDIDATE NUMBER

UNIFORM CERTIFIED PUBLIC ACCOUNTANT EXAMINATION
Accounting & Reporting—Taxation, Managerial, and Governmental and Not-for-Profit Organizations

For Proctor Use Only

November 2, 1995; 8:30 A.M. to 12:00 NOON

ARE VERSION 2

Print your **STATE** name here.

Objective Answer Sheets may vary from examination to examination. Be certain that your answer corresponds directly in number with the examination item.

QUESTION 1

QUESTION 2

407178 S

Item | Select one
80 | ① ⑤
81 | ① ⑤

Objective Answer Sheet Booklet No.

QUESTION NUMBERS 3, 4, AND 5 ARE ON PAGE 27   28

DesignExpert™ by NCS Printed in U.S.A. Mark Reflex® EM-159599-2:654321

Detach the Page at the Perforation

Exhibit 5: Sample FARE multiple-choice answer sheet

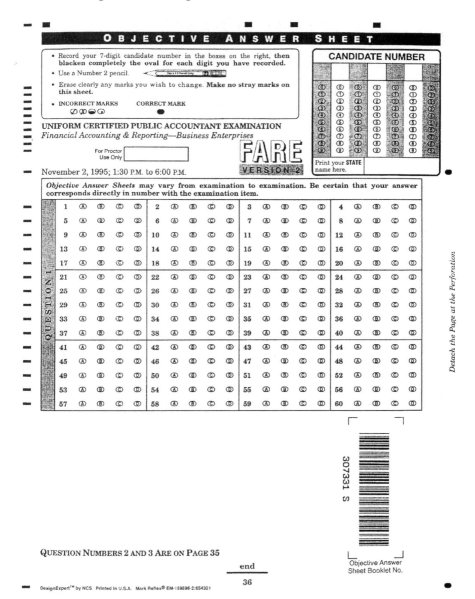

Exhibit 6: Sample FARE problem answer sheet

E S S A Y R U L E D P A P E R

UNIFORM CERTIFIED PUBLIC ACCOUNTANT EXAMINATION
Financial Accounting & Reporting—Business Enterprises

CANDIDATE NUMBER

Record your 7-digit candidate number in the boxes.

QUESTION NUMBER 4
Print your **STATE** name here. _____

a.

Baron Flowers
WORKSHEET TO CONVERT TRIAL BALANCE TO ACCRUAL BASIS
December 31, 1994

Account title	Cash basis		Adjustments		Accrual Basis*	
	Dr.	Cr.	Dr.	Cr.	Dr.*	Cr.*
Cash	25,600					
Accounts receivable	16,200					
Inventory	62,000					
Furniture & fixtures	118,200					
Land improvements	45,000					
Accumulated depreciation & amortization		32,400				
Accounts payable		17,000				
Baron, Drawings						
Baron, Capital		124,600				
Sales		653,000				
Purchases	305,100					
Salaries	174,000					
Payroll taxes	12,400					
Insurance	8,700					
Rent	34,200					
Utilities	12,600					
Living expenses	13,000					
	827,000	827,000				

* Completion of these columns is not required.

over

27

3 07331 R

Essay Ruled Paper Booklet No.

11 COPING WITH FAMILY, FRIENDS, AND COWORKERS

Studies have attempted to prove that successful people succeed only when they receive a great deal of support from the people around them. While this may be true, it is very dangerous to expect total support throughout your CPA exam study process. If you begin by expecting very little support, you will be pleasantly surprised and appreciative when someone does something nice for you. If you expect everyone to continually bolster your spirits, you will be in a constant state of disappointment, spending more time unhappy and focusing on the reasons why no one seems to understand that you must prepare for the longest and most difficult examination of your life. Get a grip--this is your goal, not their goal. Likewise, when you pass the exam, this will be your achievement, not theirs. The most important component of any relationship is communication. Begin by communicating with those involved.

FAMILY

There is no one like a family member. They can make you feel as though you are the most important person in the world and at other times they can make you feel lower than you have ever felt before. Family situations tend to run in extremes--loyal and supportive today, aloof and uncaring another day. Are they really acting aloof and uncaring, or is it just your perception of their actions? When people become stressed, they tend to overstate the situation. Whenever you feel your family is not providing the necessary support you require, stop and ask yourself, "Is it them or me?" Have you communicated with them? Have you asked for support? Explain what passing the CPA exam means to you and what it could mean to them. A CPA makes more money and can count on more job stability.

Maybe you are just so stressed out that no level of support would please you at this time. If this is the case, take a break from studying and from your family. It's time to take a walk, jog, or drive somewhere, but by all means, take some time to be alone and relax. Think about what your family is going through. They feel your stress and they want to support you. Their aloofness may just be a result of leaving you alone so that you can accomplish your goals. Stay calm and do not overreact. Give yourself a day to cool off and to allow your family members to realize that you need them. If by tomorrow things don't look better to you, call a family meeting and ask what **you can do** to improve the quality of your family life. Don't blame them for your problems and stress. If they ask you to give up on becoming a CPA, take the time to explain to them how achieving the CPA designation will make life better for everyone in the family. Remind them that the study process doesn't last forever. Look ahead to the days after the CPA exam and prepare a plan to celebrate the end of the CPA exam. Your celebration doesn't have to be elaborate. Maybe a day trip to the zoo, an outing to a movie or special play, or even a day at the park, picnicking, swimming, and playing games. Your family cares; they just need a gentle reminder of the intensity of the goal that you are attempting to complete. Try to keep family matters as calm and uneventful as possible during your study process. How does a person do this? At least one family crisis is bound to happen during your exam preparation.

When a crisis or problem arises, keep it in perspective. You did not create the problem just because you are preparing for the CPA exam. Things just happen. Avoid the guilt trip and by all means avoid pointing fingers and placing blame on yourself or others. It is a waste of time to think or say: "You know I don't need this. I am too busy and I have to study for the CPA exam. Why did this have to happen now?" A family crisis is not the time for you to be self-centered. Center your attention on dealing with the aspects of the situation that you can control. If you can't control or change anything, then you just must accept what has happened and move on.

Give troublesome situations some time. Things may look very bleak today, but the next day may be beautiful. You are very fortunate to be part of a family, however large or small. Don't begrudge family members your support. Give your family some time where you do not mention the word "CPA." They need a break from the stress and pressure too. The type of person who strives to become a CPA is often a family member that is looked up to and depended upon. Be thankful that you've earned such a reputation. Do what you can to help with the family situation and then re-vert back to your focused study plan. Consider asking relatives for some assistance. You may find that they are very happy to take over for you-- they just didn't know you needed them. Stress or no stress, you must con-tinue to study. Lack of study will stress you out more. Whatever crisis you encounter, continue to study.

Establish a structured study plan and communicate it to your family and friends. Include family time in the plan. Most family members will endure the process better when they know a certain amount of time will be set aside for them. Even if the time is 4 hours per week, it is their personal time with you. Now be careful--you must stick to the plan and you must make your family the central focus during their established time. Make the promise of time and keep it.

When it's time to enjoy family and friends, do just that--enjoy them. Periodically, you should clear your mind. Plan activities that will get you away from your study environment. Who needs reminders of the hard work ahead? Laughter is a fabulous stress reliever. Find a funny movie, play games that make you laugh, or read a funny book.

Keep in mind that your family and friends are feeling the stress too. During your scheduled family time, allow your family and friends to choose the fun activity. It is time for them to control the plan. A change of pace will provide you with a fresh outlook. Convey the feeling to those around you that you realize that they too are making sacrifices to help you achieve your goal. Be grateful for any support you receive. A simple thank you will mean much to those who have assisted you.

Be honest to yourself and to your family. If your family members are taking on additional tasks to give you time to study, then you had better be studying and making sacrifices too. When you decided to become a CPA, did you give up the weekly bowling or golf outing? Are you pretending to work on CPA preparation software when what you really are doing is playing computer card games? Are you really studying or are you surfing the net? Yes, you do need time to relax, but are you taking too much relaxation time for yourself? Every week take the time to reflect on what you did right, on what kept you studying. Also reflect upon what you did wrong, what kept you from meeting your goals. Stick with the techniques that helped keep you focused; change the incorrect behavior. Learn from your mistakes.

When it is time to study, involve family and friends in the process. They can quiz you using index or note cards. They can read materials to you while you drive. Their involvement will give them a greater understanding of the depth and breadth of the material that you must learn. After a few hours of studying with you, they will become much more supportive because they will quickly see the difficulty of mastering so much technical material. There is never an ideal time to sit for the CPA exam. There will always be distractions, crises, and family misunderstandings. It will always seem as though you don't have enough time. Manage your time to the fullest and stick to your study plan.

FRIENDS

Friends can hurt you or help you. Allow friends to give you support. When dealing with your friends becomes more draining than fun, think about changing friends. A friend is someone who helps and understands. A friend should never keep you from meeting your goals.

Friends are the "great distracters." You choose your friends because you enjoy being with them. The real struggle is to set your priorities and stick to them. If your friends have never experienced something as all-encompassing as preparing for the CPA exam, they won't really understand what you are going through. Tell them you need their help to keep you focused. It is no exaggeration that studying for the CPA exam will probably take more time than you have. Yes, friends can help by quizzing you, but this may end up in a fun outing instead of an afternoon of study. It is easy to become distracted, so avoid frequent meetings with friends. Make sure your friends understand just how difficult it is to pass the CPA exam. Show them the statistics: the first-time passing percentage is 12 –15%.

Schedule get-togethers in advance.   Avoid spontaneous invitations. Looking forward to spending time with your friends can serve as an incentive to you to accomplish your goals. Be realistic--you will not have a great deal of time to devote to your friends. Good friends will understand and will admire your dedication.

Communicate more through e-mail. When you are busy studying, you don't have to open your mail. If you are down, and need a pick-me up, e-mail your friends and ask for some words of encouragement. Avoid phone conversations since they can easily eat up valuable time and often lead to spur-of-the-moment plans to "go have some fun."

Don't let the preparation bring you down. Studying for the exam does involve sacrifice but the process does not continue forever. Limit your fun time now and enjoy your new status as a CPA later. Ask your friends for support to help you concentrate on the task at hand. Good friends will be there for you.

COWORKERS

Should you tell your boss that you are studying for the CPA exam? It depends. Look around--are most of your superiors CPAs? If the answer is yes, your boss is more likely to support you in your endeavors. If the answer is no, you might want to keep your exam preparation a secret for the time being. In most cases, your colleagues will eventually figure out that you plan to sit for the exam because you must request the 2 test days off from work. Why be so secretive in the beginning?

Your boss is a human being and as such could become intimidated by your study process. Your boss's biggest fear may be that you are learning more than he is. To retaliate, your boss may consciously or subconsciously assign you more overtime tasks, overlook you for a promotion, and just plain make your life tough. Frustration and negative feelings are not going to help you.

Assess the situation and ask yourself if your boss could be threatened by your exam preparation. This will usually occur when your boss is not a CPA. In this case, delay your announcement as long as you can be assured of getting the exam days off. Try requesting the entire week as vacation time well in advance of the exam date. Your coworkers are less likely to connect the exam with a 1-week time period requested several months before the exam.

By all means, do not lie to your boss. Don't tell your boss that you are going to Europe when you are really going to drive to the city to sit for the CPA exam. CPAs maintain a high level of integrity and should not lie in any situation. Be up-front if your colleagues confront you. You have made the commitment to bettering your future and you plan to achieve your goals. Power rests in the ability to control the situation. You don't have to act like your boss or coworkers. Don't mimic their bad behavior. Rise above the petty jealousies, the stupid misunderstandings, and the misplaced trust. You are going to become a CPA by sticking to your plan of study.

FRIENDLY ADVICE CAN HURT YOU

So your friend or coworker is a CPA. They eagerly give advice about how they studied to pass. Should you listen? Usually, the answer is no. The CPA exam has been changing every 3 years since 1990. Question formats, content changes, and question types make the exam different than what it was before. The friendly advice you receive may not even apply to today's CPA exam.

Your friends are different than you are. Each of us is an individual, and as such, should individually design and stick to our own study plan. In other words, your study plan should be tailored to fit you by helping you to correct your weaknesses. We all come from different situations. It takes a personalized study plan to be successful.

STICK TO YOUR PLAN

You spent time developing your study plan and you are well aware that the more closely you follow the plan, the better chances you have of successfully completing the task. Desire alone will not lead to achievement. In the end, will your exam score be determined by how many sporting events you attended with your friends this year or by how much knowledge you have gained? You know the answer. You know what you must do. Remain committed to your plan of attack. Study and learn the concepts.

If your boss is driving you crazy, stick to the plan. Keep your commitment to pass the exam. Passing the exam will give you greater job mobility. Spending time complaining about your boss to family and friends isn't productive. Use that time to study and learn exam concepts. Pass the exam and improve your situation. Do something about the things that you can control. Ignore what you cannot control.

PERSONALLY SPEAKING

If you look for a distraction, you will find one. Let's say you have a problem with gambling or spending too much money shopping. If you don't allow yourself to go to the casinos or the shopping malls, you don't give yourself the chance to spend money. The same situation applies to family, friends, and coworkers. If you allow them to distract you, they will.

My family is generally very supportive. I have noticed, however, that when I spend too much time requesting or demanding support, they become turned off by my attitude. Most people want to help you because it is their idea, not yours. Let them help but remember to say thank you and to tell them how much you have been able to achieve because of them. In any situation, humility will serve you well. Who likes a braggart or a big shot? Let's face it, I have achieved much in my life, and you too will achieve much in yours, but we could not have accomplished what we have without the help and support of those around us. Being humble and thankful does not mean you have turned into a meek weakling. No, you have matured to the level of understanding that most people never reach. You alone are just that--lonely. You need the people around you and it is wise to show appreciation.

I am always bothered when review candidates drive to class, walk in the door, pick up the lecture materials, and leave before class even begins. Why pay for expert lecture assistance when you don't plan to use it? Think about what you are doing before you make your decision. One evening I overheard a CPA candidate tell her friend that she must leave class early because she had to watch her team play in the World Series. Since when is baseball tested on the CPA exam? Her reasoning was that she thought her team was going to lose the game and she wanted to see the last game of the year. Think about what she was doing--her priority for the evening had nothing to do with the CPA exam. Her priority was watching a baseball team lose. When the exam results are released, is she going to be thinking about her losing baseball team or will her focus be on why she didn't pass? Ten years from now, is anyone going to remember that World Series game? Ten years from now, are you going to be earning more, working less, and receiving greater respect because you are a CPA? In the scheme of life, passing the CPA exam will have much more of an impact on your life than watching a baseball game. She was so close to making the right decision-- she was in class, almost ready to learn, close to avoiding the distraction. Think about the consequences of your actions. Think about what you are doing before you make your decision.

Do you know there is no limit to how many times you can sit for the CPA exam? I have worked with people who have sat as many as fourteen times. One person sat many times because he had never really taken accounting classes. He received approval to sit for the exam based upon economics and finance courses. The irrelevant coursework added to credit received by taking a CPA review course qualified him to sit. Imagine taking a CPA review course without ever having learned the material. He was using the CPA review to learn the material for the very first time. A CPA review should primarily be a review, not new learning. At first, I thought he was lazy and not taking time to study. Then I realized the real problem: he was learning the material for the first time. At some of the exams his brother came to the hotel to bolster his spirits. When he finally passed, his parents rewarded the entire family with a trip to Israel, a great way to celebrate a job well done. Despite the number of attempts, he completed the job. He turned all of his previous failures into one great big success. Today, he is a successful CPA with a great deal of confidence. I am sure that if his family had given up on him, he too would have thrown in the towel. His family was there for him in a very positive way. In my mind, he will always be a hero.

Another CPA candidate who has taken the exam several times still has not been successful. Each time he calls me, I ask myself what I can tell him to help him pass. He has taken the relevant accounting classes and should be a good candidate to pass the exam quickly, if only he studied. He always allows himself to become distracted somewhere during the study process. His excuses range from the birth of a child, an irrational boss or a sick wife to just not having enough time to study. After 7 years of attempting to pass the exam, his business is suffering because clients are asking why he has not yet passed the exam. He has lost large clients because he cannot perform attest work for them. Don't misunderstand me; he is one of the nicest gentlemen in the world, but he will not pass the exam until he focuses on the task of practicing and studying for the CPA exam. Several candidates have encountered stumbling blocks and still survive. There has never been a totally calm time in my life, and I would guess that you probably could say the same thing. Commitment is personal. His commitment to passing the exam is just not there.

A CPA candidate in her mid-forties approached me one evening during the class break. She looked drawn and pale, a look not unique to a person undergoing the exam preparation process. However, she was seeking advice--the following week her mother was being admitted to a nursing home. The family could no longer care for the mother at home because her Alzheimer's disease was advancing and most often the mother was not aware of her actions. The CPA candidate was undergoing a great deal of guilt, not only about studying for the exam, but also about moving her mom to a home. She said she would have to miss class next week to help her brothers and sisters admit her mom. It turned out the candidate had a total of five siblings and all five were going to be there to admit the mom. I asked a simple question: "Will your mother know if you are there?" She replied no because her mom gets very disoriented when she is surrounded by more than one person and when she is encountering new surroundings. I suggested that she come to class and visit her mom on another day when things at the home were calmer. Her mother would probably appreciate a visit at a later time and then perhaps she would have a good day and be able to communicate with her.

I will never forget that very special CPA candidate, who came to class the next week, fought hard to concentrate, visited her mother at a later date, and then went on to pass the CPA exam. Her courage and determination serve as reminders that it is up to you to assess and control the situation to the best of your ability. At first, her siblings were not happy with her decision to attend class. Later, when she was the only person who could visit the mom during the day, they realized that she could make contributions to her family at another time, in another way.

Stick to your study plan and believe in yourself, because in the end, it will be you who can change things. You will be far less stressed by doing what you ought to do to achieve your goal. You will have no reason to feel guilty if you do what is right. That student kept studying and visited with her mom at times that were different from what her family thought she should do. She did not act selfishly or badly. She acted responsibly.

The decision is yours: remain committed and pass, or make excuses for not studying and lose sight of your goal.

12 REVISING YOUR PERSONAL STUDY PLAN

Why include a chapter on revising a plan that was well-planned and all scheduled out several weeks ago? It is human nature to procrastinate and put off doing things that one just may not enjoy. Who enjoys sacrificing fun times with family and friends? It is assumed that after about 7 weeks of study, most people will realize that the CPA exam is 6 to 8 weeks away and they have not accomplished what they thought they would. This chapter helps CPA candidates revise their personal study plan to adjust for a loss of time.

HOW DID THE TIME FLY BY?

Time waits for no one and keeps on marching whether you are ready or not. People lose track of time for many reasons. They may have procrastinated (the most common problem) or they may have experienced a family crisis such as an illness. It is not frivolous to assume that people will need to adjust their study plans at least once in the 4 to 5 months before the exam. Life is complicated and for that reason time flies by. Accept the fact that you have to adjust your plans and don't waste time lamenting about lost time. Begin to make a new study plan by reflecting upon your current situation.

REFLECTING UPON THE CURRENT SITUATION

Where are you now? You might be working many hours of overtime. Maybe you just recovered from an illness. Begin by asking yourself if the things that caused you to postpone your studies have now been resolved. If you were completing a college class, and the class is now over, you will have much more time to study. Accept the fact that circumstances have caused you to fall behind. Take action to adjust the current situation.

Increase your study time from 21 hours per week to 30 hours per week. If the awful situation has occurred where you cannot control the problem that caused you to fall behind in your studies, perhaps it is time to admit that maybe you should wait to sit until the next examination. However, when you are evaluating your current situation, be honest and be very critical of yourself. For example, don't kid yourself into believing that a few hours of overtime per week caused you to fall behind by several weeks. That just shouldn't happen. Admit that you didn't utilize your time wisely.

You blew it. Now you must give up every spare minute to study. It's time to make the super sacrifice.

MAKE A SUPER SACRIFICE

A super sacrifice requires the candidate to spend less time eating and sleeping and more time studying. A super sacrifice requires that you give up everything that has been fun. Now you must study every day, including Friday and Sunday. You must study in the morning, study during every lunch hour, and study in the evening. You must give up all leisure activities --no time for sports activities, no time for charities, and no time for you.

The super sacrifice may affect you monetarily. It is time to take time off work. Take some time every week. If you have used your vacation days you may have to take the time off without pay. It's too late to fool around. Every spare minute of time must be used to learn the material.

ADJUST HOW YOU STUDY--LEARN BY DOING

In the past, you spent about 25% of the time reading material and 75% of the time practicing the concept application. Now, there is almost no time to read. Adjust your study time to 10% reading the material and 90% doing the questions. By spending 90% of the time practicing questions, you are combining the learning with the doing. You must learn by your mistakes. For example, by completing the following FARE multiple-choice question about derivatives, you can learn what a derivative is, as follows:

> Derivatives are financial instruments that derive their value from changes in a benchmark based on any of the following except
> a.   Stock prices
> b.   Mortgage and currency rates
> c.   Commodity prices
> d.   Discounts on accounts receivable

You did not take the time to read the material. What knowledge can you gain by studying this question? You read the answer explanation and see that d. was the correct answer. Here's what you have learned:

- Derivatives are financial instruments
- Derivatives derive their value from changes in a benchmark
- Typical benchmarks used are stock prices, mortgage rates, currency rates, and commodity prices

Since d. was the answer, it means that discounts on accounts receivable are not acceptable benchmarks for deriving the derivative value. If you have time, you would write out an index card for the above concepts.

You move on and attempt to complete the next question:

Which of the following is not an **underlying**, according to SFAS 133?
  a.   A credit rating
  b.   An interest rate index
  c.   A security price
  d.   All of the above could be underlyings

This is a confusing question, as you hardly know what a derivative is, let alone what an **underlying** is. That's okay. Move on to the answer explanation where you read the following explanation:

The answer is d. since the basic definition of an **underlying,** according to SFAS 133, is any financial or physical variable that has either observable changes or objectively verifiable changes.

Prepare an index card by writing out the above definition of an underlying. Then, list examples of an **underlying** as a credit rating, an interest rate index, and a security price. Think about the three examples. What do they all have in common? They all change, hence the observable changes, and they are all objective changes that are easy to verify.

If you had taken time to read all about derivatives, it is doubtful that you would remember much from your reading. By attempting to answer the question, you are thinking about the concept, reading the concept, and then reinforcing the concept by writing out the index card. Later, as you travel to work or to the mall, take the time to review the index card. You are learning by doing rather than reading. Taking action and doing serves as a powerful learning method. Chances are you won't quickly forget the concepts that you have read, wrote, and practiced.

Let's try one more derivative question:

Which of the following is **not** a distinguishing characteristic of a derivative instrument?
  a.   Terms that require or permit net settlement
  b.   Instrument that must be "highly effective" throughout its life
  c.   No initial net investment
  d.   One or more underlyings and notional amounts

Who knows what the answer might be? When you read the answer explanation you see the answer is b. The answer explanation goes on to say that as specified in SFAS 133, derivative instruments contain:

1. One or more underlyings and one or more notional amounts
2. No initial net investment or smaller net investment than required for contracts with an expected similar response to market changes; and
3. Terms that require or permit net settlement, by means outside the contract, and delivery of an asset that is substantially the same as net settlement

SFAS 133 makes no mention of the fact that an instrument must be "highly effective." The important concept to learn from this question is that derivative instruments contain the three factors listed above. Again, prepare an index card. Write it out. Learn by doing.

When time is running out, you must become an efficient and effective learner. You must learn by doing rather than reading. You should also remain calm.

REMAIN CALM

Tell yourself that if you panic and begin to doubt yourself, you will not learn anything. Anxiety and fear do not motivate. They cause you to become distracted and lose focus. With little time left to study, you must use every minute of spare time to absorb a concept. Waste no time fretting about what you don't know. Continue with your work, conscious that you must learn everything you can in the time that is left. Proceed to learn as much as you can in the time that is left. Attempt to learn something about everything.

LEARN SOMETHING ABOUT EVERYTHING

Even though time is wasting away, allocate time in your study plan to study all of your weak areas. Forget about mastering the material, since perfection is not a requirement to pass the exam. Correct the weaknesses that you can, and forget about what you are having difficulty learning. If you believe you are weak in a major area, such as corporate taxation, take some time to attempt to learn something about the topic. Learn enough to be dangerous, to answer some questions, and to make educated guesses on other questions. Use your study time wisely.

USE YOUR STUDY TIME WISELY

Go back to Chapter 6, "Developing Your Personal Study Plan," and examine Exhibits 1 and 2. Study your daily schedule. Yes, you will find time by sacrificing your fun. It's not only about finding more study time. What's important is to use all of your study time wisely. Quickly review the areas you know. Work questions, learn from the questions, and move on. Vary the topics that you study. When you are fresh, study the difficult material. As you tire, shift to your strong areas. When you find your mind wandering, take a short break by walking around the house and reading lists, definitions, or formulas out loud. Get your blood flowing by walking, but don't waste the time. Study as you walk around. When you are tired, give in and get some sleep.

IMPORTANCE OF SLEEP

Overwhelmed, frustrated, anxious CPA candidates often sacrifice sleep for study time. Giving up sleep for study can be dangerous. The more tired you become, the grumpier you get, and the more anxious you become. To absorb technical material the candidate must have adequate sleep. Your body needs sleep, so don't deprive yourself. The less sleep you get, the duller your brain becomes. Keep your brain sharp--get a good night's sleep!

CONTINUE TO BELIEVE

Even though time is short, you still can absorb more concepts, formulas, and knowledge. Continue to believe that you have the ability to learn more and continue to believe that you can pass the CPA exam. Don't ever lose sight of the end goal. You can pass the CPA exam. You will pass the CPA exam. Stay in the game for the fight. You will never know if you can pass until you try. When you try, you will want to give it your all and do the very best that you can under the present circumstances. Keep on studying, using every available minute of the day.

PERSONALLY SPEAKING

I always fall behind schedule. Even when it's something simple and fun like packing for vacation or preparing for a party. Why does this happen? For most accountants, it happens because of several reasons. Our jobs are demanding and often require overtime. We are perfectionists who spend too much time in the beginning of any project just making sure everything is perfect. Then, as time goes on, we run out of preparation time. It's bound to happen. Realize that it is normal. Accept the fact that you'll probably need to adjust your study schedule more than one time. Don't waste time worrying or attempting to place blame. Adjust and learn by doing.

In order to utilize the "learn by doing" technique, your review materials must contain detailed answer explanations. The right answer must be listed along with an explanation as to why the other answers are incorrect. Always check the materials before you purchase them. The more detailed the answer explanation, the better.

After every exam I receive phone calls and e-mails from people who gave up. They gave up long before they reached the exam--probably a month or two before the exam date. The Illinois Board of Examiners will not refund your examination sitting fee. You are out the money. Knowing this, candidates who give up usually sit for the exam, saying they want the experience. You want the experience of failure? I can't imagine anything more depressing than sitting for an exam with the certainty that you are going to fail.

I ran out of time to study for both the CPA and the CIA exam. Somehow, I managed to pass both exams. I did it because I never gave up. I kept adjusting my study plan to obtain the most knowledge in my weakest areas right up until the first exam day. I kept on studying to learn something new. I kept on reviewing to bring back what I might have forgotten. In the back of my mind, I kept telling myself that I did not know at what knowledge level a person passes the exam. Therefore, I proceeded in confidence, admitting that I wasn't perfect. Yes, I have weak areas. However, I will do the best I can to learn everything I can and I will perform to the best of my ability on all exam areas. I will do my best because it's all I know how to do.

Exhibit 1 uses the letters of the alphabet to create the "ABCs of Life." I keep these ABCs in mind when I feel depressed or overwhelmed. The letters and phrases serve as reminders that I am living my life by doing the best I can. I don't make excuses for mistakes. I just always keep trying to do my best.

Exhibit 1: The ABCs of Life

To achieve your dreams, remember your ABCs.

*A*void negative people, places, and things
*B*elieve in yourself
*C*onsider things from all angles
*D*on't ever give up and don't give in
*E*njoy life today; yesterday is gone, and tomorrow may not come
*F*amily and friends are hidden treasures; seek them and enjoy them
*G*ive more than you planned to
*H*ang onto your dreams
*I*gnore those who try to discourage you
*J*ust do it, baby
*K*eep on trying
*L*ove yourself first and foremost
*M*ake it happen
*N*ever lie, cheat, or steal--always strike a fair deal
*O*pen your eyes and see things as they really are
*P*ractice makes perfect
*Q*uitters never win and winners never quit
*R*ead, study, and learn about everything important in life
*S*top procrastinating
*T*ake control of your own destiny
*U*nderstand yourself in order to better understand others
*V*isualize it
*W*ant it more than anything
*X*celerate yourself
*Y*ou are a unique creation of God; nothing can replace you
*Z*ero in on your target and go for it!

Source: Author Unknown; Revised by Ms. Alice Brown, friend of the author.

13 HOW WILL I EVER PASS?

Feeling overwhelmed? Time is running out, you have much more to study, and you can't recall the material you studied a few months ago. Your mind is a jumble. It would be easy to give up. You can't remember the last time that you had some fun without feeling guilty. Stop and review your options. Yes, you could give up. Then you would have some free time for a few weeks before you realized you had stopped short of even attempting, let alone achieving, your goal. The second option, keeping up the fight, is still doable. It's time to enter crisis mode. You can still pass. Take control of the situation. Begin by talking to yourself and continuing to believe.

YES, I STILL BELIEVE I CAN PASS

Although that might sound like you're Peter Pan calling for Tinkerbell, it's not a bad analogy. After all, it seems it would take one small miracle for you to pass. That's what you think. How do you know what it takes to pass? Have you ever been employed to grade the CPA exam? Have you ever taken an exam where you only needed a score of 75% to pass, and probably even a raw score of 2 to 10 points less than that? You don't know anything about the level it takes to achieve a passing score. It's time to stop thinking about what you can't control and get a grip on what you can control. The AICPA controls the grading of the exam, so forget about that. You can control your attitude by remaining positive. Yes, you can still pass the exam. With a positive attitude you can go on and adjust your study plan to help correct your major weaknesses, forget about everything but studying, and sit for the exam. Now that your attitude is corrected, move on to adjusting your study plan.

ADJUSTING YOUR STUDY PLAN

Seems like you've done this before. In Chapter 6, "Developing Your Personal Study Plan," you prepared a study plan to fit your needs. Then, in Chapter 12, "Revising Your Personal Study Plan," you realized that you were no longer on target and you revised the plan. Now it's time to make an adjustment. There is not enough time to revise and apply your plan. It's time to adjust. When you are 3 to 4 weeks away from the exam, revising the study plan probably won't help. Adjust the plan to do what you can and forget about what you can't accomplish.

Take some time off work to study. Maybe you are feeling ill. After all, you probably are ill from worry and stress about the CPA exam. You could accomplish so much in just 1 to 2 days of uninterrupted study. Use some vacation time. Find some time somewhere. Sit down with your support group and explain to them that it's crunch time. Ask for their patience in bearing with you. There are only a few weeks left. Give up the fun. Stay home on weekends and study; stay in on your lunch hour and study while you eat, study all the time.

What should you study? Adjust your study plan by analyzing the areas of greatest concern. In other words, what haven't you studied and how much is it tested on the CPA exam? Let's say you have not even opened a review manual to study governmental accounting. Assess its importance: It's 30 points on the ARE section. Is the area important? Yes, 30 points are important. If you scored a perfect score on the income taxation and managerial areas you would only earn 70 points. The chances of scoring perfectly on topics as diverse and detailed as tax and managerial are slim. Yes indeed, governmental accounting is important. You must do something about it.

First, assess your entry-level knowledge. Do you know anything about governmental accounting? If the answer is yes, then you don't have to spend as much time on the topic as you would if you didn't know anything. Keep in mind the requirement to pass--a candidate must know something about everything. A candidate need not master everything. Go for the points you can learn without using all of your remaining time on one topic. Using your review manual, go to the governmental chapter(s) or module(s), and spend a short time reading. Important areas would be the eight governmental funds. The eight funds represent the big picture. Now, go to the multiple-choice questions to learn the details. Try to answer them. Expect to get questions wrong. That's okay--you will learn from the answer explanations. Exhibit 1 demonstrates how a candidate can learn from the question. In fact, some professors say that candidates remember the questions they got wrong better than the questions that they got correct. When you get a question wrong, you actually take some time to think about it.

Exhibit 1: Example of learning from the question answer explanation

QUESTION: In 1999, Joan accepted and received a $10,000 award for outstanding civic achievement. Joan was selected without any action on her part, and no future services are expected of her as a condition of receiving the award. What amount should Joan include in her 1999 adjusted gross income in connection with this award?

    a. $0
    b. $ 4,000
    c. $ 5,000
    d. $10,000

You make a guess of answer a. since you think Joan should not have to include the award at all. You don't really know the answer. You then go back to the answer explanation in your review manual and find out the answer is d. Ouch, you got the question wrong. That's okay, you can learn from the mistake. You read in the answer that prizes and awards are generally taxable. The exception to the rule is that if the award is for civic, artistic, educational, scientific, or literary achievement, and if the recipient is selected without action on his part, and if the **award is paid directly to a government or tax-exempt organization**, the award in **nontaxable**. What you learned from the answer explanation is as follows:

- Joan is an individual
- Individuals usually pay taxes on awards
- Awards are tax-exempt only when they are for a scholarly reason (civic, literary, etc.), the money is unsolicited, and the money is paid to a **governmental or tax-exempt organization**

Will you remember what you have learned? If you say yes, I won't forget, then you should not make an index card. However, if you think you will forget, take the time to write out an index card to review just before the exam. Of course, if it is 2 days before the exam, you are not going to have the time to write the index card let alone review it. Be confident, believe that you will remember.

Studying only your very weak areas by learning from the answer explanations is called the crisis study mode. You spend less time reading about the topics and more time doing the questions. Normally, of your total study time, you would spend about 25% reading and 75% practicing. When you are in crisis mode, spend only about 10% of your study time reading chapter discussions. The 10% reading is just to get a brief overview of the topical area. Then, just jump in and go directly to the practice questions to see what you can quickly learn.

The crisis mode of studying is not ideal. It is not the recommended method. However, it has been proven to work as long as the candidate does not get frustrated. Keep an open mind and let the concepts sink in. In crisis mode it is important to remain calm, learn and remember what you can, and forget about what you can't remember. There is no time to worry about what you don't know. Remain confident that you have learned something and when it comes time to use the knowledge on the exam, you will do your best. It's all a frame of mind. You still have the power to control the exam because you are not going to allow the things you don't know to get you down. You realize that you don't need to be perfect to pass the CPA exam. There is room for error.

UNDERSTANDING AND APPLYING THE CRISIS STUDY MODE

The overall goal of the crisis study mode is to do what you can. Correct your major weaknesses by working the questions. You skip the reading and jump to the doing. To most effectively use the crisis study mode, the CPA candidate must not panic. Keep your mind on the task at hand and don't think about what you don't know. Walk into the actual CPA exam as confident as if you had spent years studying and reviewing the material. Tell yourself you did the best you could. Now you are going to use what you know to answer the questions to the best of your ability.

Liken the crisis study mode to a person who has just won a contest at the grocery store. The winner is given 10 minutes to fill a grocery cart with everything that they can put in the cart. You keep it all for free. What's your plan?

First, you would analyze the layout of the store. Meat is the most expensive grocery item so plan to go directly to the meat section. Your family is allergic to turkey, so you plan to avoid that area of the meat department. Produce is also expensive, but it is very perishable. You could freeze the meat for later use, but if you don't eat the produce right away it will spoil so you skip the produce area. Cereal is also expensive and usually has a long shelf life but you know your family only eats certain kinds so before the event, you scope out the store and note where your favorite cereal is. Notice how you are analyzing the situation as it fits the contest and your individual needs. This is how you make a successful plan when studying in the crisis mode.

Now the time comes for the contest to begin. Do you walk or run down the aisles? You hurry, but you are careful not to run so fast that you might slip. You proceed directly to the meat section, grabbing some expensive items along the way. After all, make the trip worthwhile. You don't look back and worry about the food items you missed. You just keep going to the meat department. When you reach the meat coolers, you use your planned knowledge to get the maximum benefit. You select steaks and other expensive cuts of meat.

In the crisis study mode of the CPA exam, study what will benefit you the most. Forget about the knowledge you already have. Study what you don't know, not what you already know. Correct as many weaknesses as you can. Get maximum points from the situation. When it comes time for the exam, continue to believe that you can succeed. Remain calm and do not panic. Earn points along the way from what you remember of your carefully applied study plan and from your crisis study mode approach. A calm person can apply the knowledge so much more accurately than a frantic person. You wanted steaks because you enjoy the taste, but they are expensive and something you couldn't afford to buy. You corrected the weakness in your budget by throwing steaks in the grocery cart instead of hamburger. You can afford to buy hamburger. You remained calm. Study what you don't know. Fix what you can in the time you have. When the real exam comes around, you will have both hamburger knowledge (knowledge you learned a long time ago) and steak knowledge (your newly acquired knowledge). Believe that you can pass. Use everything you've got to do so.

PERSONALLY SPEAKING

Yes, the crisis study mode can produce positive results. However, avoid this mode if you can. It takes a lot of guts to use this method. You have to be a confident person who won't allow self-doubt to creep in. Many well-prepared candidates fall apart after the first exam section because they lose control of the exam. Self-doubt creeps in and takes over. Those people who have used the crisis study mode are more apt to succumb to self-doubt because they know they used an approach that was less than ideal.

I passed the exam without a review course. I basically studied for 1 week and used my guts to get through, but it wasn't that easy. I studied hard in college and had learned the material well. I used a reputable set of review manuals so I had guidance and knew what the big areas were. Because I was working very long hours in public accounting, I just ran out of study time. I had to use the crisis study mode. It wasn't easy. Frequently that little doubting voice would start to talk to me and I had to say, "Go away, I am doing my best. I believe I can pass." The worst part was controlling the self-doubt at the exam. It's hard to believe when you are stumbling over the material and guessing at answers, unsure if you have answered even one question correctly.

I knew that many people had studied more than I did. My best friend from college, now a first-year law student, had self-studied 2 to 3 hours a day. The colleague I rode to the exam with had taken a review course and seemed to have studied everything. The first day of the exam, I saw a woman who in college had always outperformed me. Did I have a chance? I believed I could earn at least 70 to 75 points and this would put me over the top. I told myself my friends and acquaintances could earn a higher score than me, but in the end there was room for all of us to pass. When I didn't know something, I first tried my educated guess and then moved on to the outright guess. I never stopped believing. If it sounds easy, think again. After the first day of testing I ran back to my hotel room and called my husband. I was crying so hard that he couldn't understand a word I said. I wanted to go home and give up. My husband was very supportive and talked me out of it, reminding me that I had no way of telling how I performed. He encouraged me to keep going so I could learn more about the exam. Then, if I had to go back, at least I would know what I was facing. Boy, did I ever need that advice! I stopped crying and started to review my material for the next day. I kept on fighting.

I passed three out of four sections. I scored 75 points in the ARE and FARE, getting as close as I could and still passing. Just think that if I had given up, I would have had to start all over. I scored in the 90s in Audit because I was an auditor and used my practical knowledge to write good essays. I scored a 69 in Law. I knew that by using the crisis mode I was cutting something short. Six months later, I returned to write off my condition.

Try your best to avoid using the crisis mode. If you find yourself in a position where it means you either give up or use the crisis study mode, you know what to do. Get going, apply the crisis techniques, do the best you can to correct your obvious weaknesses, and enter the exam room still believing that you can pass.

14 NERVES OF STEEL

How do you get nerves of steel? How do you maintain nerves of steel throughout the exam process? This chapter is about how to control CPA exam nerves by helping overcome exam intimidation. Exam anxiety can quickly send you into orbit, putting your knowledge in a hard-to-find place. Passing the exam requires a unique mix of knowledge, exam strategy, confidence, and stamina. Don't risk the chance of losing control. Be aware of how your nerves can work against you.

YOUR NERVES

The power to pass the CPA exam resides in you. Only you can walk into that exam room and answer the questions. No candidate ever earned points by being nervous. Points are earned by applying knowledge. Adjectives for nervous are jumpy, jittery, fidgety, uneasy, tense, fearful, and agitated; none of these characteristics will help you pass. It becomes very difficult to apply knowledge when you are nervous. You must remain calm to pass. Adjectives for calm are peaceful, composed, cool, collected, undisturbed, serene, tranquil, and unruffled; work to remain calm, not nervous.

GET THOSE NERVES OF STEEL

Nerves of steel are not available for purchase. No store sells them. Just like the much-desired abs of steel, you must develop nerves of steel. No one can expect to have a flat, strong stomach without a lot of hard work and exercise. Buying the exercise equipment and leaving it in the box is not going to help you. The same situation applies to maintaining nerves of steel during the CPA exam process. Simply purchasing review materials is not the answer. You must use those materials to learn. Fear is reduced by knowledge. The more you learn about the situation, the less fearful you will be. Open up the materials and study. Help yourself learn. Feed your mind with knowledge.

VISIT THE EXAM SITE BEFORE EXAM DAY

A few months before the CPA exam, go to the hotel or office building where the exam will be given. Look at the exam room. Check out the parking. Try to travel to the site about the same time you would be driving there on exam day. Note whether rush-hour traffic might be a problem. Just seeing the actual place will help keep you calm. Later, when you visualize yourself at the exam, you will have an accurate picture. Trace your route to the hotel, making note of restaurants where you might eat during the lunch hour. Walk around the hotel to find lounges and areas where you could sit and review your last-minute study packets. If available, locate express elevators. Give yourself a mental picture of the entire environment. Obtain the cost and hours of the hotel breakfast and lunch buffets. Find out when you must check out of the hotel. Make sure ice is readily available for your cooler. Inquire to find out if your room will include a refrigerator, coffee pot, and/or hair dryer. Know what to expect.

VISUALIZE YOURSELF IN CONTROL

Always visualize yourself controlling the exam. Don't see yourself jumpy, fidgety, or tense. Picture yourself so attuned to the exam material that you couldn't possibly be nervous. See yourself methodically moving through the questions, staying within the time limits, and completing all questions. Look forward to the essays as a chance to write well and show the graders what you know. Use the essays to showcase your knowledge.

BRACE YOURSELF FOR THE UNEXPECTED

Realize that you won't know everything. No matter how much you studied and how much you practiced, plenty of questions will stump you. There is no need to get agitated. Upon reading a question that you can't answer, take a deep breath and say, "Oh here is a concept that I must guess on." Use your educated guessing technique to first narrow down the answer choices. If that doesn't work, make an outright guess by selecting your predetermined outright guess letter "b." No need to waste time thinking about what letter to guess. Guess consistently and you will be correct some of the time.

Don't panic when you open the exam booklet, and see an essay question that you know nothing about. Stay in control by first reflecting on your overall knowledge. Skim the question, looking for cues and clues that will jog your memory. Release tension by chuckling to yourself. Remind yourself that if you don't have any answers, and you studied, then no one else in the room does either. This is about you and the grader. Give the grader something to grade. Write clearly to earn the writing points. Fake the knowledge by making up something that sounds relevant. Don't give up. You are maintaining nerves of steel and fighting for points by doing.

List some points in your question booklet. Stare at them for a moment, allowing a mental image to come alive in your brain. If you followed your study plan, you have studied everything and you must know something about this. Let the words speak to you. For example, a term such as accounting for uncompensated absences provides you with clues. An employee is absent from his job and has not been compensated. At least now you know something. You can discuss some concepts such as the compensation has been earned and must be accrued for by debiting an expense account and crediting a liability account. Remain calm to bring knowledge back to the front of your brain where it can be more easily accessed. Expect some questions to throw you.

TAKE SOME RISKS

Even the best athletes aren't going to keep winning without taking some risks. Don't be afraid to take some risk. Every now and then, decide that you must "go for it." Taking risks on the CPA exam means answering the question to the fullest. Leave no problems or essays blank. Put down what you know first. Then, keep on fighting by listing those concepts that might be correct. After all, the grading method is positive; points are not deducted for incorrect statements. When in doubt, write it down. If the graders don't want the concept they will ignore it.

USE YOUR FAVORITE RELAXATION TECHNIQUES

Athletes will often go to a corner and meditate or pray before an important game. Others will listen to their favorite music. Some might call home to talk about something other than the event coming up. Before the exam, think about what works best for you and what techniques you could do in such a situation. Maybe your favorite relaxation method is to sit in a bubblebath and read. Unfortunately, you won't be permitted to take the CPA exam while bathing. However, taking a bubblebath the night before would relax you. Don't schedule a massage before an exam section, as you will probably be too relaxed and fall asleep in the exam. Schedule a massage the night before to help you sleep. Don't bring your CD player to the exam to listen to music outside the room or your cell phone to make last-minute calls, since you are prohibited from taking CD players and cell phones into the exam room. Use these techniques the night before to relax. The day of the exam, keep your relaxation techniques simple. Some suggestions are as follows:

- Chew gum
- Close your eyes and picture a peaceful waterfall
- Drink water, but remember the restrooms are usually closed the first 30 minutes of each exam section.

- Do some jumping jacks
- Go outside and take a breath of fresh air
- Give your study buddy a high-five or a hug
- Sing or hum to yourself
- Use the restroom outside of the exam room
- Wish others good luck
- Complement people on their clothing or hair style
- Talk to yourself saying you are proud of you for making it to the exam
- Take deep breaths
- Smile

Notice that most of the activities in the list are easy to do and are very low key. Why? You don't want to get yourself stirred up before the exam. Avoid making the common mistakes that can contribute to additional stress and tension.

DON'T CRAM

Don't study up until the last minute before the exam. Clear your mind. Leave your exam materials in your car or hotel room. If you must bring along your afternoon study materials, check them at the coat check. Last-minute study points probably won't stay with you until the end of the exam.

STAY CALM, NOT ACTIVE

Pacing around the room will only contribute to more tension. Your heart will beat faster and you might become more nervous. Keep your pre-exam activities to a minimum. To be peaceful one must utilize peaceful activities like prayer or meditation.

FORGET THE OFFICE

Your colleagues know it's exam day. Don't call them; they will just remind you of the many problems and deadlines that are coming up. You can't do anything about work issues now. Save them for your return.

WATCH WHAT YOU EAT AND DRINK

Eat foods that won't upset your stomach. Having greasy sausage and bacon for a preexam breakfast will lead to trouble later on. Stuffing yourself at the hotel breakfast buffet leads to a drop in blood-sugar levels a few hours later. Drinking too much coffee or caffeine beverages not only leads to many restroom trips but can also bring on a decrease in energy level when the caffeine wears off. On the other hand, if you're used to consuming morning caffeine, don't try to go without it. The best idea is to stick to your normal routine. Now is not the time to experiment, diet, or overeat. Do what you normally do.

Try to eat breakfast at least 90 minutes before the exam begins to give your digestive tract a chance to work before you enter the exam room. Plan on a light lunch that includes some protein. Avoid hot, spicy foods and alcoholic drinks. Give yourself the best chance possible to think clearly. Stress levels decrease by utilizing rational thinking methods.

DON'T TRY TO SHOW OFF

Outside of the exam room, don't try to impress the candidates around you by reciting concepts out loud. You just might make a mistake and become really flustered. Keep your technical thoughts to yourself. Clear your mind. Engage in light conversation about the weather, a person's outfit, or the color of the walls. If a candidate asks you how to do something, tell them you don't remember. You could become more confused. There will not be time to go back to your room and check your notes. Now is not the time to be helpful. Focus on the business of concentration.

FORGET ABOUT WHAT YOU DON'T KNOW

So what if there are areas you did not study? Sure there are topics that you don't fully understand. The exam is going to begin in a few minutes. There is no time to improve the situation. Nerves of steel require you to keep that positive attitude out in front of you at all times. Go ahead and admit that there are areas in which you are still weak. That's to be expected with an exam of this technical breadth and depth. You are ready to face the exam. Predict that you will respond to each and every question to the best of your ability. Trust that the knowledge you have will be enough to get you a 75% on every section.

REMIND YOURSELF THAT YOU DON'T NEED
TO BE PERFECT TO PASS

Tolerate an average performance because an average performance on the CPA exam will get you a score of 75% or greater. Nerves of steel will carry you through this exam. Cut yourself some slack and be forgiving if you don't know something. Think about all of the material you do know.

PERSONALLY SPEAKING

All this talk about nerves of steel might make you think you have to be superhuman to take the exam. What if you just lose it all right before the exam begins? I know candidates that react to every pressure situation by bursting into tears or cussing and swearing before the event begins. It is their method of releasing tension. It's okay to do this. Of course you won't want to cuss out loud. You might want to walk away from the group to cry alone. Don't worry--you will have tissues because I listed them on the packing checklist shown in Chapter 15, "CPA Survival Kit," Exhibit 1. If you must, go ahead and release the tension. Do it your way, but, once you are in the exam, it's show time! Time to keep your cool and demonstrate nerves of steel.

Maintaining nerves of steel requires you to forget about what others think. Let's say you feel pressure because everyone from your boss, to your college professors and your family think you will pass. In fact, they not only believe that you will pass, they think you could win an Elijah Watts Sells award, which is the award given to the three highest average scorers for each exam. Admit it--their belief in you is flattering, but it also could lead to disaster if you start to doubt yourself. One of my colleagues likes to take bets on who might win an award. He even goes so far as to encourage certain students to go for a top score. Who needs this pressure? If someone is placing this kind of pressure on you, don't accept it. You risk the chance of feeling you must be perfect to pass. Then, when you run into problems during the law exam that you have never seen before, or you experience time pressures, you could get so upset that you can't concentrate. I have seen it happen many times. Don't expect too much of yourself. Tell the well-wisher that while an award would be nice, you are going to be thankful just to pass all four parts the first time. After all, with a 12-15% pass rate, you would still be in the upper 85th percentile of the nation.

15 CPA SURVIVAL KIT

CPA SURVIVAL KIT

Are you beginning to think the CPA exam is similar to a survival outing where you must learn how to exist in a vast wilderness for 2 days without food, water, and the comforts of home? Just like a wilderness adventure, you will survive better if you are properly prepared and trained for the outing. Through the study process you are building stamina every day. You have spent 4 to 6 months preparing for the event. Your knowledge base of concepts is growing stronger. You can almost feel your brain growing with all that newly acquired knowledge. Still, you could commit a treacherous mistake by arriving at the exam without the proper materials, attitude, and commitment. Simple things like knowing what to wear, what to bring, and how to act at the exam can make a big difference in your performance.

WHAT TO WEAR

Wear comfortable, loose clothes. So what if you gained weight during the study process? Break down and buy yourself some new jeans or sweatpants that feel comfortable. Work on your new improved image after you complete the exam. Now it's time to do whatever it takes to make you feel comfortable.

Wear clothes that are layered. Temperatures can vary greatly depending on the time of day. You could be hot during Law and freezing during Auditing. A special word about temperatures--if you find yourself seated under an air duct and it bothers you, ask the proctors for a new seat. The blowing air will only bother you more as the time progresses. Wear sweatshirts that you can take off and sit on if your seat is uncomfortable, or if you need some cushion for your aching back. Watch the type of sweatshirt. For security reasons, most exam sites do not allow you to wear hooded or pocket sweatshirts. The exam proctors control access to the exam. The proctors could ask you to check your sweatshirt.

Leave your contact lenses at home. Who needs to be beautiful at the CPA exam? Wear glasses that have been prescribed within the last year. Be sure you can read well. Under the stress and pressure to read so much information, your eyes could dry out. Purchase some lubricating drops to use between exams.

All coats and hats must be checked at the coat checks. Candidates who wear blazers that look like a coat may be asked to check them. Keep it simple--wear a crew neck sweatshirt over a tee shirt and wash your hair so you don't have to wear a hat.

Wear shoes that could accommodate swollen feet. Sitting in one position for long periods of time can cause swelling. Anything that is tight may distract you. Sandals with socks that you can slip off while taking the exam work well.

Wear barrettes, bows, or whatever it takes to tie or clip hair back out of your eyes; constantly fixing your hair takes time and may cause loss of focus. Keep it out of your way.

Should men shave? If you are used to a clean-shaven face, a growing stubbly beard could cause you to itch, and/or fiddle with your face. If you normally shave, then shave for the exam. If you are used to an unshaven face over weekends, go ahead and be grubby.

Ladies, what about your purse? Most exam sites allow ladies only (sorry, gentlemen) to bring a **small** purse into the exam. Realize that a proctor could search your purse. Remove all study notes, index cards, and calculators. Note the emphasis on small. The examiners understand that you may need to conceal some personal feminine items in your purse, but the purse should be small. Candidates are not allowed into the exam room with purses that resemble tote bags or suitcases. All purses are to be kept under your chair.

Avoid wearing tee shirts with lewd sayings. Keep it clean. The examiners could ask you to leave if they believe you are inappropriately dressed.

Wear a watch and bring another along. Clocks are not always visible from your exam seat. Do not bring alarm-type clocks. Keep to a simple watch that you are very familiar with because you have been using it during your study time. Familiarity is the key. Use a watch that allows you to tell the time at a quick glance. Who needs to waste valuable time figuring out what time a watch is registering. Replace the watch battery about 1 week before the exam to allow you time to buy a new battery if the replacement battery is not working.

Leave backpacks, tote bags, or briefcases in your hotel room, car, or at the coat check. You will enter the exam with only a small purse (if you are a lady) and a small bag of materials.

CPA EXAM BAG OF MATERIALS

A clear plastic bag that fastens with a zipper lock closure is perfect to hold the materials to take into the exam. You probably wonder what the world is coming to as you walk into a room with a plastic bag. Why a clear bag? The proctors must check what you are bringing in with you. A clear bag allows them to tell at a quick glance just what you are bringing in. Place the following items in your bag:

- Exam permit
- A picture ID such as a driver's license
- The questionnaire to be turned in during the first exam section that you sit for
- Plenty of sharpened Number 2 pencils--mechanical pencils are acceptable as long as the lead is as hard as a Number 2 pencil
- A good pencil sharpener
- A soft eraser
- Tissues
- Aspirin or pain relievers
- Antacids for an upset stomach
- Nasal spray, atomizers, and other medications which you routinely use and are likely to need during the exam
- Your hotel and/or car key
- Earplugs only if you have tested them during your studies at home. Unless you are used to earplugs you could be distracted by the internal noises you hear
- Comfort foods
- Money to buy your lunch before you go back to your hotel room to study and relax for the next section

Notice that you are not allowed to bring rulers, calculators, notes, cellular phones, beepers, laptop computers, or firearms into the exam. May you use a pen on the exam? You may use a pen to write your essay or problem answers only. Complete all questions where you darken in ovals and items on an answer sheet using a Number 2 pencil, as they will be scanned. Leave your pens at home. Orderly papers help earn points. Erase and make your answers look organized and neat.

Acceptable comfort foods are small food items that can be consumed quickly without making a big mess. Obviously you aren't going to bring in the leftover cold pizza from last night's review session. Things like hard candy, gum, granola bars, candy bars, and other prepackaged foods are fine. Keep the food items to a minimum, as you won't have much time for eating.

Notice that you are not allowed to enter the exam room with beverages. The risk is that you could spill liquid substances on your exam papers and ruin them. There will be watercoolers in the exam room. Standing up and walking to the watercooler will help you wake up and get the blood flowing for maximum thinking capability.

Leave the heartfelt keepsakes at home. Bringing pictures, stuffed animals, dolls, and rabbits' feet into the exam is a waste of time. You won't have time to even think about these things since you have much work to do. Who wants to worry about accidentally forgetting the keepsake at your exam seat? Your knowledge and your attitude will serve as your good luck charms.

Leave the expensive jewelry at home. You might be tempted to play with your jewelry and interrupt your concentration. Remain preoccupied with the exam, not your accessories. Don't risk losing precious items by being careless or forgetful.

There will be restrooms in the exam room. You must not leave the exam area until you have completed the exam. Be sure you understand the boundaries of the room. While you are waiting for the first exam to begin, look around to locate the nearest restrooms and watercoolers.

WHAT TO BRING TO YOUR HOTEL ROOM

Bring whatever it takes to keep you happy. Some typical items a candidate could bring to the room are as follows:

- Your friend or spouse--only if they comfort you. Otherwise, go alone.
- That special pillow you always sleep on. If you are used to sleeping on a special down-type pillow, you had better bring it to the exam. Hotels usually provide foam or polyester-filled pillows. You must do everything to help get a good night's rest.
- A cooler with lunch meat, beverages, and items you are used to eating. Getting an upset stomach because you are eating hotel food won't help you.
- Your review manuals, software, index cards, and calculator. You never know what you might want to consult. Having your materials handy will help keep you calm.
- A windup or battery alarm clock. Hotel clocks are sometimes hard to figure out. Wake-up calls are not always reliable. You will sleep better if you know you have help to wake up on time.
- A candle or two, to burn while you study and relax. Don't fall asleep before you blow it out!
- Cards, posters, banners, flowers, and other motivational "well-wishers" that your supporters have made for you.
- The above-mentioned plastic bag of materials for the exam room.
- A wonderful attitude!

WATCH YOUR MEDICATIONS

I once helped a very stressed-out candidate who suffered an asthma attack 1 hour before the CPA exam began. She had not had breathing problems for years. I calmed her down and had her call her doctor. He called in a prescription to a pharmacy nearby. I sent the candidate into the exam. I ran to the pharmacy, paid for the prescription, and delivered it the exam proctors to take to her seat. Chances are you won't have a friendly review-faculty person attending the exam with you. Think about all of your past medical problems. Be prepared. The extreme stress of the CPA exam can bring out old illnesses.

ABOUT YOUR ATTITUDE

You can make or break your day just by the way you act. Leave the bad attitude at home. Come to the exam site with confidence. Believe that you are here to do your best. Refer to Chapter 14, "Nerves of Steel," for specific tips to help control the exam. Know that you will fight, scratch, and crawl for every point that is available. Smile at others in the elevator. They too, are afraid and uncertain. Accept the wish for you to have "good luck." Although many say there actually isn't anything in the universe such as good or bad luck, a strong belief in either one or the other may produce a particular "attitude" that almost ensures one or the other. Maintaining a positive, confident attitude could make "good luck" more likely. Surely, a positive attitude will keep you happier and calmer. You are here. You are ready to go. It's show time!

PERSONALLY SPEAKING

Packing for the CPA exam makes the exam seem real. Refer to the checklist in Exhibit 1 to ensure that you are ready. Arrive at the exam site early and make yourself as comfortable as you can. I love to watch people check into the hotel room. Many have three or four boxes of textbooks and are accompanied by the entire family. As much as I love my family, I actually checked into the hotel 3 days before the CPA exam all by myself. In other words, I left home to study. Yes, I was behind schedule and I was getting very grumpy. Who wanted me at home anyway? Assess the situation and leave when you need to. I used the extra time to acquaint myself with the exam area. I actually got to meet some of the exam proctors the day before the exam. I had found the fast-food court and other areas before they became overrun with nervous CPA candidates. If your budget doesn't allow you to check in early, find peace and quiet by going to a relative's house who is out of town, or just by locking the bedroom door and asking your family to pretend that you are not there. Use the checklist to guide you in your packing. Use luggage on wheels so you won't waste time waiting for bellhops. Comfort and simplicity is the name of the game.

If your hotel has a pool or other water recreation, take a bathing suit. I brought my swimsuit because the hotel had a hot tub. It felt great to unwind and relax my tense muscles. This aided in my sleep and provided me with some time to rest my brain. Remember, being sleepy is a good thing when it's time to give up the last-minute reviews and get some rest.

I will never forget the exam where one of my candidates wore a lewd tee shirt to the exam. She claimed she didn't realize what impact that might have on other people. She just wore it because it was comfortable. Look at what you plan to wear. Read what it says. Think about other people's reactions when they have to stare at your back for 15½ hours of exam time and read that saying over and over again. No, I can't print what that tee shirt said. However, I do know that the Board of Examiners did consider throwing her out of the exam. Instead they opted to have her go to the bathroom and turn her tee shirt inside out so other candidates wouldn't be forced to read the saying. You see, about 15 minutes into the exam, many people around her, both male and female, complained to the proctors. They said the tee shirt distracted them and broke their concentration. Expect some distractions.

During the middle of my Auditing exam, the hotel speakers got turned on and we could hear the phone ringing and every conversation that was going on in the hotel office for about 10 minutes. Did the examiners give us extra time to complete the exam? No, they did not. Be ready to use your powers of concentration, as you may need them. Other examples include subway trains going close by a window, jackhammers being used in a nearby street, and rush-hour traffic with horns honking and people yelling. Shut out extra noise by using such focus techniques as writing in the exam booklet, mumbling to yourself, and using highlighters to note the key points.

Eat normally at the exam. Don't try new foods. Avoid greasy and spicy foods. Watch your beverage intake--you won't have much time to use the restrooms. Relax and try to assume some of your normal schedule by eating and exercising as you would if you were at home. If you can afford it, book a massage at the hotel the night before each exam day. If money is tight, bring some bubble bath and take a hot bath. Review some last minute study sheets while you soak.

You are ready to show those graders what you know. I know you can do it. I believe in you!

Exhibit 1: CPA survival kit checklist

Check off the following items as you pack:

1. CPA plastic bag containing:

   - Exam permit
   - Picture ID
   - Exam questionnaire
   - Number 2 pencils
   - Eraser
   - Pencil sharpener
   - Tissues
   - Earplugs
   - Money for lunch
   - Hotel and/or car key
   - Watch
   - Necessary medication
   - Comfort food

2. Pack for the hotel room:

   - Special pillow or blanket to help you rest easy
   - Exercise clothing such as swimsuit or tennis shoes
   - Food or beverages to keep you happy (I always bring my own coffee, mug, and coffeepot)
   - Three comfortable, layered outfits
   - Review materials for comfort
   - Last-minute study packets
   - Your own alarm clock
   - Candles to burn while relaxing
   - Bubble bath to soak in a warm bath
   - Your positive attitude--the "I believe I can do it attitude!"

16 SHOW TIME

Yes, the time has finally arrived to perform at the exam. The final dress rehearsal is here. This chapter explains what to do during the week and days preceding the exam and when to arrive Wednesday morning.

ONE WEEK BEFORE THE EXAM

Get some sleep. Do not attempt to make up for lost study time by pulling all-night study marathons. This method just does not work. Attempt to get at least 7 hours of sleep each night. If you're waking up due to exam nightmares, get out of bed and study. Studying CPA materials is the quickest way to cure insomnia. Don't fight against your body's will. When you are tired, rest.

Some people turn to sleep when they become anxious. If you find you're sleeping too much, use exercise, proper diet, and an active study plan to pull yourself out of the CPA preexam doldrums. Sleep is necessary, but there is no need to overdo it. With 1 more week to go, there still is plenty of material to learn and review.

As suggested in Chapter 6, "Developing Your Personal Study Plan," you should try to take off the week before the exam, yes, even if you must take a leave of absence without pay. Explain to your boss that you will be much better off at home studying instead of at work getting grumpier and more anxious as the hours fly by. Use your vacation time to study. Future vacations will be so much more enjoyable when you know you've used every available resource to pass all four exam sections the first time. Make passing the exam your priority. Enjoyment and self-gratification can only truly be experienced upon accomplishment of your goal. The week before the exam is prime review time as you are now entering the "crisis mode."

CRISIS MODE

Seven more days to go and it's time to enter the crisis mode. This means you must stop and take stock of the key areas that you have absolutely left untouched. Divide each of the remaining 7 days into time for studying the areas you have not yet worked on and give yourself time for reviewing previously studied areas. Let's say that at this time, with 1 week left, you still have not studied deferred taxes, leases, pensions, and bonds. Although you really have some large holes to fill at this late date, all you hope to do is to fill in as many gaps as you can. Total knowledge is not necessary. Since these four areas were listed on the top 10 FARE items to study, they are important. What should you do? You must attempt to study all of the above areas. Since it is so close to the exam, simply remain calm and attempt to reap as much knowledge as you can. Try to learn something about all of the areas. There will be no review time since the exam is just days away. Again, trust your memory to remember the concepts that you studied a few days ago.

What's your best time of the day to study? Morning person or not, get up early and study one of the four areas listed above for about 6 hours per day. That's all you can give it. Normally, you would study by reading about 25% of the time and practicing questions about 75% of the time. Adjust this time frame to crisis mode. Crisis mode means you will decrease the reading time to about 10% reading and increase the practice to about 90% doing. When you answer the questions, you are practicing, and practice increases the long-term retention.

One morning should be devoted to the study of deferred taxes. Do what you can to learn something about everything. After you spend the 6 hours studying, it is now time to review old study concepts.

The best way to review old areas is to test your memory by answering questions. If your review course included software, use the computer to generate an exam for yourself. If you are self-studying, look to see if your review manuals have practice exams. Work the exams, attempting to follow the techniques listed in Chapter 8, "Time Management." Have your study buddy bring some essays, problems, and other objective answer format questions to the study session. Exchange papers and work each other's questions. Take the rest of the day to go over the exam, learning from your mistakes.

Realize that in order for the crisis mode to work effectively, you can only expect to study five to six areas the week before the exam. The crisis mode also requires that you do not work that week. You must make the CPA exam your priority. The week before the exam can be your most productive study time, especially if you can remain calm.

REMAINING CALM

You cannot help yourself if you are nervous, tense, and uptight. Reassure yourself that a calm, cool, and collected state of mind will allow you to absorb and retain more knowledge. Face your worst fear. Talk to your family, friends, and coworkers and tell them that you are scared; you are afraid that you might disappoint them by failing. Get all of your worries out in the open. If you talk about your fears, you will find that the worst situation, total failure, won't make you less of a person. It will just mean that you scored like the majority of people who take the exam. About 84-88% of the people fail. Spend no more than 15 minutes per day thinking and talking about failure. Get the idea out in the open but don't dwell on the negative. After 15 minutes of discussion, stop and move on. Go back to your studies with a clear mind, ready to absorb the material. There is no time for self-pity. There is still plenty of time to fight for points and to learn new areas. Limit your complaint time to 15 minutes per day because you have better things to do with your time. Spend about 6 hours studying new material and about 4 hours reviewing previously studied areas. Take short (about 15 minutes) study breaks every 2 to 3 hours.

STUDY BREAKS

No phone calls during study breaks. A short phone call often turns into a discussion of great length or, worse yet, the struggling CPA candidate decides to run off with a friend or family member for "just a short while." This does not work. Use your study breaks to organize what you will take to the CPA exam. Begin setting aside items to pack. Use the checklist in Chapter 15, "CPA Survival Kit." Obviously grocery store trips are allowed, but make them short and always be sure you are purchasing the items you want to take to the exam. For example, some pain medication, cough drops, purse-size tissues, and/or your prescriptions. One week before the exam, all activities must center on preparing for the big event. This is one weekend where you will do nothing but study.

WEEKEND BEFORE THE EXAM

All time must be spent studying, so your family reunion will have to get along without you. All energy and time must be spent getting ready. If your family members scheduled a big event such as a wedding or baptism, and you are a major part of the party, obviously you should go. Hopefully you planned for this well in advance and knew that you could only afford to have two to three areas left to study the week before the exam. Life does go on even if you are taking the exam. Do only what is absolutely necessary.

If you are one of the rare accountants who has kept to the personalized study plan and you really are caught up, you have more time for reviewing and even some time for fun. Reward yourself by spending some time shopping, watching a movie, or doing anything else that isn't too taxing. Running a marathon the weekend before the exam might get your mind off the exam, but it might also make you so tired you won't function clearly on Wednesday when the exam begins. Everyone has a different situation. Realize that in the upcoming week you must face one of the most challenging and grueling experiences of a lifetime. Take it easy--pace yourself.

ONE DAY BEFORE THE EXAM

It's Tuesday and tomorrow you will begin the final leg of the CPA journey. Perhaps you must pack and travel to the site today. If Tuesday travel is required, leave early in the morning, arriving at the exam site just in time to check into your hotel room. Upon checking into your room and making sure that the room meets with your approval, take a walk to the exam site. Note restaurants, heavy traffic areas, and restroom locations. Read signage that the proctors and building personnel may already have posted. If necessary, locate the CPA exam coat-check area. Spend no more than 1 hour touring. You still have time to learn some material or to review some old areas. Stay off the phone. The phone is your enemy, since it gives you an excuse to waste time. Forget about the office. They know where you are and what you must do. Save your call home for later in the evening when you need a short study break. Continue to believe in yourself. You are so smart that you could learn a 10-point essay topic today. Yes, people have studied areas the day before the exam and have been pleasantly surprised as the area was tested the next day. You never know just how valuable the study process is. Remain focused on the task at hand.

If you are planning to travel to the exam site the day of the exam, set two or three alarm clocks. Take no chance of getting a late start. If it normally takes 20 minutes to travel to the exam site, budget 40 minutes. Always double the time. Who knows what obstacles might detain you? The AICPA does not grant extra exam time to any participant, even in hardship cases such as being detained by a car accident or train derailment. To avoid the problem, travel to the exam site the day before. It's beneficial to take time to get acclimated to the exam environment. Just seeing the site will relax you, and Tuesday evening will be so much more relaxed if you can fall asleep knowing where you must go in the morning and being able to picture what the room looks like.

If you are staying at a hotel the night before, set your alarm and call the hotel desk for a wake up call about 5 to 10 minutes after the alarm is scheduled to go off. Set your exam outfit out. Put the clear plastic bag with the exam permit and all other important items in a place where you will be sure to easily locate it. Pretend you are a parent setting out the clothing and materials needed by a child leaving for the first day of kindergarten. Although this might all sound absurd, activities like this will not only help you if you wake up late, but this planning will also help you to realize that the event is almost here and you are prepared and eager to tackle the exam sections one by one.

Before you fall asleep, say a meditation or prayer. Tell yourself that you have done your best and there is no turning back now. You believe in yourself. You believe that you can pass the CPA exam.

GOOD MORNING--IT'S WEDNESDAY!

Good morning indeed, as you will now begin the final miles of the CPA journey. Jump out of bed ready to go. Begin the day with a positive outlook. Here you are, ready to take the test. No, you may not be ready for all of the questions, but you are happy that the test day has finally arrived. You are ready to battle with the exam.

Take a deep breath and go get something to eat. It is dangerous to count on room service the morning of the CPA exam. Many times the food arrives too late to eat. Take your last-minute Law study packet and walk to a nearby restaurant. The walk will help to wake you up. As you wait for your food, look over the materials. Spend a few minutes acquainting yourself with the Law time management techniques. You will spend 1½ minutes per multiple-choice question, hoping to complete 20 questions every 30 minutes. Remind yourself to check the front of the question booklet for the point values of the essay and other objective answer format questions, budgeting 2 minutes per point.

Don't call home, or anywhere, for that matter. Phone calls may cause you to lose focus. Right now, you don't want to be worried about something back home or at the office. You can't do anything about those situations now. Postpone phone calls until the day of testing has ended. At 6:15 Wednesday evening you will need a friendly voice to talk to. Phone conversations right now could easily upset you. Keep your thoughts focused only on the CPA exam.

Smile at people in the halls. If you engage in conversation, keep it light. Talk about the weather, the latest sports event, or your last vacation. Don't quiz each other. It is not the time to ask your mind to recall things. If you are in a public area, spend your time silently reviewing. If you are in your car or a hotel room, talk out loud. Recite lists and check them to see what you remember.

Take Your Final Smoke

Smoking is not permitted at the CPA exam site. If you must, chew some nicotine gum. However, as discussed in Chapter 5, "Assessing Your Strengths and Weaknesses," smoking is a weakness that can dull your brain. If you didn't quit during the study process, forgive yourself and say you will quit after the exam. Just be prepared to sit for the entire exam time without smoking.

Check Your Non-CPA Items

Items such as coats, hats, beepers, cell phones, laptop computers, hand-held computers, calculators, and firearms are not allowed in the exam room. Leave such items in your car, hotel room, or at the coat check outside of the exam area. Rules are rules. There is no use getting upset attempting to enter the exam room with an ineligible item. The instructions you receive from your state board of accountancy will remind you what to bring and what not to bring. Take these rules seriously, as the state boards will enforce them. Leave all note cards, crib sheets, and review materials outside the exam room. You must go it alone. Scrap paper is not allowed. Use the margins of your examination question booklet to write on. Take your watch, exam permit, and the plastic bag of items into the room. Smile at the proctors as you enter the examination room. This is it--you are ready to show the AICPA what you know.

Arrive at the Exam Room Early

The Law examination begins at 9:00 a.m. Make a restroom stop before you enter. At most exam sites, the restrooms inside the examination area are closed 30 minutes before and 30 minutes after the exam begins. Enter the room no later than 8:45 a.m. Locate your assigned seat, which is usually the last three or four digits of your candidate number. Even before the exam begins, the proctors will be making last-minute announcements. Listen carefully to what they have to say.

Greet Your Tablemate, Take Control

Introduce yourself to your tablemate(s). Smile and shake hands, wishing everyone good luck. You will be surprised at just how much a little conversation helps you stay in control. As soon as your exam booklets arrive, remain totally quiet. Use the 15 minutes before the exam begins to look around. Locate the water cooler, restrooms, head proctor table, and exits. Read the material that you can. In other words, don't open booklets until you are told to do so. However, use the opportunity to read the information that's out in the open. If the proctors say you may complete the attendance record, go ahead and do so. See Exhibit 1 for a sample attendance record. Do not use pen. Use your Number 2 pencil.

Exhibit 1: Sample attendance record and instructions

EXAMINATION QUESTION AND ANSWER BOOKLET

CANDIDATE NUMBER

Record your 7-digit candidate number in the boxes.

ATTENDANCE RECORD
(To Be Retained by State Board)

Print your **STATE** name here.

Name _____
(please print)

Home Address _____

City _____ State _____ Zip Code _____

Signature   Date

LPR

VERSION 3

203912 S

Attendance Record Booklet No.

Detach the Page at the Perforation

UNIFORM CERTIFIED PUBLIC ACCOUNTANT EXAMINATION
Business Law & Professional Responsibilities

November 1, 1995; 9:00 A.M. to 12:00 NOON

INSTRUCTIONS TO CANDIDATES

(This *Examination Question and Answer Booklet* contains an *Attendance Record, Examination Questions, Essay Ruled Paper,* and *Objective Answer Sheet*)

1. Do not begin writing on this *Booklet* until you are told to do so.

2. Complete the *Attendance Record* and your 7-digit candidate number above. Detach the page at the perforation so it can be collected and retained by the State Board.

3. Turn the *Booklet* over and record your 7-digit candidate number and state on the *Objective Answer Sheet.*

4. The *Objective Answer Sheet* is on pages 27 and 28. The objective portion of your examination will not be graded if you fail to record your answers on the *Objective Answer Sheet.*

5. See instructions 3 and 4 on page 3 for instructions on how to record your answers to Question Numbers 4 and 5.

6. In order to grade your *Objective Answer Sheet* and essay answers, the Booklet No. above must be identical to the Booklet Nos. on pages 3, 19, and 28.

over

1

E X A M I N A T I O N　Q U E S T I O N S

UNIFORM CERTIFIED PUBLIC ACCOUNTANT EXAMINATION
Business Law & Professional Responsibilities

The point values for each question, and estimated time allotments based primarily on point value, are as follows:

	Point Value	Estimated Minutes Minimum	Maximum
No. 1	60	90	100
No. 2	10	10	15
No. 3	10	10	15
No. 4	10	15	25
No. 5	10	15	25
Totals	100	140	180

CANDIDATE NUMBER

Record your 7-digit candidate number in the boxes.

Print your **STATE** name here.

LPR

November 1, 1995; 9:00 A.M. to 12:00 NOON

INSTRUCTIONS TO CANDIDATES　*Failure to follow these instructions may have an adverse effect on your Examination grade.*

1. Do not break the seal around *Examination Questions* (pages 3 through 18) until you are told to do so.

2. Question Numbers 1, 2, and 3 should be answered on the *Objective Answer Sheet*, which is pages 27 and 28. You should attempt to answer all objective items. There is no penalty for incorrect responses. Since the objective items are computer-graded, your comments and calculations associated with them are not considered. Be certain that you have entered your answers on the *Objective Answer Sheet* before the examination time is up. The objective portion of your examination will not be graded if you fail to record your answers on the *Objective Answer Sheet*. You will not be given additional time to record your answers.

3. Question Numbers 4 and 5 should be answered beginning on page 19. If you have not completed answering a question on a page, fill in the appropriate spaces in the wording on the bottom of the page "**QUESTION NUMBER ___ CONTINUES ON PAGE ___.**" If you have completed answering a question, fill in the appropriate space in the wording on the bottom of the page "**QUESTION NUMBER ___ ENDS ON THIS PAGE.**" Always

begin the start of an answer to a question on the top of a new page (which may be the reverse side of a sheet of paper).

4. Although the primary purpose of the examination is to test your knowledge and application of the subject matter, selected essay responses will be graded for writing skills.

5. You are required to turn in by the end of each session:

   a. Attendance Record Form, page 1;
   b. *Examination Questions*, pages 3 through 18;
   c. *Essay Ruled Paper*, pages 19 through 26;
   d. *Objective Answer Sheet*, pages 27 and 28; and
   e. All unused examination materials.

   Your examination will not be graded unless the above listed items are handed in before leaving the examination room.

6. Unless otherwise instructed, if you want your *Examination Questions* mailed to you, write your name and address in both places indicated on page 18 and place 55 cents postage in the space provided. *Examination Questions* will be distributed no sooner than the day following the administration of this examination.

Test Cover 2

over

3

Examination Questions Booklet No.

2 03912 Q

The example is from the November 1995 CPA exam, the last exam to be disclosed. The attendance sheet may look slightly different, as candidates must now sign a statement of confidentiality. Begin by reading the attendance sheet carefully from top to bottom. Note the instructions for completing the ovals on the Scantron answer sheet. Just like the ACT or SAT exams, the entire oval should be darkened using a Number 2 pencil.

Write your candidate number in and then blacken the ovals. Your candidate number will be on the exam permit that served as your entrance permit to get into the exam. As you are waiting for the actual exam to begin, read as much as you can see. Do not break the seal on the question and answer booklet until you are told to do so. The general instructions to the candidates about what they are allowed to complete before the exam begins usually read as follows:

> The Examination Question and Answer Booklet (Booklet) will be distributed shortly before each session begins. Do not break the seal around the Examination Questions portion until you are told to do so.
>
> Prior to the start of the examination, you are permitted to complete page 1 of the Booklet by recording your 7-digit candidate number in the boxes provided in the upper right-hand corner of the page and by filling out and signing the Attendance Record. You are also permitted to turn the Booklet over and carefully and accurately record your 7-digit candidate number and State on the Objective Answer Sheet portion of the Booklet.
>
> You must also check the booklet numbers on the Attendance Record, Examination Questions, Objective Answer Sheet, and Essay Paper. Notify the proctor if any of these numbers do not match.

Based upon the above instructions, you are to do three things before the examination begins

1. Complete the *Attendance Sheet* which includes signing the confidentiality statement
2. Turn the booklet over, and record your 7-digit candidate number and state on the Scantron answer sheet
3. Check the booklet numbers

Instructions 1 and 2 are self-explanatory. Instruction 3 means to check all booklet numbers to be sure that they are the same. The booklet number will be in the lower right-hand corner of the front page, just below the bar code. This is an important step, as it assures the proctors that you have not exchanged booklets with nearby candidates. If any of the booklets do not match, notify your proctor immediately. Don't be afraid. It is better to discover the problem before the exam begins rather than after. An exchange of booklets constitutes cheating, and of course, cheating is out of the question. You want to be a CPA, so promptly report any booklet discrepancies to the area proctor.

Time to Begin

This is it! You just heard the proctor say, "Good luck, you may begin." This is really it. You have worked hard and thought about this day for months. Now is the time to control the exam. As soon as the proctor tells you to begin, take a deep breath. Tell yourself that you will begin when you are good and ready to begin. What you have just done is taken control. Now we all know that you really don't have time to waste, but by talking to yourself and reminding your brain that you can begin when you want to, you will control the exam--the exam will not control you.

Take some time to look through the entire exam. This might take you about 3 minutes and no more. Hopefully you have thought about whether you will begin with the multiple-choice, the other objective, or the essay(s). At the top of each problem, write down the total point value and the total time. A sample time allocation for Audit may look like this.

Question number	Point value	Question type	Time allocation	Total time allotted
1	50	Multiple-choice	2 minutes per question x 90 questions	180 minutes
2	10	Other objective	2 minutes per point x 10 points	20 minutes
3	10	Other Objective	2 minutes per point x 10 points	20 minutes
4	20	Essay	2 minutes per point x 20 points	40 minutes
5	10	Essay	2 minutes per point x 10	20 minutes
Total				**280 minutes**

Add up your total time and ask yourself if your time allotment fits the total minutes that you have. In the above example the candidate must go back and adjust the time allocation, as the Audit exam is a total of 270 minutes. The time allotment is over by 10 minutes. The 10 minutes could be deducted from essay number 4 and number 5. It is not wise to rush the multiple-choice questions. Looking through the exam and budgeting time should take no more than 5 total minutes. The time budget for the multiple-choice questions includes the 5 minutes it took you to acquaint yourself with the entire exam and to budget your time.

Once you've determined that your time allocation fits the total minutes, go ahead and write down the time you expect to complete the questions. Recall, for Law this usually is 20 multiple-choice questions every 30 minutes. Write down 9:30 by question number 20, write down 10:00 by question number 40, and 10:30 by question number 60, assuming you begin with the multiple-choice questions. For Audit, the candidate plans to complete 15 multiple-choice questions every 30 minutes.

See Chapter 17, "Law--You've Only Just Begun," for more tips on how to stay cool and calm while writing the Law exam. Yes, you can do this. Once you see the actual exam, you will realize that you can pass the CPA exam. You will believe that you can pass. The end is near.

PERSONALLY SPEAKING

My knees were knocking, my stomach was sick, and I was sure I would fail. Yes, that pretty much describes how I felt when I woke up the morning of the first section of the CPA exam. You had better believe that I was talking to myself! I looked at myself in the mirror and just started to laugh. I looked awful. I didn't look like a gutsy, in-control woman. I took a few minutes and actually put on some makeup. Now don't misunderstand me. I would rather have you spend time reviewing some last-minute study tips than applying makeup or shaving. But, if it helps you gain control, do it. For me, it was like therapy.

Before you leave your car or hotel room, take a big, long, deep breath and remind yourself that if you walk in looking like you are somebody who knows what they are doing, with your shoulders back and your head held high, you will psych out more than one nervous candidate. I know you are not trying to be mean to the people around you, but the more you look in control, the more you will be in control. This is not about the other guy or gal. This is about competing only with yourself to do the very best you can. The event has arrived and it is your event. Only you can go in the room and do what you must do. There is no time to look back and certainly no time to think about what you don't know. All focus must be on what you do know and how you can use your knowledge to be successful. Go in ready to do battle with the exam. Battle through the tough parts, coast through what you know, and complete the exam on time. Fight, scratch, and crawl for every point and every concept. Answer all questions, leaving nothing blank. Give the graders something to grade. Give the exam a very good fight.

17 LAW--YOU'VE ONLY JUST BEGUN

Suddenly you realize that this is real. You are taking the CPA exam at last. The exam question booklet is far less intimidating than you ever dreamed of. It's just a paper booklet with several questions. You have an answer booklet section that contains the essay paper, multiple-choice answer sheet and other objective question answer sheet. Your job has just begun. This chapter provides the candidate with tips to handle the stress of the first exam section, Business Law and Professional Responsibilities, hereafter referred to as Law.

TAKE CONTROL--BUDGET YOUR TIME

The informed candidate understands that there is considerable time pressure on this exam section. There is no time to relax, hyperventilate, or have a panic attack. After all, what good would it do to panic? Apply the time-management techniques that you have spent time learning. Mark the multiple choice off in sections, taking the time to indicate when each section should be completed. Glance through the other objective questions, perhaps noting the topics tested. Don't let them scare you. If you see that one of your strong areas is tested in the essays, breathe a sigh of relief. This is good. If at first glance you don't remember much about an area, don't let it worry you. You will deal with the question when the time comes. Right now, you must list the time constraints and begin reading the multiple-choice questions.

LAW MULTIPLE-CHOICE QUESTIONS

Expect 60 to 70 multiple-choice questions with a 4-option answer choice as the letter a, b, c, or d. As you work the questions don't try to keep score. It's a waste of time to tally how many questions you think you have answered correctly. Your job over the next 2 days is to provide the answers, not the grade. Paid graders will evaluate your paper over the next 6 weeks, so stick to your job.

Read each question deliberately. Write in the margins of the question booklet and on the actual test question. Your question booklet will be shredded shortly after the exam ends, so feel free to mark it up. Writing and marking on the exam booklet helps you to remain in control and focused. Use your highlighter to mark key words. Read and think, don't try to hurry.

Take the time to recall what you know about the area. For example, consider the following negotiable instrument question:

> To the extent that a holder of a negotiable promissory note
> is a holder in due course, the holder takes the note free of
> which of the following defenses?
>
> a. Minority of the maker where it is a defense to
>   enforcement of a contract
> b. Forgery of the maker's signature
> c. Discharge of the maker in bankruptcy
> d. Nonperformance of a condition precedent

Recognize the key phrases, such as "holder in due course." Recall what a
holder in due course is and the requirements that must be met to be a holder
in due course. To be a holder in due course, the individual must be a holder
of a negotiable instrument and fulfill certain requirements. Negotiability is
not a problem here since the question states that the promissory note is negotiable. Step 1 out of the way. Now, it is necessary to recall the defenses.
The two categories of defenses are real and personal. A holder in due
course takes negotiable instruments free of personal defenses and therefore
is subject only to real defenses. Another way to restate the question is to ask
which of the above listed defenses are personal defenses. The answer is d.
since nonperformance of a condition precedent is a personal defense, the
only situation listed in which a holder in due course is free of personal
defenses.

EXPECT TOUGH QUESTIONS

The negotiable instruments area is one of the toughest sections of the
Law exam. While you might struggle to answer questions like the one
above, don't despair. At most, the number of questions won't exceed 10 and
more than likely will only be about 5 to 6. You can't afford to allow your
confidence to slip just because you have hit a rough patch of questions.
Take your time with these, making educated guesses. The next section
might be one you know.

On both the Law and the Audit exam, it seems the AICPA groups the
questions by topical areas. This is comforting when it is one of your strong
areas. Enjoy the ease with which you can proceed through the questions.
Tell yourself this is how you will pass the exam--by correctly answering
what you know. When you hit one of your weak areas, recognize that this is
all part of the process. If you have studied to learn something about everything, you will know some of the material. Don't fight the questions.
Simply admit your shortcomings, answer the question to the best of your

ability using the knowledge that you have, and move on. You can't fix it now.

Expect to guess on some questions. Say to yourself, "Yes, this is what I expected, I don't know everything." Spending time thinking about what you didn't study or don't understand is not helpful. This is the real exam and there is no time to go back and correct your weaknesses now. Now is the time to remain alert. You can't sleepwalk through your performance. You will have to deal with the easy as well as the difficult questions.

OTHER OBJECTIVE LAW QUESTIONS

Of all the other objective answer format questions, Law is the easiest. Many of the objective formats are similar to true or false questions. Allowing 2 minutes per point will give you adequate time to read, understand, and complete the question. Blacken in your ovals as you go. Be careful not to get off track. Don't ponder too long over one question. Continue with the essays. You can always go back to the unanswered areas.

LAW ESSAYS

Use all of the essay techniques described in Chapter 9, "Writing A Beautiful Essay Answer." Mark the completion time on the top of the question. Read the question requirements first. List the key words that come to mind as you read the question. After you've finished listing the key words, read the entire essay looking for hints and clues to incorporate into the answer.

At this point in the exam, your stomach has calmed down and you feel almost comfortable. Don't relax too much. Time is an enemy on the Law exam. Continue to work at a steady pace. Label the requirements and use lead-in sentences. If you make a mistake, erase or cross out.

It is easy to make a false start. If you just spent 5 minutes writing two pages of points and then discover you have taken the wrong approach, don't waste time erasing your work. Simply cross out what you have written and start over. The graders are aware that you are under considerable pressure and could easily make a mistake.

The most important step in an essay is to proofread your answer. Before you begin reading your answer, reread the question requirements. Then read your answer. Did you address the question requirements? Did you tell the graders everything you know about the situation that might be relevant? Did you take a stand?

A candidate cannot afford to sit on the fence. In other words, the question must be answered. You must answer the question and defend your reasoning. For example, study the essay question shown in Exhibit 1. The requirements clearly ask the candidate to state whether a corporation is correct about a certain situation. There is no room for debate. The candidate must begin the answer by stating that the corporation is correct in its contention or it is not.

Some candidates believe that it's okay to sit on the fence. In other words, they attempt to take both sides by first answering why the corporation might be correct in the situation and then going on to compromise by saying the corporation could also be incorrect. The graders are not allowed to make judgments. They are not going to pick your best reasoning and support. If you try to take both sides of the argument you will not earn points. Bite the bullet and take a stand. Answer the question and provide the reasoning to support your conclusion. Once you take a stand, don't look back. You have made your choice.

Examine the essay answer shown in Exhibit 2. Note how clearly and concisely the answer is presented. All requirements are labeled and each answer begins with a direct answer to the question asked. The candidate is clear and to the point. This is the proper technique for Law questions.

CONTINUE TO WATCH YOUR TIME

At most exam sites, an announcement is made stating that there are 10 minutes left. At every site, an announcement is made stating that there are 5 minutes left. At the 5-minute point, stop what you are doing and blacken any ovals that you have left untouched. Pick your lucky letter and consistently use it. An outright guess is better than leaving the question blank. Who knows just how lucky your lucky letter might be? After all ovals have been filled in, continue completing the essays until the proctors tell you the exam is over.

PUT YOUR PENCILS DOWN

When the law exam has ended, an announcement will be made that the exam time has expired and you are now to put your pencils down. Don't fool around and try to keep on writing. Disregarding exam rules is a serious offense that could result in your exam being confiscated and not counted. Follow the rules--put your pencil down and turn your materials in to the proctor. The Law exam is over.

You may not leave the examination room with any exam materials or notes. At the end of the Law exam, you are required to turn in the following items:

- Attendance Record and Statement of Confidentiality
- Examination Question Booklet
- Essay Paper, both the used and unused paper
- Objective answer sheet

Note that you are not to turn in your examination permit. Take your permit with you. Don't take chances. Ask the proctor if you have turned in all necessary items. Thank them and walk out of the room with a smile. You have just completed 3 hours of testing. The Law section is over.

Exhibit 1: Law essay example

Perry, a staff accountant with Orlean Associates, CPAs, reviewed the following transactions engaged in by Orlean's two clients: World Corp. and Unity Corp.

WORLD CORP.

During 1998, World Corp. made a $4,000,000 offering of its stock. The offering was sold to 50 nonaccredited investors and 150 accredited investors. There was a general advertising of the offering. All purchasers were provided with material information concerning World Corp. The offering was completely sold by the end of 1998. The SEC was notified 30 days after the first sale of the offering.

World did not register the offering and contends that the offering and any subsequent resale of the securities are completely exempt from registration under Regulation D, Rule 505, of the Securities Act of 1933.

UNITY CORP.

Unity Corp. has 750 equity stockholders and assets in excess of $100,000,000. Unity's stock is traded on a national stock exchange. Unity contends that it is not a covered corporation and is not required to comply with the reporting provisions of the Securities Exchange Act of 1934.

Required:

a.   1.   State whether World is correct in its contention that the offering is exempt from registration under Regulation D, Rule 505, of the Securities Act of 1933. Give the reason(s) for your conclusion.

2.   State whether World is correct in its contention that on subsequent resale the securities are completely exempt from registration. Give the reason(s) for your conclusion.

b.   1.   State whether Unity is correct in its contention that it is not a covered corporation and is not required to comply with the reporting requirements of the Securities Exchange Act of 1934 and give the reason(s) for your conclusion.

2.   Identify and describe 2 principal reports a covered corporation must file with the SEC.

Exhibit 2: Law essay answer

a.   1.   World is incorrect in its first contention that the offering is exempt from registration under Regulation D, Rule 505, of the Securities Act of 1933. World did not comply with the requirements of Rule 505 for the following reasons: the offering was sold to more than 35 nonaccredited investors; there was a general advertising of the offering; and the SEC was notified more than 15 days after the first sale of the offering.

2.   World is also incorrect in its second contention that the resale of the securities would be completely exempt from registration if the offering were exempt. Securities originally purchased under a Regulation D limited offering exemption are restricted securities. They must be registered prior to resale unless sold subject to another exemption.

b.   1.   Unity is incorrect in its contention that it is not required to comply with the reporting requirements of the Securities Exchange Act of 1934. Unity must comply because it has more than 500 stockholders and total assets in excess of $5,000,000. Alternately, Unity must comply because its shares are traded on a national securities exchange.

2.   A covered corporation must file the following reports with the SEC: Quarterly Reports (10-Qs); Annual Reports (10-Ks); and Current Reports (8-Ks). These reports are intended to provide a complete, current statement of all business operations and matters affecting the value of the corporation's securities.

DON'T LOOK BACK

The first exam section is over. There is no going back to change answers. Hang on to that positive attitude. Look forward and concentrate on the next business at hand--food, exercise to stretch those cramped muscles, and a last-minute review of the Audit area.

Don't talk to others about your performance. They will only confuse you and make you feel inadequate. No doubt they encountered problems that you didn't, but there is no need to discuss your problems or their problems. There is no way you can fix it now. The graders at the AICPA will grade your exam. Your job is not to grade--your job is to move on and get ready for the Audit exam.

PERSONALLY SPEAKING

My nickname for the Law exam is the exam of tears. Candidates shed tears before and after the exam. Some people release their tension by crying. Since Law is the first exam section, it is inevitable that you will see some people crying or at least very upset. Don't let it bother you. This is your performance and you must remain in control.

After the exam, people cry because they believe they have failed. The sobbing people are usually the kind of people who have extensively prepared for the exam, and are shocked by the detail and rigor of the actual Law exam. The more prepared you are, the more likely you are to be upset by Law. Yes, it's going to be difficult. Yet the Law pass rate is usually the highest or second highest pass rate per section. The tears are needless. You will see them and you must ignore them. Tell your crying study buddy or friend that they probably didn't perform as poorly as they think. Leave the grading up to the AICPA.

I dread dealing with the person who walks out of the Law exam and informs me that they did not complete the exam because they ran out of time. The odds of passing are against them. Candidates who leave essays blank and other objective questions unanswered have little or no chance of passing this section. However, the person has a chance to condition. If you fail to properly manage your time, don't contemplate giving up. There are three more sections to pass. Law is an easy one to repeat after you have conditioned on the other sections. Move on--you have only just begun.

18 THE ART OF AUDITING

The Audit and FARE exams are the two longest sections, testing 4½ hours of material. Both exams are given in the afternoon from 1:30-6:00 p.m. Afternoon exams are always tough, as a candidate tends to tire after lunch. The adrenaline rush of the morning Law exam has worn off and now the candidate must dig deep to stay focused. This chapter deals with the unique challenge that such a long afternoon exam presents. Begin by watching what you do during the lunch break.

THE BREAK BEFORE AUDIT

Law is over. The first leg of the journey is complete. There is no time to lament about wrong answers. As mentioned many times before, it is a waste of very valuable time for the candidate to attempt to grade the Law exam. Whatever you do, don't look back. Move forward by getting some exercise. Wake up the brain, stretch the muscles, and reward your body with some food. If you normally eat pizza or greasy hamburgers from a fast-food restaurant, go ahead and eat them now. If you normally eat yogurt and fruit, go ahead and eat yogurt and fruit. Do what you normally do for lunch. However, do keep in mind that if you normally skip lunch because you eat a big meal at 3:00 p.m. every day, then don't skip lunch. You won't be leaving the exam room for a big meal break at 3:00 p.m. The point is, do what you normally do by keeping the constraints of the exam in mind. Don't talk about the exam.

Hide from the people who just won't stop talking about the exam. Your performance is your performance and their performance is theirs. Neither party can change their performance. Talking about questions and answers is fruitless. Be firm and let the talkers know you don't want to talk or think about Law. You are moving on to Audit.

Arrive at the Audit exam by 1:15 to 1:20 p.m. with your exam permit and plastic bag of materials. There is no mystery now. You know where you sit and who your seatmate is. Greet the people around you, sit down, and begin completing your attendance sheet. Read the instructions that are visible. Complete the confidentiality statement. Don't open the seal until you are told to begin. You know what to expect.

AUDIT EXAM EXPECTATIONS

Expect 85 to 100 multiple-choice questions, 1 to 2 other objective answer format questions, and 1 to 2 essays. Sometimes, Audit uses one long, 20-point essay with multiple parts related to one set of information. More often, however, there will be two essay questions, worth 10 points each. When there are two essays, expect one to be quite straightforward, such as asking the candidate to read and answers questions about a particular internal control process. Another typical Audit essay is a question that asks a candidate to prepare the substantive audit procedures for a particular account or to examine an audit report and identify deficiencies in the written example. The straightforward essay is probably the question that will be graded for writing points. Remember that the examiners do not identify which questions or sections will be graded for writing points. A wise candidate always operates under the assumption that all essay responses will be graded for writing points and will exercise great caution when preparing all writing responses. When there are two Audit essays, expect one to be straightforward and one to be vague and unfamiliar.

Another way of describing a vague and unfamiliar essay is to say that the essay question appears to come from outer space or from off the wall. In other words, expect that one essay will appear to be almost unanswerable. This is where you, the candidate, must begin your fight. Here is where we separate the men from the boys, the women from the girls, and the potential CPAs from the plain accountants. The real CPAs will talk to themselves, work on writing points, and say everything that they possibly can about the subject. The real CPAs will keep on fighting until they can fight no more. The real CPAs will keep the little voice that says, "I can't pass this exam. This is just too hard--I give up." bottled up inside. The successful CPA candidates jump in and give it their best shot. You see, if the question is difficult for you, the prepared candidate, then it is almost impossible for the candidate who hardly even studied. Sure, you didn't study everything, and you admit that you far from mastered any one area. However, you studied to learn something about everything. You have some tools in your head and some fight in your body to give it your best. You will put down anything that appears to be relevant. After all, isn't the Audit section of the exam the area where you can be most creative?

THE CREATIVE AUDIT CANDIDATE

Let the title of this chapter speak to you. The art of auditing should tell you that there is room for some creativity. Unlike the Law essays, the Audit essay questions allow you to say anything you can think of. For Law you had to be precise, answering a definitive question and then going on to provide the support for your answer. Here you can be very creative and artistic. If in doubt, put the concept in your answer. Part of the creativity can come from your real-life experiences. Think about what you do in your job. Try to draw on some of your work experiences to help you. If in doubt, put it down. This is no time to be shy.

Spend the allotted time on your essay questions. Why hurry to complete the exam? Don't look ahead to this evening. You can begin preparing for ARE and FARE after 6:00 p.m. The successful candidate will utilize every minute of the 4½ hours. If you find yourself losing focus, get up and go to the watercooler. Get a drink of water and come back to your seat ready to fight. Continue to carefully manage the time element.

AUDIT TIME MANAGEMENT

The typical candidate does not have too much time pressure on Audit. However, never take extra time for granted. For example, there are times when a difficult other objective answer format question can eat up extra time. Keep the time guidelines in mind. Leave difficult questions blank, and come back after you complete everything you can.

The biggest time-management problem on Audit tends to be using all of the allotted time. Force yourself to use the entire block of time. It is tempting to hurry so you can go back to your room or begin your journey home. This is not the time to hurry to watch your favorite television program or go to your favorite restaurant. Unless you are a condition candidate who does not need to sit for ARE and FARE, your evening is not your own. Why hurry through the exam? It's like speeding. Often driving a few miles per hour faster will only get you to your destination 10-12 minutes earlier. Is this really an advantage? Use all of the 4½ hours. When you utilize the full amount of time, you can say that you really tried to do the best you could. If you leave early, you may really hate yourself when you receive a score of 73 or 74. You will always wonder if the extra 15 or 30 minutes would have helped you. You probably could have earned the additional one or two points just by proofreading your essays and making corrections and additions. You could have improved your writing presentation by changing the spellings of misspelled words or by adding a few concepts to your bulleted lists. Don't cut yourself short. Stay in the examination room until you have fully exhausted every possible technique. There will be plenty of time later this evening to phone your family and friends, eat dinner, relax, and get ready for the next day's events. Spend the time you need to do your best. Allow plenty of time for the multiple-choice questions, as they are often quite tricky.

AUDIT MULTIPLE-CHOICE QUESTIONS

The Audit multiple-choice questions are the most difficult of all four exam sections. The Audit multiple-choice questions are difficult for three reasons.

1. With the exception of the statistical sampling and analytical procedure ratio areas, the candidate is not using a formula or algorithm.
2. Many of the Audit questions have more than one correct answer. However, the "best" answer is what the graders are looking for.
3. Several questions require the candidate to know the definitions of numerous words and phrases, and then require that the candidate apply these concepts, definitions, words, and phrases to real-world examples. In other words, the candidate must act like an auditor.

There is nothing a candidate can do to change reason number one. The majority of the Audit questions are not numerical in nature and that is just a fact. The candidate should recognize this fact and change study habits accordingly. Using different study techniques for the Audit multiple-choice questions leads us to reason number two--candidates must work to find the "best answer."

The best answer is the one that gives the auditor the most assurance. Auditors just know the reason is good, just because they have audited and they understand the concepts. To reach the level where you can select the "best" answer, you must spend considerable time practicing.

Reason number 3 is difficult for most candidates. The majority of the candidates sitting for the CPA exam have never audited before. How can a candidate compensate for this deficiency? Practice makes perfect. As you learned in Chapter 10, the candidate doesn't really need to be perfect to pass the exam, they just need to be somewhere around 70-72% perfect for Law and Audit, and 60-65% perfect for ARE and FARE. The curve points will help you. To solve an experience deficiency, most candidates must go out in the real world and obtain some experience. This is not possible since typical CPA candidates will want to sit for the CPA exam as close to the time they have completed their college coursework as possible because most of the exam is a college textbook exam. Audit is the exception. To compensate for the lack of real-world experience, candidates will just have to practice more. Work as many multiple-choice questions as you can. Use the review materials and use the review software, but don't use old exam questions that your friend or colleague gave you. When you work Audit multiple-choice questions, read each answer response. Don't select the first answer you believe is correct. Choosing the "best" answer takes time. For example, take the following Audit multiple-choice question:

Which of the following most likely would give the most assurance concerning the valuation assertion of accounts receivable?

a. Tracing amounts in the subsidiary ledger to details on shipping documents.
b. Comparing receivable turnover ratios to industry statistics for reasonableness.
c. Inquiring about receivables pledged under loan agreements.
d. Assessing the allowance for uncollectible accounts for reasonableness.

The candidate must first recognize the key words in the question. "Most likely" is very important. Write a big "YES" next to the question to remind you that you are looking for the procedure that the auditor is most likely to perform. Valuation is the financial statement of concern here. There are basically five financial statement assertions as follows:

1. **Presentation and disclosure**--Deals with presenting the account on the proper financial statement in the proper section and requires that the client prepare the proper footnote disclosures to explain the various relevant accounting methods and policies.
2. **Existence and occurrence**--Requires the client to only list assets that exist and liabilities and revenues and expense accounts that have occurred.
3. **Rights and obligations**--Recognizes the fact that the financial statements should include items only if the client has the right to them and only if the liabilities are the obligation of the entity. For example, a mortgage payable shown on the balance sheet of XYZ Corporation must be a mortgage on a building owned by XYZ, and not owned by XYZ Corporation's CEO's mother-in-law for her vacation home. All obligations (liabilities) on the corporation's balance sheet must be for the company.
4. **Completeness**--All transactions must be included and presented.
5. **Valuation and allocation**--All account balances on all of the financial statements should be valued properly, in accordance with generally accepted accounting principles.

Keeping the above assertions in mind, the candidate answers the question by reading each answer choice. Answer a. is an activity an auditor would perform. However, the auditor traces from a ledger back to a source document such as a shipping document to satisfy the assertion of existence, not valuation. Answer b. might indicate valuation. Turnover ratios are analytical procedures. Most analytical procedures are performed to satisfy the assertion of completeness. The candidate should put a pencil dot by this answer, just in case a better answer cannot be found. Continuing with answer c., inquiring about receivables that have been pledged indicates rights and obligations. If the receivables have been pledged, they are not free for use by the client. This fact must be disclosed in the footnotes. So far in the analysis, answers a. and c. are clearly not valuation. Answer d. is the very best example of valuation since accounts receivable are to be valued in accordance with generally accepted accounting principles at net realizable value. Net realizable value indicates that uncollectible accounts have been estimated and the value is subtracted from the overall receivable balance. It may be an exhausting experience to read each and every answer response. While reading each answer response takes time and energy, it is the only way a candidate can say for sure that they have carefully considered all answer possibilities and have selected the best answer for the circumstances described.

Remember that your study materials must be current. While Law seldom changes, the content of the Audit exam has changed greatly over the last 10 years. Don't buy old CPA exams. The only exams that are now available are several years old, as the last open CPA examination was in November 1995. Since that time, the Audit knowledge has changed in total by at least a third. Yes, one-third of the Audit material has been revised. Follow the 1-year rule, making sure that your materials are no older than 1 year. Don't forget to check the software copyright date. Some review providers are slow to update software.

As you practice the multiple-choice questions, note that the same concepts can be tested using other objective answer format questions. The Audit exam will contain one to two other objective answer format questions, probably each worth 10 points. Don't let the form of the question scare you. Other objective answer format questions are really quite similar to multiple-choice questions.

AUDIT OTHER OBJECTIVE ANSWER FORMAT QUESTIONS

Here's where the prepared candidate will shine. Recognize that while the form of the other objective answer format question can be very intimidating, the knowledge needed to answer the questions is the same knowledge needed to answer the multiple-choice questions.

The other objective answer format question that scares a candidate most is a flowchart or an example of an audit working paper. Don't let this scare you. These types of questions can be broken down into bite-sized chunks that fit your knowledge bank. Take the flowchart question shown in Exhibit 1. At first glance this questions looks almost impossible. Stop and take a deep breath. Remind yourself that you must know something about

Exhibit 1: Sample Audit Essay Question

The following flowchart depicts the activities relating to the sales, shipping, billing, and collecting processes used by Newton Hardware, Inc.

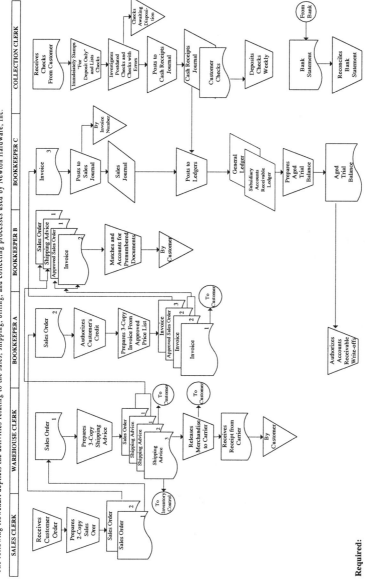

Required:

Identify the weaknesses in the internal control structure relating to the activities of (a) the warehouse clerk, (b) bookkeeper A, and (c) the collection clerk. Do **not** identify weaknesses relating to the sales clerk or bookkeepers B and C. Do **not** discuss recommendations concerning the correction of these weaknesses.

this. Take control by first marking down the time that you will complete the question. If the exam booklet indicated that this question was worth 10 points, you would allocate 20 minutes for completion time. Add 20 minutes to the current time and write the completion time at the top of the question. Now you know when you must stop working on this question and move on to other areas. Next, read the requirements. The requirements ask you to identify the internal control weaknesses for the following people:

- Warehouse clerk
- Bookkeeper A
- Collection clerk

Note that the examiners want the weaknesses for only three out of the six people shown on the flowchart. If the candidate were to describe weaknesses for all six people, he or she surely would not earn the full number of writing points. As discussed in Chapter 9, "Writing A Beautiful Essay Answer," addressing the requirements of the question is very important. Do not discuss items that the examiners have not asked for. The flowchart question requirements make it very clear that the candidate is not to discuss the recommendations concerning the correction of the weaknesses. Do not discuss means just that, don't make mention of how to correct the weaknesses, just identify and list the control weaknesses. Remain calm and take your time to read the entire flowchart. As you read, make a list of the weaknesses as you note them.

A candidate who has practiced this type of question will not be intimidated because they know the answers are similar to the items a candidate would provide for an essay question. Study the answer in Exhibit 2. Note how the answer is presented. The answer begins with a lead-in sentence that simply repeats the requirement question in a statement form (e.g., "The weaknesses in the internal control structure activities of Newton Hardware are as follows"). This shows the graders that the candidate can read and respond to the question. The answers are presented in excellent form--the three areas, warehouse clerk, bookkeeper A, and collection clerk are listed separately with the applicable weaknesses given under each heading. The answer also uses the technique of listing the answer in bullet-point fashion, making the response easy for the graders to grade. When a candidate practices, the candidate becomes more familiar with proper technique. Use this essay example as a model for other responses. When a candidate works on presenting his or her exam answers in the proper form, there will be no time for the candidate to panic or to think about just how tired he or she may be.

Exhibit 2: Sample Audit Essay Question Answer

The weaknesses in the internal control process of Newton Hardware, Inc. are as follows:

WAREHOUSE CLERK

- Clerk initiates posting to inventory records by preparation of shipping advice.
- Clerk releases merchandise to customers before proper approvals of customers' credit.
- Clerk does not retain a copy of the shipping advice for comparison with receipt from carrier.

BOOKKEPER A

- Bookkeeper authorizes customers' credit and prepares source documents for posting to customers' accounts.
- Bookkeeper prepares invoices without notice that the merchandise was actually shipped and the date it was shipped.
- Bookkeeper authorizes write-offs of customer accounts receivable and authorizes customers' credit.

COLLECTION CLERK

- Clerk receives directly and records customers' checks.
- Clerk does not deliver checks excluded from the deposit to an employee independent of the bank deposit for review and disposition.
- Clerk initiates posting of receipts to subsidiary accounts receivable ledger and has initial access to cash receipts.
- Clerk does not deposit cash receipts promptly.
- Clerk reconciles bank statements and has initial access to cash receipts.

FIGHTING AFTERNOON FATIGUE

The Audit and FARE exams are tiresome. Fight the urge to think about just how tired you might be. When a candidate is well focused, fighting for points, there will be little time to think about fatigue. Therefore, it is so important for candidates to use the entire set of exam-taking skills they have learned. A few of the more important skills are

- Manage your time.
- Read each multiple-choice question answer before you select the correct response.
- Blacken in the ovals on the answer sheet as you go.
- For essays, problems, and other objective answer format questions, read the question requirements first.
- Keyword the essays.
- Proofread your essay by first rereading the question requirements and then rereading each answer.
- Don't panic over the format of the other objective answer format questions. Remain calm and read the entire question before you begin.

Now the exam is over for today. Pick up your exam permit and your plastic bag of materials. You did your best to control the exam. You didn't even feel tired this afternoon. Candidates who control the exam by using proper exam procedures do not tire during the exam. These candidates are too busy managing the entire exam experience to begin thinking about how they feel. They won't feel the fatigue until after the exam.

AFTER THE AUDIT EXAM IS OVER

Now the candidate will succumb to the exhaustion. When a person has worked hard and expended all of his or her energy toward completing something as comprehensive as the first day of the CPA exam, he or she is bound to feel tired. However, if you tried your very best, you will also feel proud that you have completed the first day of the CPA journey. Like any traveler in a journey, you need rest. A suggested timetable for the evening's events is shown in Exhibit 3.

Exhibit 3: Timetable after the Audit Exam is completed

Time frame	*Tasks to complete*
6:00 – 7:00 p.m.	• Walk back to your hotel room or drive home • Call your family and friends, laugh, cry, and ask for sympathy, but don't talk about the exam
7:00 – 8:00 p.m.	• Get something to eat • Watch some television • Do some stretching exercises • Take a hot bath or go for a swim in the hotel pool
8:00 – 10:30 p.m.	• Review the ARE and FARE topics • Review the time-management techniques • Work some other objective tax questions • Look over some FARE problems selecting the areas that you fear the most
10:30 – 11:00 p.m.	• Lay out your clothes and exam materials • Put your FARE last-minute review materials in a bag to check at the CPA coat check • Set two alarms and ask a friend or the hotel desk to give you a wake-up call. Recall that the ARE exam begins at 8:30 a.m. and you must arrive by 8:15 a.m. to test your calculator • Pack your bags
11:00 p.m. – Midnight	• Continue to review and study only if you are unable to sleep

Notice that the schedule includes time to relax and time to study. There is limited time available to make phone calls or to go back over the day's activities. Stop thinking about what you can't change. You did your best; let the graders do their work. Your focus is now on tomorrow, when you must check out of the hotel and complete the last leg of your CPA journey. Your focus is now the ARE and FARE sections.

PERSONALLY SPEAKING

Isn't it great when you know you gave your all to completing a task? Isn't it a great feeling when you know you did your best? While you probably won't feel like you did your best, you did. You do your best when you stay in the exam room fighting for points. You do your best when you do not give up. You do your best when you complete the task. Don't be sorry--give it your all.

The greatest mistake I see candidates make the first day is that they spend too much time fretting over what they did wrong or what they didn't know. Didn't I tell you that you would not know everything? Didn't I tell you to expect an Audit essay that was really "off the wall"? Didn't I tell you that you would really have time pressure on the Law section? Didn't I tell you that some people would cry after the Law exam? Didn't I tell you that some people would leave very early in both sections of the exam? Yes, I told you, but that still doesn't make it any easier. The uniform CPA examination is so tough that it's almost hard to describe. But look at it this way--you are a success so far because you remained in the exam room and fought for every point you could.

Did you notice that in the evening schedule of events, I did not include any time for discussing the Law or Audit exam with your friends? I also did not include much time for phone calls home. The less you know about what's going on at home, the better off you will be. Problems at home and work can wait until after the exam. Why spoil your best chance to continue? Discuss this philosophy with your family and colleagues before you leave for the exam. Tell them you care about work and home activities, but right now that cannot be your primary focus. Make yourself and the CPA exam your primary focus.

You have completed one-half of the CPA journey. Go forward with confidence that tomorrow will be even better because not only do you now know what to expect, but you also will have the benefit of a huge curve. You will be working with numbers, and most accountants enjoy that. Leave today's events behind. Move on and work to get prepared for the next day. After all, there is still time to learn something about ARE and FARE. If you remain calm, who knows? What you review tonight could show up on the exam tomorrow. Keep on believing that you can pass this exam. Know that you gave it a good fight. Don't waste valuable time on the phone complaining about what you can't control. Go for the points and keep on studying right up until the bitter end. That's what I did, and it really paid off. I received a score of 75 on two exam sections. Just think, if I had given up, I might not have passed. You know what you must do. Go and do it.

19 ARE--A TAXING EXPERIENCE

It's Thursday, the second and last day of testing. Yesterday was a short day, testing only 7½ hours. Today's exam sections, ARE and FARE, will last a total of 8 hours, 3½ hours for ARE and 4½ hours for FARE. This chapter deals not only with completing the ARE exam but also with the many details you must think about on your last day, such as checking out of the hotel, packing your bags, and testing your calculator.

LAST DAY--TIME TO CHECK OUT

Most hotels set early checkout times of 11:00 a.m. to noon. Since the ARE exam begins at 8:30 a.m. and ends at noon, candidates should check out of their rooms before they go to the exam. Plan to check out early. If the hotel offers express checkout with your credit card, take advantage of the offer. Lines can be long and few people understand the pressure that you are under. The CPA exam waits for no one. The proctors will not give you extra time just because the hotel was slow in checking you out. Pack your bags and get on your way. Worrying about paying a late charge because you didn't get back to check out on time can be a great distraction. Do it right--check out on time or arrange to pay an extra fee for late checkout.

Late checkout is an option that usually costs more money. Sometimes the extra fees are worth it. Checking out at the lunch hour can be less crowded and it will give you a chance to go back to your room, brush your teeth, splash some cold water on your face, take a nap, and review some FARE last-minute study areas. Be prepared, however, to pay extra for this convenience.

If you must check out in the morning, think about what you might need during the day. At lunch, it is a good idea to review your FARE index cards or last-minute study packet items so do not pack them in your suitcase. Put the FARE items in a bag. Use one of the hotel laundry bags. Take your luggage to the car or check it with the bellhop. Check your FARE bag at the CPA coat check.

Allow for plenty of time to check out, eat breakfast, review your ARE notes, and pack your bags. The activity will be good for you. It will keep your mind off of the long day. Don't waste time thinking about yesterday.

YESTERDAY'S PERFORMANCE

Yesterday's performance is just that--a job you did yesterday. It is too late to change anything. The law and audit exams are **not** meant to boost your spirits and make you feel good. They are tough exams and should be respected. Your job is to continue on, doing the very best that you can today. Use your experiences from yesterday to prepare for today.

What did you learn yesterday? Now you know where your seat is, who you share your table with, and you probably even know some of the proctors by name. The procedures for entering the exam room are familiar. You have located the restrooms and the watercoolers. The whole exam environment is something that you now know. What's going to be different today?

TODAY'S PERFORMANCE

Today, the exam is going to begin at 8:30 a.m. instead of 9:00 a.m. The morning ARE exam will have no essays. The multiple-choice and other objective answer format questions will be machine graded. Expect 80-90 multiple-choice questions and 2 to 4 other objective answer format questions. The ARE exam contains no essays and no problems.

Proctors distribute calculators the morning of ARE. Before the exam begins, candidates should test the AICPA calculator for possible malfunctions.

TEST YOUR CALCULATOR

Each candidate receives a calculator at the examination site to use on ARE and FARE. Candidates may not bring calculators to the exam even if the candidate ordered the calculator from the AICPA. At the end of the day, all calculators must be returned to the proctors.

It is the candidate's responsibility to test the calculator to ensure that it is functioning properly by using the test calculations printed in the examination booklets. Candidates are usually allowed to test the calculator before the ARE exam begins. Hence, it is wise to arrive at the ARE exam and be seated as early as 8:15 a.m. See Exhibit 1 for the calculator test. Understand that the instructions are distributed to the candidates, so there is no need to memorize the details. Calculator malfunctions are to be reported to the exam proctors as soon as they are discovered. Replacement calculators are available.

As mentioned in Chapter 10, "Practice Makes Perfect," **it is very important to hit the "CCE" button before beginning a new calculation** as stored data might affect new calculations. The examiners state that the candidate usually uses only the calculator's four primary functions.

1. Addition
2. Subtraction
3. Multiplication
4. Division

It is unlikely that the candidate will use the other function keys of square root, memory, and percentage.

Since about 1% of the calculators malfunction, don't take the calculator test lightly. Follow the directions and immediately inform the proctor of any problems. Typical calculator malfunctions include such problems as the display board showing only part of the number or the CCE clear key sticking. Be aware that a calculator could work well at the beginning of the exam and malfunction later. If you are having problems getting a correct answer, stop and check your calculator. Again, no additional time is granted because of calculator failure. Simply take your malfunctioning calculator to the proctor and get a new one. Return to your seat and spend a few minutes testing the new calculator's functions. Relax, as more than 99% of the calculators work just fine. Spend more time on the technical issues needed to pass ARE and FARE. Continue to manage your time.

TIME MANAGEMENT FOR ARE

There is seldom time pressure on ARE. The format of all multiple-choice or other objective answer format questions leads to quick decisions. Continue to play it safe by applying the time-management techniques of budgeting 1½ minutes per multiple choice and 2 minutes per point for the other objective format. Write your time allotments next to the questions.

Use the extra time wisely. Fight the urge to let your mind wander to the afternoon when the exam is finally over and concentrate on the task at hand. Write in the margins of the booklet, use a highlighter to mark keywords, and read each question slowly. When necessary, make educated guesses. Take the time to do your best and don't be distracted by the people who leave early.

EARLY DEPARTERS

ARE and FARE are the worst sections for early departures. Many candidates just give up. Don't let them bother you. You paid the exam fee, so get your money's worth by utilizing all of the time. Make a careful first pass through the exam, taking the time to think about what you've learned. Leave troublesome questions blank. Return to them after you have completed what you know. Answer the blank questions and don't go back to change the first answers unless you are absolutely sure they are wrong.

CHANGING ANSWERS

Should candidates use the extra time in ARE to reread questions and check over answers? Checking your exam for obvious errors is a good thing to do. However, exercise caution when changing answers. A person's first response to a question is usually correct. Change answers only when you are absolutely positive that your first response was incorrect. Leave any questionable answers as they are, assuming that you read the question thoroughly the first time through. The variety of tax topics can be overwhelming.

INCOME TAXATION--60 POINTS

Some candidates believe that ARE is the toughest section because it tests a candidate's weakest areas. The combination of subjects--taxation, governmental/not-for-profit, and managerial--results in a difficult exam. Recall the tax law rule:

- May exams test the previous year's tax laws
- November exams test the current year's tax laws.

Either you know the tax laws or you don't. As you work through the exam, you may feel you are getting more answers wrong than right. It may seem as though you are guessing on every other question. You are probably far more critical than you ought to be. Take a deep breath and recall the curve. ARE and FARE are often curved in the double digits. As many as 10 to 15 points could be added to your overall raw score. Take heart and continue to believe that you can pass, even when you hit the other governmental objective questions.

GOVERNMENTAL AND NOT-FOR-PROFIT--30 POINTS

The thirty points of governmental and not-for-profit questions usually include at least one other objective question. Expect the objective question to be very involved and expect the actual layout of the other objective question to be confusing. Don't think you are the only person in the room who is struggling. Remain in control of the situation. There is extra time so use it to read the other objective question from start to finish before you even attempt to answer one concept. Increase your comfort level with the question format by reading the entire question through again. Take the time to understand where the question is going. Use the extra time to take hints from the transactions.

Accountants are born to achieve and become very unhappy when they encounter snags. Slow down and work one question at a time. Upon completion of a question, don't look back. If you allow your confidence level to dissipate, you will hit "rockbottom." Appease your brain by admitting that you are tired and struggling. Take a break and get a drink of water or use the restroom. This isn't as bad as it seems. Keep on fighting, scratching, and crawling for points. One answer can make a big difference between a score of 74 and a score of 75. Move on to the managerial questions.

MANAGERIAL--10 POINTS

As you studied cost accounting, also called managerial accounting, it all seemed to be so simple. How could 10 points hurt you? Now, after wrestling with the tax and governmental areas, the managerial topics appear to be very involved. The increase in difficulty level can be attributed to your tiredness. It's now midmorning of the last day and it's easier to look forward to tonight and total freedom from the CPA exam than it is to expend energy reading cost graphs. Force yourself to sit there and concentrate. Focus all of your attention on the concepts. Managerial accounting is quite logical. Use your calculator to help test different formulas. No candidate can afford to overlook 10 points. Attempt to earn as many of the 10 points as you can. Strong cost accounting knowledge can help offset a major governmental weakness. Don't make a hasty exit. There is plenty of time to check your answer sheet.

CHECK THE ANSWER SHEET

Check the direction of the multiple-choice answer form. Recall there could be as many as four different forms. Typically a candidate receives at least two if not three different forms over the course of the two days of testing. Check to see that you've blackened the ovals in the correct direction. Small details can make a huge difference in helping you to remain in control.

REMAIN IN CONTROL

The step of verifying the answer sheet keeps you in control. You still have the power to pass the entire exam, so repress doubts about your knowledge. It doesn't matter if you are perfect. It only matters that you perform as well as or better than the other candidates.

After you have answered and reviewed the responses, leave your calculator on the table, pick up your exam permit and plastic bag of supplies, and quietly leave the room. Walk out of the room with your head held high and your shoulders back. You did your best. If it's only 11:00 a.m. that's great. Forget about ARE and begin preparing for FARE, the long haul.

PERSONALLY SPEAKING

Income taxation has always been my worst area so I would dream that I opened the exam and it was all taxation. This isn't going to happen, as only 60 points can be income tax topics. If it seems as though they are testing more than that, it may be because they are pretesting 10-15% of the multiple choice in the tax area. See Chapter 10, "Practice Makes Perfect," for a discussion of pretesting.

Now I understand that I passed the CPA exam because it was curved. The typical candidate does not know this and often becomes very depressed upon completing an area where the topics seem to be so unfamiliar. If you have a fear of taxation like I did, don't give up. The best way to improve your CPA tax knowledge is by working the tax questions in your review manuals over and over again. In the case of tax, practice really does make you almost perfect. There are only so many variations the examiners can use to test the tax knowledge. If you study, you will find they repeat many of the tax questions.

Governmental accounting is one area where candidates learn the basic knowledge level and are tested at the application or evaluation level. It's hard to predict just how the examiners will test governmental concepts. You can almost count on an other objective question but the form will often be very different from what you have already seen. Don't let the form of the question scare you. Answer what you can, make educated guesses, and then move on. All the preparation in the world probably wouldn't improve your knowledge level. Completing the exam is the most important task, not attempting to grade your performance.

Managerial accounting will either be very easy or very difficult, depending upon your skill level. Prepared candidates who spent time learning the material perform better when the exam is difficult. Either way, if you spent time studying, it will pay off.

The best advice I can give you is to never give up. I will never forget the candidate who suffered chest pains in the FARE exam. The exam proctors, aware of the candidate's distress, brought in the paramedics to examine him. He told them that he was not leaving until he had completed the FARE exam to the best of his ability. He knew that if he gave up, he might score less than 50 on FARE and miss the chance of conditioning.

The candidate felt pretty good about his performance on the other areas. I had never before witnessed such determination. After the exam, the paramedics took him to a local hospital where he was admitted for tests to determine if he had in fact suffered a heart attack. I called his wife and explained that he had postponed the hospital trip to finish the exam. She couldn't understand why he acted the way he did.

Those of us who have taken the exam understand why he waited to finish FARE. To him, a heart attack was easier to deal with than the thought of failing. He certainly did not give up. The story has a very good ending. He was found to have suffered a mild heart attack but recovered quickly. Three months later he learned he had passed not just three parts of the exam, but had also successfully completed the FARE exam. He really used his powers to concentrate on the task at hand.

When you find yourself feeling like you want to give up, remember the gentleman that fought through the pain of a heart attack to do his best. Surely you can fight through the discomfort of some tough material. There is no time to feel sorry for yourself. You must go on to pass FARE!

Exhibit 1: AICPA instructions to the calculator test

To turn the calculator on press ⓒⒸⒺ. Display will read "0." The calculator automatically turns itself off approximately 8 minutes after the last entry. All data in the calculator will be lost once the calculator is off. When you complete a calculation, we recommend that when you press ⊂=⊃, you press ⓒⒸⒺ before beginning a new calculation. The basic key descriptions are as follows:

ⓒⒸⒺ   **On and Clear**--Turns the calculator on and clears the display. To clear the calculator of all entries, press ⊂=⊃, then press ⓒⒸⒺ

⊂0⊃. . . ⊂9⊃   **Numericals**--Inputs that number.

⊂·⊃   **Decimal**--Indicates that all numbers to follow are decimals.

⊂+⊃ & ⊂-⊃   **Add & Subtract**--Adds the next number entered to, or subtracts the next number entered from, the displayed number.

⊂x⊃ & ⊂÷⊃   **Multiply & Divide**--Multiplies or divides the displayed number by the next number entered.

⊂=⊃   **Equal**--Displays the results of all previously entered operations.

⊂+/-⊃   **Change sign**--Changes plus (minus) to minus (plus).

⊂%⊃   **Percentage**--When performing a calculation, converts the displayed number to a percentage and completes the calculation. It is unlikely that you will need to use this key during the exam.

⊂√⊃   **Square Root**--Calculates the square root of the displayed number. It is unlikely that you will need to use this key during the exam.

ⓡⒸⓂ   **Recall/Clear Memory**--Pressed once, displays the balance in memory. Pressed twice in a row, eliminates the balance in memory but not the displayed number.

ⓜ-   **Memory Subtract**--Subtracts the displayed number from the balance in memory.

ⓜ+   **Memory Add**--Adds the displayed number to the balance in memory.

Test Calculations

Keystroke					*Display*
ⓒⒸⒺ	53000	⊂+⊃	47600	⊂=⊃	100600
ⓒⒸⒺ	125000	⊂-⊃	98300	⊂=⊃	26700
ⓒⒸⒺ	5000	⊂x⊃	1.667	⊂=⊃	8335
ⓒⒸⒺ	39000	⊂÷⊃	1300	⊂=⊃	30

20 FINANCIAL ACCOUNTING AND REPORTING--THE LONG HAUL

Financial Accounting and Reporting (FARE) is administered from 1:30 – 6:00 p.m. on Thursday, making it the last exam section. Talk about the long haul! Here you're dealing with the most difficult and diverse subject matter at a point in time when you've already spent 11 hours of testing over a 2-day time period. One might think the AICPA Board of Examiners is sadistic. Not really, it just seems like it when you're enduring the event. It makes good sense to put both calculator exams on the same day so the exam administrators don't have to take the time to distribute and collect calculators on different days. Accounting and Reporting (ARE) is tested Thursday morning because it is shorter than FARE and can be completed before lunch. Don't spend time feeling sorry for yourself. Think about it as the last leg of a marathon. Everyone else has an aching head, sore muscles, and tired eyes; you aren't the only one who is fighting to stay fresh. The trick is to fight for concentration and to resist the urge to leave the exam early. Control the urge to give up and continue to control the exam until the very end. Don't lose hope. The more you understand about the FARE exam, the better you can manage the long haul.

FARE--CURING THE COMMON MISTAKES

The statistics are pretty grim. Nationally, FARE has the lowest pass rate of all sections, sinking as low as 28% on the November 1998 exam. While the pass rate seems grim, there is a bright light at the end of the tunnel--the low pass rate doesn't have to apply to you. You don't have to be in the over 70% category of failures, you can be in the 28% pass category. Some factors contributing to the low pass rate are

- Exam fatigue
- Loss of focus
- Lack of technical breadth
- Misunderstanding essay and problem requirements
- Omitting the all important proofreading step
- Inability to dissect other objective questions

FIGHTING EXAM FATIGUE

Staying awake the night before to study for ARE and FARE is counter-productive. The best cure for exam fatigue is to get a good night's rest. How does one do this? Try turning out the lights, closing your eyes, and picturing yourself taking a walk in a beautiful park. What you picture is not important. What's important is that you work at getting **rest**. Without a good night's sleep, you will be a "basket case," incapable of concentrating. Begin planning for that peaceful rest immediately after you complete the Audit exam on Wednesday. Plan to get a good night's rest by doing everything you can to help yourself relax. Do not drink or eat caffeine products. Hot chocolate or tea may be your favorite bedtime beverages, but stay clear of these items the night before the test. When a person is under considerable stress, the usual effects of caffeine products tend to become exaggerated. Avoid the use of products that could leave you groggy in the morning. The more wide awake you are Thursday morning, the longer you can continue to feel awake and fresh.

What should you do if you didn't get a good night's sleep on Wednesday evening? Try **not** to think about it. Get up and eat your normal breakfast. Proceed through the day as though you got the best night's rest of your life. Making a big deal about not sleeping will only distract you. It's too late--you just have to deal with the lack of sleep. Throughout the day, go to the restroom and splash cold water on your face. The water and the walk will give your body a jolt. Hopefully you will have some spare time to take short breaks. As was mentioned in the time management chapter, candidates that can retain their focus will probably not experience time pressure on the FARE section.

Arrange for late checkout on Thursday so that during the lunch hour after ARE, you can return to your hotel room, brush your teeth, and take a short nap. Since ARE takes about 2½ hours, you can take a 45-minute nap as long as you wake up on time. Have a buddy check on you, in addition to setting an alarm and placing a wake-up call. You will be surprised how energized you can become from a 30- to 45-minute nap. But be careful to avoid the disastrous situation of forgetting to wake up on time to take FARE. Even if you can't sleep, simply stretching out and closing your eyes will help. Listen to some soft music. Don't turn on the television. You might find yourself wrapped up in the latest soap opera or news crisis and forget that you are there to rest your mind and body, especially your eyes. Don't phone home or the office--you need time to relax and your office or work matters will wait. Now is the time to stay focused and get some rest. If you did sleep well Wednesday evening, you might be wide awake. Still it is best to meditate, relax, and allow your mind and body to zone out.

After your restful period, eat a light lunch, and try some exercise. Go outside and get some fresh air. A walk around the building will get those cramped muscles stretched out and help settle your food. Do some jumping jacks or stretches. Who cares what you might look like? When you are a successful CPA no one will recall you jumping around at the exam site. Exercise and fresh air between exam sections are a must. Get the blood flowing again and act kind to your body by helping it cope. No one is used to sitting in a stressful situation for 15½ hours.

REMAIN FOCUSED AS THE END APPROACHES

FARE serves as a reminder that the end is near. Candidates begin to think about how great it will feel to walk out of the exam room and once again become a free person. You must work to remain focused--it won't just happen. Don't hurry through the questions. Is it better to become a free person at 4:00 p.m. or at 6:00 p.m.? At the moment you might say 4:00 p.m. Three months from now when you receive your exam scores and you are staring at a low score you will no longer feel free, you will feel sick; you will never forgive yourself if you leave early only to find out you received a score of 74. Ouch! You paid for the full 15½ hours of testing--stay in the exam room and get your money's worth. To keep your focus use the following techniques:

- Cover up the answers to the multiple-choice questions. Work the formulas through using the numbers in the problem. Write the formula out on your exam booklet. Plug the numbers in on your calculator. Write down each intermediate step. Upon completion, pull your hand away and look for your answer. If it is there, wonderful! Another question complete. If the answer is not listed, read the question again. Go over your steps, verifying the numbers and math computations one more time. Don't doubt yourself. You are tired and can easily transpose numbers. Calmly work through the data a second time.
- Continue to use highlighters. Use your brightest color for the FARE exam. Highlight the key words in the question. Read each question as if it holds the clue to a famous treasure. You are an explorer on a mission looking for the treasure and you must precisely complete all tasks or you will be stabbed to death or eaten by wild bears. Sound stupid? If candidates would read each question that carefully, the pass rate on FARE would probably double.
- Don't schedule an airplane flight to Las Vegas or to any other place that evening. Don't take a gamble. Worrying about making it to the

airport on time will drive you crazy. Your mind will keep wandering to the activities going on later in your life, causing massive loss of concentration. First things first--complete the exam, checkout of the hotel, and go home for a good night's sleep. You can pack and depart on Friday. You shouldn't be packing for a trip before the exam anyway--you should be studying.

• Don't pay any attention to the people who leave early. There will be plenty of early departures. At 5:00 p.m., the exam room will look deserted. Only you and the rest of the diehards will still be fighting for points. If your concentration powers are working like they should, you won't even be aware of the people leaving the exam. You are a trained CPA candidate. Your exam conditioning calls for you to stick it out and fight for points!

• From the very beginning, plan to stay until 6:00 p.m. No other time will do. If you plan all along to stay until the very end, you won't even think about leaving early.

MANAGING THE VAST TECHNICAL BREADTH

FARE is the most diverse exam section. One minute you're answering a question about capital leases and the next minute the subject is pension accounting. The technical breadth on this section is overwhelming. Preparing and following a study plan to guide you through the maze of numerous topics is almost a requirement for passing FARE. Candidates must know something about everything.

A common mistake is to study some topics very well and to overlook other subjects entirely. You are asking for failure. You must be well-versed in numerous areas. The top-ten list of all-important subject areas for the FARE exam is as follows:

1. Bonds
2. Pensions
3. Leases
4. Investments and Financial Instruments
5. Multiple-step Income Statement
6. Classified Balance Sheet
7. Converting Information from Cash to Accrual Basis of Accounting
8. Statement of Cash Flows
9. Other Comprehensive Income
10. Deferred Income Taxes

A successful candidate must have considerable knowledge about how to calculate, account, and report for all of the above items. There are also other areas like inventory, accounts receivable, and the statements of financial accounting concepts. You will be asked questions about these too, but the top-ten list identifies the key areas that have been tested in great depth and breadth exam after exam. They are the classics. Don't leave home without your top-ten list of FARE knowledge.

WATCH THE QUESTION TYPE

FARE uses all four forms of question types:

1. Four-option multiple-choice
2. Other objective answer format
3. Essays
4. Problems

Each question type requires its own techniques.

FARE MULTIPLE-CHOICE QUESTIONS

First, check your answer sheet to make sure you understand how the sheet is flowing. Typical choices are vertically, horizontally, or diagonally. Be alert, the forms do change from section to section.

When studying FARE, you were taught to cover up the answer choices, work the formulas, and then uncover the answers to see the amount you just calculated. The idea here is to first visualize the formula, write it down, and then plug in the numbers. Errors occur in FARE because you don't have the right formula, you are mathematically applying it incorrectly, or you did not understand the requirements. Most candidate mistakes are of the application variety. Usually the person knows the formula, but he or she did not plug the numbers in correctly. If your answer does not appear to be one of the choices, you should first check the math. Resist the urge to believe that little voice inside of you that keeps saying, "You're going to fail. You don't know what you are talking about." Continue to believe in your abilities. Cut yourself some slack, after so many hours of testing, you are tired and can easily make a mistake. Calmly punch the numbers again. If you still are not getting one of the answer choices, review your formula. Carefully examine what your formula is telling you to do. If it is telling you to add two numbers together and then divide, are you doing that? Maybe you are dividing each number separately and this is causing your error. If you are well-studied, you do know how to compute this problem--it's just a matter of methodically applying your knowledge.

Finally, if you are still not obtaining the correct answer, review the entire question. Chances are the question contains some information that you do not need to use. Persistence and focus will guide you to success.

FARE OTHER OBJECTIVE ANSWER FORMAT QUESTIONS

Why is it that candidates begin to answer the questions without preparing journal entries, computations, and a full analysis of the material at hand? To answer a FARE other objective answer format question, you must be patient and take the time to read and compute **before** you answer. The other objective answer format questions often contain a combination of financial statement presentation issues, computations, and theoretical issues. Divide the question into chunks and deal with each piece of the question one item at a time. Take for example, the question shown in Exhibit 1. At first glance, you see there are actually two sections to this question because you see "**Required**" being used two times. Skim the entire question first, checking to see if the sections are independent of each other or if you will use the information throughout the entire question. Here, there are really two separate question sets. The first set, numbers 1-6, is a theory set. Theory questions should take you about 1 minute each. Question set number two requires computations. Allow yourself more time here. Answer the theory first, working fairly quickly to save time for the more complicated computations.

Items 1-6 are asking you to make a decision about expensing the item or capitalizing. Now is the time to recall the applicable concepts. If you choose **expensing**, present the item as an expense item on the income statement. **Capitalizing** leads to presenting the item on the balance sheet. Ask yourself if the item will benefit more than one accounting period. If it does, you capitalize the expenditure as an asset. Recall that you capitalize all costs involved in getting the asset ready for its use. Next to the question, jot down the basic concepts that you believe apply. Some of the concepts that come to mind are

- Capitalize all costs required to ready the asset for its intended use
- Costs that "attach" themselves to the asset are directly connected with getting the asset ready for its intended use
- Expense items that will benefit only one accounting period

Take time to reflect and remind yourself of the definitions before you plunge in. Since you know the first set is different from the second, answer the first set of questions in its entirety, keeping your definitions and focus in tact. Talk to yourself and think about the hints given in the question.

Exhibit 1:   Example FARE other objective answer format question

Problem 1

This problem consists of 10 items. Select the **best** answer for each item. Use a No. 2 pencil to blacken the appropriate ovals on the Objective Answer Sheet to indicate your answers. **Answer all items.** Your grade will be based on the total number of correct answers.

Items 1 through 6 represent expenditures for goods held for resale and equipment.

Required:

For **items 1 through 6,** determine for each item whether the expenditure should be capitalized ⓒ or expensed as a period cost Ⓔ and blacken the corresponding oval on the Objective Answer Sheet.

1. Freight charges paid for goods held for resale.
2. In-transit insurance on goods held for resale purchased FOB shipping point.
3. Interest on note payable for goods held for resale.
4. Installation of equipment.
5. Testing of newly purchased equipment.
6. Cost of current year service contract on equipment.

Items 7 through 10 are based on the following 1999 transactions:

•   Link Co. purchased an office building and the land on which it is located by paying $800,000 cash and assuming an existing mortgage of $200,000. The property is assessed at $960,000 for realty tax purposes, of which 60% is allocated to the building.

•   Link leased construction equipment under a 7-year capital lease requiring annual year-end payments of $100,000. Link's incremental borrowing rate is 9%, while the lessor's implicit rate, which is not known to Link, is 8%. Present value factors for an ordinary annuity for seven periods are 5.21 at 8% and 5.03 at 9%. Fair value of the equipment is $515,000.

•   Link paid $50,000 and gave a plot of undeveloped land with a carrying amount of $320,000 and a fair value of $450,000 to Club Co. in exchange for a plot of undeveloped land with a fair value of $500,000. The land was carried on Club's books at $350,000.

Required:

For **items 7 through 10,** calculate the amount to be recorded for each item. To record your answer, write the number in the boxes on the Objective Answer Sheet **and** blacken the corresponding oval below each box. Write zeros in any blank boxes preceding your numerical answer, and blacken the zero in the oval below the box. **You cannot receive credit for your answers if you fail to blacken an oval in each column.**

- **Question 1, freight charges paid for goods held for resale.** Goods held for resale are inventory. Inventory is an asset that could benefit more than one time period so this expenditure must be capitalized.

- **Question 2, in-transit insurance on goods held for resale purchased FOB shipping point.** Again, the hint is about the goods held for resale. The company is incurring costs to insure inventory. The FOB shipping point concept is telling you that the title for the goods passed to you; it was your inventory the minute the supplier shipped the goods from his or her loading dock. If the shipping terms had been FOB destination, the supplier (vendor) would have been responsible for the goods until the goods reached you at your destination, and it would not be necessary to insure the goods while in transit. Capitalize the cost of insurance since the costs were necessary to ready the goods for resale. Insurance costs are treated like freight costs--they are capitalized because they are a necessary cost incurred to receive the goods.

- **Question number 3, interest on a note payable for goods held for resale.** Time to recall your interest capitalization cost concepts. Capitalize interest costs only on internally generated assets, not for those assets purchased from outsiders. You purchased fully completed assets. These goods were ready for resale, so all interest costs should be expensed.

- **Question number 4, installation of equipment.** A shift from inventory items to fixed assets. Capitalize all costs necessary to ready the equipment for its intended use. Obviously uninstalled equipment is not ready to use so capitalization is required.

- **Question number 5, testing of newly purchased equipment.** You must recall the basic concept: capitalize all costs required to ready the asset for its intended use. Is testing required to prepare the equipment for its intended use? Definitely, the machine has to be set up and tested before it's ready to use. Capitalize the costs!

- **Question number 6, cost of current-year service contract on equipment.** It's easy, expense the expenditure. The equipment is already being used, the service contract is not part of the costs necessary to prepare the equipment for its intended use, and a service contract provides no tangible evidence of future benefits.

You are now ready to answer the second set of questions. Before you do, go ahead and darken in the ovals for the questions you have just completed. Carefully check the correspondence between the question number in your question booklet, and the question number on the answer sheet. Always complete the Scantron sheet as you go along answering the question. Never wait until you have finished the entire exam as you could slip off a line, forget to answer a section, or run out of time before you complete the ovals.

Treat the second question set as if it were a brand new question, applying your best solutions approach methods which include reading the question requirements first. You will waste time if you begin reading the data. You are asked to compute the dollar amount to be capitalized for four items. It's time to read the data and prepare some journal entries. Treat each of the bullet points as a separate situation. Journalize transactions and write formulas in words first and then plug in the numbers. Always record the portion of the journal entry you know first, then later complete the entry. For example, you know that in the first transaction, Link would credit Cash for $800,000 and credit Mortgage Payable for $200,000. Now you know the debit has to be a total of $1,000,000 so it matches the credit total. Do you really need the $960,000? No, this is a distraction. Recall that assessed value is used to calculate the property taxes and does not usually reflect the fair market value. Land and buildings are recorded at historical cost on the date of purchase. Link paid $1,000,000, of which 60% was allocated to the building. This is easy--take 60% of $1,000,000, allocating $600,000 to building and $400,000 to land. Write down the journal entry. Don't trust your memory! You must deal with many more situations before you have completed this question. Your journal entry is as follows:

Land	400,000	
Building	600,000	
Mortgage payable		200,000
Cash		800,000

In the second situation, they are really giving you hints. No need to think about whether the lease is a capital lease because they clearly state it is. What about the interest rates? The concept you learned was to use the **lesser** of the incremental borrowing rate or the lessor's implicit rate, whichever is **known**. That's right, Link doesn't know the lessor's incremental borrowing rate so the computation of the net present value of lease payments must use the 9% rate. Before you begin multiplying, think about all of the rules applying to a capital lease--the lessor cannot capitalize the equipment at an amount greater than the current fair market value of $515,000. When you take the lease payment of $100,000 times the 5.03 factor (the 9% rate) you will get $503,000. Great, this is below the fair market value so the journal entry will debit the leased equipment account for $503,000.

In the third situation, Link is giving away land. Whenever a company gives away something in exchange for something else and little or no cash is involved, the situation is called a **nonmonetary** exchange. Once you recognize the situation, you must recall that two important concepts are relevant.

1. Link and Club are exchanging **similar** assets so the earnings process is not considered to be complete
2. When the earnings process is not considered to be complete, gains and losses will not be recognized

When gains and losses are not recognized, Link records the land acquired from Club at the book (carrying) value of the land given away plus the boot given ($320,000 + 50,000 = $370,000). Link paid boot (cash), Club received boot. In a nonmonetary exchange, no gain or loss is recognized for the company that **pays** the boot. However, the company **receiving** the boot is in effect saying the earnings transaction is complete for the portion related to the asset received. Therefore, a gain must be recognized for the portion that applies to the boot received. How complicated can it get? You probably practiced the above concepts in a multiple-choice question. Why does it seem so hard here? It really shouldn't be difficult. Apply what you have practiced--use your concepts. Compute the recognized gain. The formula for the recognized gain is as follows:

$$\left(\frac{\text{Boot}}{\text{Boot} + \text{Fair value asset received}}\right) \text{ x Total gain } = \text{ Gain recognized}$$

What's the total gain? Club received $50,000 cash plus $450,000 fair value of land, or a total of $500,000 worth of assets by giving up land it had carried on its books for only $350,000. This was a great deal to receive $500,000 by giving only $350,000, making the total gain $150,000 (the difference between what was given up and what was received). Now, compute the amount that the land should be recorded on Club's books. The formula is the book value of the land Club gave away ($350,000) less boot Club received ($50,000) plus the recognized gain ($15,000) = Cost to record Club's land ($315,000).

Notice how important it was to read and understand the data. The data must be understood before it can be plugged into the formulas. Ever wonder how you're going to remember all of the concepts? You developed your personalized study plan to allow you time to practice applying the concepts. Did you practice or did you just read the information? I hope you took the time to practice so the concepts have been crammed into your brain for later recall and use.

It is time to transfer your answers to the answer sheet. When you transfer numbers to an answer sheet, it is important to write in your answer as well as to blacken the ovals for zeros. Your answer sheet will show a separate box for each answer. The cent columns are usually omitted. For this particular question, the AICPA also preprinted the ones, tens, and hundreds columns as zeros. See Exhibit 2 for the completed answer sheet.

Exhibit 2:   Example of completed Scantron answer sheet other objective answer format questions

Uniform Certified Public Accountant Examination

VERSION 3
FARE

Item		
1	C	E
2	C	E
3	C	E
4	C	E
5	C	E
6	C	E

Zeros have already been preprinted for the ones, tens, and hundreds columns. Write zeros in any blank boxes preceding your numerical answer, and blacken the zero in the oval below the box.

7.

8.

Zeros have already been preprinted for the ones, tens, and hundreds columns. Write zeros in any blank boxes preceding your numerical answer, and blacken the zero in the oval below the box.

9.

10.

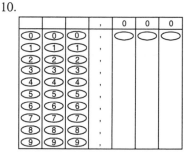

FARE ESSAYS

Use the basic essay techniques discussed in the Chapter entitled, "Writing the Perfect Essay." A brief overview of the steps is as follows:

- Control your time! For FARE essays, allow 2 minutes per point
- At the top of your question booklet, write the time you expect to complete the essay
- Read the requirements
- Recall the relevant concepts
- Key word the essay in your question booklet
- Write the answer in the answer booklet on the lined paper, beginning each essay section with a lead-in sentence and labeling each new part
- Write neatly, using short, concise sentences to obtain the maximum grade of 5 points for your writing
- Proofread the essay by first rereading each individual question requirement and then rereading your answer, making sure your answer addresses the question

What's unique about FARE essays? FARE essays often contain three types of situations.

1. Definitional, requiring the candidate to define and explain
2. Accounting-based, requiring the candidate to explain how to account for a given situation
3. Report-based, requiring the candidate to explain how to report a transaction

Each situation requires individual treatment.

DEFINITIONS AND ESSAYS

When they ask you to define a term or phrase, they really want more than just a definition. What the examiners are really looking for is a solid definition supported by examples and a discussion of the theoretical issues involved. Say what you know. Don't stop short--say everything you know about the situation. A recently released 1997 FARE exam question asked the candidate to "define *off-balance-sheet risk of accounting loss* and give an example of a financial instrument having off-balance-sheet risk of accounting loss." Even if you didn't know what off-balance-sheet risk was, you could earn points by writing well and allowing the words to speak to you. Let's say you really don't have the faintest idea how to define this term. Begin by rewriting the question into a statement form: Off-balance-sheet risk of accounting loss is the risk of accounting loss resulting from *something*. Now your job would, of course, be to say what that something is. You are not going to earn points by being afraid of saying something wrong. In fact, you will probably make plenty of incorrect statements, but it's all about keeping up the fight. You want writing points so go for it! Make up something that could happen because of an off-balance-sheet situation. The real answer involves a discussion of financial instruments. Off-balance-sheet risk of accounting loss is the risk of accounting loss from a financial instrument that exceeds the amount recognized for the financial instrument in the balance sheet. Examples of a financial instrument having an off-balance-sheet accounting loss are

- Letters of credit
- Noncancelable operating lease with future minimum lease commitments
- Options
- Interest rate caps and swaps
- Repurchase agreements
- Purchase commitments
- Futures contracts

Hopefully, after all of your hard work and study, you will know the definitions and the concepts. In the case of the above question, many candidates probably left the answer blank. When you leave an answer blank, not only can't you earn concept points, but you will also not earn writing points. The description, "off-balance-sheet" should have told you something.

HOW TO ACCOUNT

When an essay requirement asks you to describe "how to account" for a particular transaction, you will think of journal entries and write the entries down in words. You don't want to show the actual debits and credits in a journal entry form in the body of your answer. Just talk the grader through the journal entry by discussing what account should be increased and what account(s) should be decreased. For example, if the question asked you how to account for a bad debt write-off, you would answer by saying: "To account for the write-off of the bad debt, the accountant would increase the valuation account, allowance for uncollectible accounts, and decrease the accounts receivable account." You told the grader what accounts to use and you identified whether the accounts were increased or decreased. Your key words showed debits and credits, but in your answer you used the terms increased or decreased. This is what the graders are looking for.

HOW TO REPORT IN A FARE ESSAY

When a FARE essay asks you how to report a particular situation, the requirement is actually asking you to name each account involved and to identify the proper financial statement. A typical question might ask how the legal expenses incurred in defending a patent should be **reported** in a company's statement of cash flows under the direct method. Your answer would state that the legal expenses incurred in defending this company's patent should be reported on the statement of cash flows under the investing activities section in the period in which the expenses were paid.

When the balance sheet is involved, be sure to specify the specific asset, liability, or equity section. For example, equipment should be shown on the balance sheet, in the asset section, under the property, plant, and equipment caption. A prior period adjustment should be shown on the balance sheet, in the retained earnings section, as a restatement to the beginning period's retained earnings balance. Pretend you are preparing a map to get an accountant to the correct financial statement. Once he or she is looking at the correct financial statement, use your map to guide the person to the exact place where that account would be shown. Reporting questions are easy and fun. Just use your financial statement knowledge.

SOME GENERAL FARE ESSAY CONCEPTS

Positive grading implies that extra concepts can't hurt. For example, if the essay is asking about a revenue issue, why not include a discussion about matching. Matching refers to the process of expense recognition by associating costs with revenues on a cause and effect basis. Other generic terms to mention are as follows:

- Accrual accounting--recording expenses when incurred and revenues when earned
- Earnings process complete--refers to an exchange that has taken place

- Benefits future periods--refers to assets
- Valuation and allocation--refers to accounts like depreciation and amortization where the accountant uses a systematic and rational method to allocate costs to the appropriate time periods

FARE PROBLEMS

Here's your chance to show off. Read the entire problem, using the question booklet margins to write your journal entries, classifications (asset, expense, liability, etc.) and making any special computations. You must tear apart the problem and break it down into bite-sized chunks of information. Some basic problem techniques are as follows:

- Every worksheet and financial statement you prepare must contain a heading. The typical heading is

Company Name
Name of Schedule (e.g., Computation of Net Present Value of Lease Payments)
Date (As of or For the Year Ended)

Watch the date--Use for the year ended for all income statement items and any balance sheet accounts where you are scheduling the account activity (e.g., statement of cash flows shows the difference between the cash balance last year and this year.) The schedule is "for the year ended" because it shows the entire year's activity. The balance sheet just shows the balances as of that date.

- Use subschedules to show how you computed something. For example, if you are asked to present a multiple-step income statement that requires you to compute the cost of goods sold, show the total amount of cost of goods sold on the income statement and then refer the grader to "Schedule A, Computation of Costs of Goods Sold."
- Label all subschedule items. In other words, write the subschedule formulas in words so the graders can trace what you are attempting to do. Fill in the numbers next to the words. If you make a mistake in math, the graders will at least know that you were aware of the concepts.
- Proofread your schedule. Proofread a problem? Yes, begin by rereading the requirements one at a time and then look at your answer. Did you address the question? Did you prepare the proper form of the question? For example, a single-step income statement is different from a multiple-step income statement. Recompute

your math. The graders will be quickly looking for correct answers. A simple math mistake can result in loss of points.

- Make your schedule answers look pretty. Use dollar signs and double rule amounts.

- Look at a problem as just a bunch of little multiple-choice questions. The only difference is that you must document the formulas and the results for the graders. This is your chance to show the graders what you know.

What if the problem asks you to do something you know nothing about? The chances of this happening are slim, but you should be prepared to do your best. If you don't know, and you studied and practiced using current materials, you are not alone. There are many candidates in the exam room who are scratching their heads. You will move ahead of the other candidates in points, if you make an attempt. Begin by scheduling out a heading. Once you have a heading, write in what you do know. Take the time to think about everything you studied in this area. At the very minimum, make an attempt by at least writing in on your schedule some of the information in the question. You never know how many other candidates in the room are leaving questions blank. You are a trained CPA candidate who knows how to fight for points and you will leave no essay or problem blank. You will give the graders something to grade. You believe you should be a CPA so you will show them why.

YES, FARE IS DIFFICULT

Yes, FARE is the most difficult exam section. If you are having trouble answering the questions, so is everyone else. Remember you studied, you practiced, and you reviewed. Here you are and the material seems foreign. What happened to all of your knowledge? Stop. Take a reality check. It's almost over. Do you still believe that you can pass? Yes! You can pass the FARE section with some help. The big surprise is that the AICPA Board of Examiners is actually going to help you by curving the exam. Points are added to each candidate's scores based on the modified Angoff passing standard study. In plain English, this means you will receive curve points. In the past, it appears that as many as 10 to 15 points are added to the candidate's raw score. Do you realize that if this is true, you only have to receive a raw score of 60% to pass FARE. While the AICPA no longer releases actual curve points, it is apparent from candidate's diagnostic reports that points are being added. Relax, take a deep breath, and keep on fighting. The FARE exam is passable. You will pass if you remain confident. Believe in yourself and believe that you know more than the average candidate. In the final tabulation you just have to perform better than the rest. Use Exhibit 3 to help keep you focused on FARE, the last exam section.

Exhibit 3

FARE Reminders

- Continue to budget your time. As soon as you receive the exam, take control and allocate your time to the multiple-choice questions, other objective questions, essays, and problems.
- Tell yourself you will stay in the exam room until 6:00 p.m., using extra time to proofread essays and problems.
- Think about the concepts, not about how tired you are.
- Write all over the question booklet. Highlight keywords. Cross out extraneous information. Writing helps to keep you focused.
- If your mind starts to wander from the subject at hand, go to the bathroom, splash some cold water on your face, and go back to your seat refreshed.
- Read every question as if your life depends on you understanding the question in its entirety. Take the situation seriously.
- Do not spend time evaluating your knowledge level. The graders will grade your exam papers. Your job is to provide answers. The grader's job is to score your exam.
- Remember that if you are suffering, everyone is suffering. You studied, you practiced, and now you are doing the best you can.
- Stay for the fight. Fight, scratch, and crawl for points. Accumulate points one concept at a time.
- Resist the urge to change your other objective and multiple-choice answers. Change answers only when you are very sure you have made a mistake.
- Be more careful than ever when transferring your answers to the answer sheet. You are tired and must be careful.
- Continue to believe in yourself for the entire 15½ hours.

PERSONALLY SPEAKING

Because of its technical breadth, FARE is the exam section that candidates seem to fear the most. Yet in the end, this section is highly curved to compensate for the technical breadth. You should expect to see questions that you cannot answer. You should expect to make educated guess on some questions. Accept the fact that you will be tired and will have to fight to stay focused. Don't waste time thinking about what you don't know. Forge ahead and do the best you can.

Over the years I have found that people give up too early. About 1 to 2 hours into the exam, candidates begin to self-grade. This is very dangerous since we are much more critical of ourselves than of others. Self-grading the FARE exam will really hurt you. You will always give yourself a much lower evaluation of your progress than the performance warrants. Your FARE raw score could be as low as 62% and you still might have a chance to pass. When was the last time you took an exam in college, scored a 62%, and felt good about it? You have no way of knowing just how low you can sink and still pass the exam. Don't even try to predict the results. Answer each question, one at a time. After you have done the best you could, blacken in the oval on the Scantron sheet and move on. Leave the question behind. You are finished with it. The best words of advice I can give you for FARE are

- Keep on fighting
- Don't give up
- Don't leave early
- Don't grade your work
- Don't change answers

When I mention focus, please understand that you must work to remain focused. It doesn't just happen. You know this is going to be a long haul--2 days, 15½ hours. Don't set yourself up for failure by scheduling a big event immediately after the CPA exam. I listen to candidates tell me that they are going to rush to the airport to catch a plane to spend the weekend in Paris, Las Vegas, or with their in-laws in Iowa. The destination doesn't matter. The problem is that you can't help but think about the trip while you are taking the exam. I always wonder why a person would want to travel right after the exam. If you put up a good fight, you will be so tired after the exam that you might not even be able to drive home. Do yourself a favor for the exam and for the enjoyment of your trip--postpone your reward for a few weeks. You will enjoy it even more when you are not tired, and you will know that you performed the best that you could at the time.

Don't give up--such a simple statement, yet many people don't heed the advice. Do not grade yourself. Let the AICPA grade your exam. You are there to take the test. Someone else will grade it. Wouldn't it be awful if you knew you gave up, guessed on questions without even trying, and left the exam early, only to find out you received a 74 in FARE? Take my advice--stay in for the long haul. Stay there for the fight. Leave the grading to the graders. Your job is to answer the questions to the best of your ability. At the end of the exam, I want you to say, "I've done my best." Who can fault that? You will find out about your grades in 3 months. Sit back and enjoy life while you wait.

21 THE WAITING GAME

The CPA exam is over. You have done your best. Now you must wait 3 months to receive your scores. Why the long wait? It takes about 6 weeks for the graders to grade the exams at the AICPA offices in New Jersey. Then the exam scores and information must be mailed to each individual jurisdiction for recording and further tabulation. Finally, it is the jurisdiction that will mail the letters to the CPA candidates, informing them of the results. The purpose of this chapter is to help you cope with the stress of waiting and to inform you of your rights when you are concerned about possible errors in questions while taking the exam.

CONCERNS ABOUT EXAMINATION QUESTIONS

Since the CPA exam is a closed exam and the candidate is precluded from discussing exam questions with fellow candidates, professors, and other knowledgeable professionals, what happens when you feel there is an error on the actual exam? Candidates who believe they have identified a possible error in a question should notify the AICPA within 4 days of the completion of the exam administration. For example, if a candidate believes that the Law exam contains an error, the candidate would have 4 days from the Wednesday of the exam to notify the AICPA of the concern. The 4 days are assumed to include business and nonbusiness days. Therefore, for law and audit concerns, the candidate has until Sunday to notify the AICPA and for ARE and FARE the candidate has until Monday to inform the AICPA of the concern. The tight deadline is to ensure that all comments are received and given consideration before the grading guides are fully developed and before the grading bases for the examination are approved.

To date, fax is the only method of communication accepted by the AICPA. The fax number as of the writing of this book is 201-938-3443. The communication should include the following:

- The candidate's 7-digit candidate identification number
- A description of the precise nature of any error
- The rationale used to support your concern
- A citing of possible references to support your concern

The procedure should assure candidates that all technically accurate answers are considered in the grading guides.

The AICPA does not personally respond to the candidate. However, the AICPA promises that they will review and consider every request received by the deadline. Therefore, it is very important to meet the 4-day deadline.

USE OF GRADING GUIDES

The high-quality grading process of the AICPA Board of Examiner's Advisory Grading Service includes the use of a grading guide for each section. The grading guides are first developed during the exam preparation process and are approved by the preparation subcommittee and the Board of Examiners at the AICPA. The grading guides for the machine-graded areas, multiple-choice, and other objective answer format questions consist of the answer key and the point value assigned to each answer. Do not assume that each multiple-choice or other objective answer format question is worth one point. A question may be worth a fraction of a point. For the essay and problem question formats, the grading guide consists of the model answer, each concept being elicited, and each concept's assigned point value. Again, don't assume a one-to-one correlation. Essays may require a candidate to identify 16 concepts to receive only 10 points. See Exhibit 1 at the end of this chapter for an example of a grading guide prepared by the author. The AICPA does not release the actual grading guides. Exhibit 1 is just a hypothetical guide developed to illustrate what concept(s) might be considered to be valuable and how the points may be allocated.

After the exam, a sample of papers is selected to be used as a check on the application of the grading guides. The Standards Setting Subcommittee of the Board of Examiners of the AICPA may make modifications to the grading guide based upon the sample responses. This sample review assures that a quality grading process is utilized. For example, if the sample papers show that a substantial number of candidates select an answer response that is different from the answer shown in the grading guide, the question is submitted for review to a panel of independent experts. If other answers are found to be acceptable, the grading guide is adjusted accordingly and all papers are regraded using the revised answer key. For essays and problems, additional concepts may be found to be appropriate. The sample review may also identify additional question interpretations and approaches. If the alternative approaches and interpretations are deemed to be acceptable, the guide is adjusted. The final grading guides are not approved until after all changes are complete. After the final adjustments have been made and accepted, the grading guide is then consistently applied to all candidate papers. It is time for the grading process to begin.

GRADING PROCESS

What does the grader know about you? The grader only knows your candidate number and the state in which you sat for the exam. The grader does not know if you have sat for the exam one time or more. The grader does not know if this is the last time before you will lose condition status. As a result, the candidate should always assume that the grader knows nothing about him or her and what he or she is attempting to explain. On all essay and problem formats, the best approach is for the CPA candidate to assume that the grader is a monkey for which every fine detail must be explained. Don't leave knowledge in your head where it will not earn you points. If in doubt, put it down. You can't go wrong by writing down what you think is right because the CPA exam is positively graded. No deductions are made for wrong statements. Since the graders really know nothing about the candidate, the candidate's performance is measured solely on the basis of the answers submitted on the exam. The idea is to achieve a score of 75% or greater on each examination section. If a candidate comes close, he or she may receive as many as two additional reviews of his or her performance. The first grading is called the initial production grading.

In the initial production grading, an optical scanner is used to grade the multiple-choice and other objective answer format questions. A sample of papers is used to test for scanner malfunction. A staff of CPAs and attorneys grade the essay and problem questions. All graders receive extensive training in how to identify the concepts that count as points earned. Graders also receive training in how to consistently apply the techniques so that they are proficient both in the subject matter and in the evaluation of candidates' answers. In addition to concepts, the essay question formats are graded for writing skills using the holistic grading method. See Chapter 9, "Writing a Beautiful Essay Answer," for a description of how the graders apply a holistic grading approach to grade for writing points. The initial production points are totaled and studied to determine if another review is necessary.

When a candidate receives an adjusted initial grade of 65-79, a *first review* is performed. The purpose of the first review is to confirm the initial score and to provide a quality control check on the consistency and application of the grading process. Here, reviewers compare the work of different graders, thereby checking for consistent application of all grading concepts. Based on this first review, scores are corrected for any scoring errors. For all papers now receiving an adjusted score of 72-74, a *second review* is performed.

The second review process is administered using a two-step approach:

1. The accuracy of the objective answer sheet is manually verified

2. A reviewer who did not grade the paper in the first process verifies the accuracy of the essay and problem grading

Adjusted scores are corrected for any scoring errors. The grades are then reported to the jurisdiction for tabulation and grade notification. As a result, candidates who receive final scores of 72–74 can rest assured that a very stringent grading process has been applied to their paper. However, the candidate may receive one more review if they so request.

REVIEW SERVICE

Upon receipt of the final score, a candidate may ask their board of accountancy to submit a request to the AICPA for review of their papers. The review service cost varies from jurisdiction to jurisdiction. As of the writing of this book, the state of Illinois charges $50 each to review the Law, Audit, or FARE sections. A review of ARE costs only $30 since it is all machine graded.

The AICPA Advisory Grading Service reviews a candidate's paper by manually checking the accuracy of the objective answers and by verifying the original scoring of essays or problem solutions. A qualified individual who did not participate in the original grading evaluates the paper. The final total score is then recomputed.

A "no change" is issued to the board of accountancy unless a failing grade has been increased to a passing grade or to a minimum grade required on a failed section to earn or retain condition status. The review service rarely results in a grade change and the process takes about 6 weeks. Therefore, the candidate who receives a score of 72-74 should request a review and regrade service only if he or she feels committed to do so. However, the best way to spend your time and money is to purchase the latest review manuals and to begin the study process for the next exam. Knowing that grade changes are rare and take time, don't waste time waiting for a change. Assume that there probably will not be a change because the papers were already reviewed three times as follows:

1. Initial production grading
2. First review
3. Second review

Note that a grade change, if it were granted, would probably not be received until after the application deadline date to apply for the next exam. Waiting for a rare event to occur can cost you time and may cause you to lose the momentum you had gained. If you feel you must, send the money in for a review, but as you wait for the results, continue your study plan.

KNOW THAT YOU DID YOUR BEST

As you're waiting, know that you did the best you could. You prepared a detailed study plan and followed that plan. There is no need to fret and worry about what you cannot change. The graders are busy scoring your paper. Let them do their job and continue on with your life. The positive thing about waiting for scores is that while you are waiting there is always hope. Hope that you passed. With an exam as detailed and comprehensive as the CPA exam, it is very difficult to predict at what level one must achieve to pass. Liken the CPA waiting game to a gymnastics performance. The performer may complete a less than satisfactory performance personally, but who knows just how that score may hold up in the final tally. Don't ever give up as you just might be surprised at how low your knowledge level can fall and still allow you to end up with a passing score. You do not need to be perfect to pass the CPA exam.

REPORTING OF THE SCORES

Your state board of accountancy will mail your scores directly to your home. The dates grades will be mailed in the new millennium are as follows:

Examination date	Date grades will be mailed
May 3 and 4, 2000	July 31, 2000
November 1 and 2, 2000	January 29, 2001
May 2 and 3, 2001	July 30, 2001
November 7 and 8, 2001	February 4, 2002
May 8 and 9, 2002	August 5, 2002
November 6 and 7, 2002	February 3, 2003

Some state boards post the names of the people who passed the latest CPA exam on an Internet site. Exam scores are not posted. Most states, however, mail the scores directly to the candidate. It is very important to notify your state board of all address and name changes. You don't want to increase the waiting time beyond the traditional 3 months.

It is hard to wait. It is also difficult to know that in most states the names of those people who passed the last CPA exam is public knowledge. Yes, people can find out whether or not you successfully completed the last CPA exam. Do not lie about your results. This only makes matters worse. If you did not pass, the world isn't going to fall in. Remind your friends and acquaintances that only 12-15% of the candidates successfully complete all four sections the first time. It is expected that you take the exam more than one time. Don't waste energy worrying about what other people think. You know just how difficult this exam is. That's all that matters.

PERSONALLY SPEAKING

I was too busy to worry about my CPA exam scores. It wasn't until I heard that all my friends and coworkers were receiving their scores that I began to tremble. My husband called the public accounting firm where I was working late and told me that the scores had arrived. I can't tell you how nervous I was. I wasn't sure if I wanted him to open the envelope and tell me over the phone or if I should drive home to open the letter myself. I took so long deciding what to do that my husband just ripped open the envelope and blurted out that I had **successfully** completed three sections. I needed to repeat the Law section. Wasn't that nice of him--he did not call me a failure. He told me I was super and that I only had one more section to go. I was elated, as the results were really much better than I had expected. I thought that I would be required to repeat all sections. I had conditioned and to pass Law would be a breeze. It was--I passed the final section at the next exam. I was proud of my accomplishment.

I know of people who have copied another person's CPA certificate, typed their name in, and hung the falsified document on their office wall. Why pretend to be something that you are not? Claiming to be a CPA when you are not could result in the loss of a good job and a messy lawsuit. Do it the right way. Because you must work hard to achieve your goal, when you finally pass, you will feel justifiably proud of your accomplishment.

Never lie about your achievements. A very good friend of mine says, "Always tell the truth, as it is easier to remember when you are in a pinch." The truth needs no embellishment and no story telling. The truth stands alone.

I am often asked if I believe that the CPA exam is fairly graded. Over the many years that I have helped candidates, I have found the grading process to be very reliable. The AICPA subjects the papers to strict quality-control checks. I do believe your reported score is accurate. If you do not pass, spend little time complaining about your scores and much time regrouping to pass the next exam.

The worst is over. You showed up and took the exam. You fought for points. Now it is time for rest and relaxation. Should you begin studying before you receive your scores? No, because you probably performed much better than you thought you did. Work hard at your job, spend some time with your family, and just get caught up on the things you left behind while you were studying. If you must repeat one or more sections of the exam, you want to be well-rested and organized. Spend these 3 months enjoying the beautiful life that you have. Each day is a precious jewel; appreciate your life and the people with whom you share your days.

Exhibit 1: Example grading guide

The following example grading guide was prepared by the author to illustrate how a grading guide might be developed for an audit essay. The AICPA does not publish the actual grading guides. To illustrate the grading of essay concepts, question Number 3 from the November 1993 audit exam was used with permission of the AICPA. The question and AICPA unofficial answer as modified for today's standards is as follows:

NOVEMBER 1993 REPORTING ESSAY QUESTION

Number 3

The auditor's report below was drafted by Miller, a staff accountant of Pell & Pell, CPAs, at the completion of the audit of the consolidated financial statements of Bond Co. for the year ended July 31, 1993. The report was submitted to the engagement partner who reviewed the audit working papers and properly concluded that an unqualified opinion should be issued. In drafting the report, Miller considered the following:

- Bond's consolidated financial statements for the year ended July 31, 1992, are to be presented for comparative purposes. Pell previously audited these statements and appropriately rendered an unmodified report.
- Bond has suffered recurring losses from operations and has adequately disclosed these losses and management's plans concerning the losses in a note to the consolidated financial statements. Although Bond has prepared the financial statements assuming it will continue as a going concern, Miller has substantial doubt about Bond's ability to continue as a going concern.
- Smith & Smith, CPAs, audited the financial statements of BC Services, Inc., a consolidated subsidiary of Bond, for the year ended July 31, 1993. The subsidiary's financial statements reflected total assets and revenues of 15% and 18%, respec-

tively, of the consolidated totals. Smith expressed an unqualified opinion and furnished Miller with a copy of the auditor's report. Smith also granted permission to present the report together with the principal auditor's report. Miller decided not to present Smith's report with that of Pell, but instead to make reference to Smith.

Independent Auditor's Report

We have audited the consolidated balance sheets of Bond Co. and subsidiaries as of July 31, 1993 and 1992, and the related consolidated statements of income and retained earnings for the years then ended. Our responsibility is to express an opinion on these financial statements based on our audits. We did not audit the financial statements of BC Services, Inc., a wholly owned subsidiary. Those statements were audited by Smith & Smith, CPAs whose report has been furnished to us, and our opinion, insofar as it related to the amounts included for BC Services, Inc., is based solely on the report of Smith & Smith.

We conducted our audits in accordance with generally accepted auditing standards. Those standards require that we plan and perform the audit to obtain reasonable assurance about whether the financial statements are free of material misstatement. An audit includes assessing control risk, the accounting principles used, and significant estimates made by management, as well as evaluating the overall financial statement presentation. We believe that our audits provide a reasonable basis for our opinion.

In our opinion, based on our audits and the report of Smith & Smith, CPAs, the consolidated financial statements referred to above present fairly, in all material respects except for the matter discussed below, the financial position of Bond Co. as of July 31, 1993 and 1992, and the results of its operations for the years then ended.

The accompanying consolidated financial statements have been prepared with the disclosure in Note 13 that the company has suffered recurring losses from operations. Management's plans in regard to those matters are also discussed in Note 13. The financial statements do not include any adjustments that might result from the outcome of this uncertainty.

Pell & Pell, CPAs
November 4, 1993

Required:

Identify the deficiencies in the auditor's report as drafted by Miller. Group the deficiencies by paragraph and in the order in which the deficiencies appear. Do **not** redraft the report.

NOVEMBER 1993 REPORTING ESSAY ANSWER

UNOFFICIAL ANSWER
Number 3

Deficiencies in Miller's draft are as follows:

Within the opening (introductory) paragraph:

- The statement of cash flows is not identified in this paragraph or in the opinion paragraph.

- The statement of other comprehensive income is not identified in this paragraph or in the opinion paragraph.

- The financial statements are not stated to be the responsibility of management.

- The magnitude of the portion of the consolidated financial statements audited by the other auditors is not disclosed.

- Smith may not be named in this paragraph or in the opinion paragraph unless Smith's report is presented together with Pell's report.

Within the second (scope) paragraph:

- The statement that "an audit includes examining, on a test basis, evidence supporting the amounts and disclosures in the financial statements" is omitted.

- It is inappropriate to state that an audit includes "assessing control risk."

- Reference to the audit of the other auditors as part of the basis for the opinion is omitted.

Within the third (opinion) paragraph:

- Use of the phrase "except for the matter discussed below" is inappropriate.

- Reference to "conformity with generally accepted accounting principles" is omitted.

Within the fourth (explanatory) paragraph:

- The terms "substantial doubt" and "going concern" are omitted.

HYPOTHETICAL GRADING GUIDE
November 1993 Audit Number 3
Modified for Audit Standard Changes

Grading concept:	*Check box if candidate mentioned*
Opening paragraph:	
• Statement of cash flows not identified	☐
• Statement of Other Comprehensive Income is not identified	☐
• Management responsibility is not listed	☐
• The magnitude (amount) of consolidated financial statements is not disclosed	☐
• Smith, the other auditor, should not be named unless his report is attached to Pell's report	☐
Second (scope) paragraph:	
• Omitted "audit includes examining on a test basis"	☐
• Should not mention "assessing control risk"	☐
• Omitted reference to the other auditors	☐
Third (opinion) paragraph:	
• Inappropriate use of "except for matter discussed below"	☐
• Omitted reference to "conformity with generally accepted accounting principles"	☐
Fourth (explanatory) paragraph:	
• Omitted "substantial doubt about going concern"	☐
Subtotal of grading concepts mentioned	———
Writing points earned*	———
Total grading concepts and writing points	═══

CONVERSION SCALE

Concepts Mentioned	16	15	14	13	12	11	10	9	8	7	6	5	4	3	2	1	0
Grade	10	9.375	8.75	8.125	7.5	6.875	6.25	5.625	5	4.375	3.75	3.125	2.5	1.875	1.25	0.625	0

*Writing points	# Points
• Paper blank or almost blank	(0)
• Writing **very** weak	(1)
• Writing weak	(2)
• Writing average	(3)
• Writing good	(4)
• Writing **very** good	(5)

The CPA candidate receives a check for each concept correctly identified. A subtotal is taken and the total writing points are added. If a candidate had correctly stated 7 of the 11 required concepts and was given a 3 for average writing, the raw score would be 10 (7 plus 3). Referencing the conversion chart, the final score would be 6.25 points out of a total of 10 points. Hopefully, the candidate performed well on the other essay(s), multiple-choice, and other objective answer format questions. It would have been better if the candidate had earned 12 raw points so the converted score would have been at least a passing score of 7.5.

22 REGROUPING AFTER AN UNSUCCESSFUL ATTEMPT

It happens--you fail the CPA exam. Does this mean that you are a failure? No, you are not a failure. Register to sit for the CPA exam again. A failed attempt is only a temporary setback. Continue to believe you can pass the CPA exam. Turn the failed attempt into success. You tried the CPA journey and your road map took you on a few detours, but you have learned from the trip. When you try the journey again, you will know where the roadblocks are. You will improve your route and steer clear of problems. Does this sound ridiculous? It shouldn't because you do know more now about the CPA exam than you did before you took it. You can use your knowledge to assess what you did right and what you did wrong. Correct the errors and make the right moves on the next exam. Determine how close you are to achieving your goal.

EVALUATING YOUR RESULTS

Look at your overall scores by exam section. Did you pass any one section? In most jurisdictions, a 75 or higher in one exam section will not qualify for condition status. However, the results prove that you can pass the exam. You performed up to the expectation level once so you can do it again. If you received scores in the 60s or 70s, you are very close to passing. Register to take the next exam. Begin preparing by working to correct your weaknesses.

Scores in the 50s or below indicate that you have some work to do. It may not be a good idea to sit for the exam so soon. By the time you receive your results, you have only 3 months to prepare for the next exam. If you are not working and can find substantial study time between now and the next exam, go ahead and register, but realize that you need to improve. Improvement takes time and considerable effort. Consider taking a review for those areas in which you received a score of 50 or less.

See Exhibit 1 for a sample Candidate Diagnostic Report. The diagnostic report is mailed to you with your scores whether you pass or not. See how the subdivision of topics for each exam section matches the "uniform candidate specifications" as given by the AICPA. The detail for Audit and FARE is sketchy. The Law and ARE detail give you a good idea of the areas where you are weak. Is there one area that you should improve, or are you weak in all areas? Analyze your results honestly. Now is not the time

Exhibit 1

Uniform CPA Examination--Sample Candidate Diagnostic Report

JURISDICTION: **ILLINOIS**
CANDIDATE NUMBER: **SAMPLE**
EXAMINATION DATE:

AUDIT — GRADE 67

SECTION	CONTENT AREAS AND PERCENT COVERAGE		PERCENTAGE OF AREA EARNED					
			≤50	51-60	61-70	71-80	81-90	>90
I	Plan the Engagement	40%					*	
II	Obtain and Document Information	35%			*			
III	Review Engagement	5%			*			
IV	Prepare Communications	20%	*					
		100%						

LPR — GRADE 72

SECTION	CONTENT AREAS AND PERCENT COVERAGE		PERCENTAGE OF AREA EARNED					
			≤50	51-60	61-70	71-80	81-90	>90
I	Professional and Legal Responsibilities	15%				*		
II	Business Organizations	20%				*		
III	Contracts	10%				*		
IV	Debtor-Creditor Relationships	10%				*		
V	Government Regulation of Business	15%			*			
VI	Uniform Commercial Code	20%				*		
VII	Property	10%				*		
		100%						

Exhibit 1 (cont'd)

FARE — 54

			≤50	51-60	61-70	71-80	81-90	>90
I	Concepts and Standards for Financial Statements	20%			*			
II	Typical Items in Financial Statements	40%		*				
III	Specific Transactions and Events in Financial Statements	40%		*				
		100%						

ARE — 68

			≤50	51-60	61-70	71-80	81-90	>90
I	Federal Taxation – Individuals	20%				*		
II	Federal Taxation – Corporations	20%		*				
III	Federal Taxation – Partnerships	10%			*			
IV	Federal Taxation – Other	10%			*			
V	Governmental and Not-For-Profit Organizations	30%			*			
VI	Managerial Accounting	10%			*			
		100%						

to pretend that you have no weak areas. When you fail, you are obviously weak in one or more areas; figure out which area and work to improve it. See Exhibit 2 for an idea of how to evaluate your strengths and weaknesses now that you have sat for the exam.

Exhibit 2: Interpretation of Sample Diagnostic Report

The following discussion is an example of how the sample data from Exhibit 1 could be interpreted.

OVERALL RESULTS

The candidate is very close to passing Audit, Law, and ARE. A score of 54 in FARE indicates that some major weaknesses must be corrected. Perhaps the candidate should consider taking a review course for FARE and self-studying the other three sections. The candidate should definitely sign up to sit for the next exam before the knowledge base erodes with time.

AUDIT ANALYSIS

The candidate performed very well in the area of planning, earning 81-90% of the points. Since this is 40% of the exam, this is a good start. Little study time should be allocated to engagement planning, risk assessment, errors, fraud, and illegal acts. Tie the categories to the actual candidate content specifications available on the AICPA website at www.aicpa.org/edu/candspe. An average amount of time should be spent on the second and third categories. Scores of 61-70 mean that some work must be done. Spend more time working actual questions rather than reading about how to these areas. Learn by doing. The candidate performed very poorly on the fourth category, prepare communications. Since this area represented 20% of the points, the candidate must spend considerable time correcting the weaknesses by reading for understand and by working the questions. If the candidate remembers struggling with an reporting essay or other objective answer format question, then the format of the question may have hurt the score as much as the lack of technical knowledge. If this is the case, extra time should be spent working more essays and other objective answer format questions. However, keep in mind that the essay questions are seldom repeated on the next exam. If reporting were an essay on this exam, it probably will not be an essay on the next exam.

LAW

Oh so close with a 72%. More time should be spent studying government regulation of business that includes the Securities and Exchange Commission laws. If an essay tested the government regulation area, it could be that the candidate did not earn the writing points and did give the graders enough discussion of the topic. Because Law is the first section, the candidate may have been nervous or forgot to carefully manage his or her time.

FARE

Here the candidate needs work. Since the candidate diagnostic report is so sketchy, the candidate should take some time to review the detailed FARE topics and identify the areas that they remember as being the most difficult. For example, if the candidate remembers the statement of cash flows as being something that gave him trouble, the candidate should begin the study program with this area. The candidate would greatly benefit by a targeted review to help demonstrate some problem-solving techniques.

ARE

Corporate taxation was a problem. If the candidate remembers that the topic was tested in an other objective answer format question, then more practice time should be allocated to working other objective answer format questions. Do a quick review of individual taxation since the score was high. Do an average review of the other areas.

IN SUMMARY

This candidate should sign up to take the next exam. If the candidate's review materials are now older than 1 year, new materials should be purchased. This candidate should go back to Chapter 6, "Developing Your Personalized Study Plan," and establish a schedule that helps him or her correct his or her weak areas first. This candidate should not give up! He or she is very close to passing.

Whenever you fail an area, you may ask your board of accountancy to submit a request to the AICPA for a review of your papers. Request for such reviews are accepted up to 90 days after the examination has been given. This would be until September 20 for a May exam and March 20 for a November exam. The service is not free. For example, sample fees currently charged in the state of Illinois are $30 for reviewing the ARE section and $50 each for the other three sections. Chances are that the review will result in a "no change" in the grade status. Do not count on receiving a grade change. Statistics show that grade changes are rare. For a candidate who receives a 74 on one or more exam sections, the reality is tough to face. You came within one point of a passing score. This is especially sad when a candidate receives four scores of 74, resulting in an outright failure by the loss of four total points. Another equally sad situation is where a candidate passes one section and misses a condition by one point on another section. While the statistics are grim, the situation is real. Face the reality and move on. Keep in mind that the AICPA has already applied careful grading techniques throughout the grading process. Chances of a grade change are rare. Take some comfort, however, in the fact that you came close to passing.

When a candidate comes close to passing by receiving scores in the 70s and 60s, it is an accomplishment. The results show that you are almost there. Take the time to think about where you felt weak. Use your review manual to identify topical areas and then rank the topics as to how you felt about them when you were taking the test. For example, most review manuals show that there are six important areas in the Audit exam.

1. Audit planning
2. Understanding and evaluating internal control
3. Performing substantive tests
4. Communication and audit reporting
5. Statistical sampling
6. Auditing with technology

Do you remember trying to answer questions on these areas and feeling inadequate? Perform a simple ranking of the individual areas using the following scale:

1. Very weak and needs considerable improvement
2. Remember having some trouble with the more difficult areas
3. Don't recall having problems, knowledge level seems to be adequate

Where do you go from here? Design a study plan to spend more time studying the areas that you ranked "1." and less time on the areas you ranked "3." Plan to begin your studies with your weak areas first. Spend little time studying the areas you ranked "3." The best way to study areas that you ranked as "3." is to skip the reading entirely and go directly to the questions. Review the material by working the problems. You'll be surprised at how quickly these concepts come back to you. That's because you know these areas and have reinforced the concepts by practicing the questions. Once you truly understand a concept you will never forget it. Spend your time studying areas that you ranked "1."

What if you ranked most of the areas "1?" You have considerable work to do. It might be wise to forgo the next exam and spend much more time preparing. Perhaps you should join a reputable review course. If you know you did poorly because you did not make the commitment to a study plan and you believe you will change that level of commitment this time around, then go for it. The decision to sit or not sit is up to you. Be careful though; don't set yourself up for failure. For example, if you are entering a busy season at work and won't have time to study, then sitting for the next exam will just result in another disappointment and much frustration. Postpone taking the test until next year. Begin your study process 6 to 7 months before the exam.

When making the decision to sit or not to sit, recognize the general tendency to forget. The longer you wait, the more you will forget. If you ranked your exam knowledge level a "2.," you are so close. Register to sit for the next exam and make every attempt to find time to study. You have already achieved a very high knowledge base and you need so little to perfect what you already know. If you wait, not only could you forget concepts, the material could also change.

Study materials must be up-to-date. Don't assume that accounting never changes. In the last 3 years, as much as 30% of the Audit concepts have changed. Major recent FARE changes include a new financial statement entitled "other comprehensive income." FARE is also undergoing numerous changes as the accounting profession decides how to account and report for derivatives and financial instruments. Terms such as swaps and hedging are new areas within the last few years. Look for a major change in governmental accounting. Every year expect several tax law changes. Spend the time and money to obtain information about the latest changes. Don't waste your time studying old material. Study old material and almost always count on failure. Spend the cash to obtain new materials. Make the investment in the future. The return on your investment will be great. Money spent on new materials will seem a small investment to make to help boost your chances of success. Give yourself every possible chance to successfully complete the exam.

TO REVIEW AGAIN OR NOT TO REVIEW

Do you need an organized review? If you have already taken an organized review and have up to date materials, it is probably best to stay home and spend your time studying--unless you have trouble disciplining yourself to stick to the plan. A good review course not only helps increase your knowledge, but should also help psych you up. Look for a review course that helps you identify and understand the reasons for your failure. Look to the review course to provide you with sound, practical advice about the corrections that you should make to pass the next exam. If you scored 50 or less, you have a lot to learn. Enroll in a review course to accelerate the learning process.

If you decide to repeat a review course, don't forget to make the commitment and keep the commitment. Attend every class and listen to the instructor as if it were brand new material. You never know when the instructor is going to insert new material or make changes to concepts that you previously learned. Repeat takers tend to zone in and out, believing that they have already heard this story before. Work to concentrate. Hang on every word. Pretend this is all new to you. Focus on the task at hand.

Often a review course is not a review because the candidate has never learned the material. If you found you were learning material for the first time in the review, you have discovered one of the reasons why you did not pass. It is tough to learn and review at the same time. Take the course again and you will see that the second time through, the concepts will be much clearer. Think about why you might have failed.

REASONS CANDIDATES FAIL THE EXAM

Lack of technical knowledge may not be the only reason why you were not successful in passing the CPA exam. Did you manage your time correctly, or did you find yourself running out of time? Did you panic and let the exam control you, or did you control the exam? Did your nerves of steel turn soft halfway through? Did the little voice of doubt rise up and scare you? Did you find yourself changing answers without knowing why? Did you leave an essay or problem blank? Did you take the time to proofread your work, making sure you addressed the question requirements? Did you leave the exam early, thinking that there was no way you could have passed? Did you grade yourself as you progressed through the exam? Did you forget to fight, scratch, and crawl for points? Yes, there are many factors that could have contributed to your failed attempt. Think about them. The little things like time management really do make a big difference. Maintaining your confidence level is crucial. That's right, you must always believe that you can pass the CPA exam.

GO BACK TO CHAPTER 6

You know where you might have gone wrong. Now is the time to go back to Chapter 6, "Developing Your Personal Study Plan," and develop a new study plan to fit your new situation. Follow the techniques to develop a schedule. An exam condition reduces the amount of review material. You have more time now, so use it wisely. Condition candidates beware-- discipline and commitment are still important success factors, but procrastination can be your enemy. Don't waste time. Prepare your plan and stick to it. Maybe this time through you will not have to revise or adjust your study plan. Let's hope you can develop it and closely follow it.

FAILURE VERSUS SUCCESS

You are only one more exam away. Failure is temporary. The only way you can truly be a failure is if you give up. Try and you will succeed. Give up and you will never become a CPA. Being a CPA is not a requirement for happiness, but once you have made the attempt you realize that although this exam is difficult, it is also passable. Keep on trying and you will make it.

PERSONALLY SPEAKING

People don't ask you how many times you have taken the CPA exam. They only ask: "Are you a CPA?" Cut yourself some slack--this exam is not easy. Going in you knew that upon the first attempt, most people fail. Some say that on the average it takes 4½ attempts to pass. While I have no statistics to back up that number, I do know that it is not uncommon to sit more than two times. I really believe that the number of failed attempts could be greatly reduced if people would first take the time to understand what the exam tests, and second to realize that these concepts must be practiced. Michael Jordan always practiced his free throws, dribbling, and even his jumps. He was the master of basketball, but he did not stop practicing until the day he retired. Don't stop studying until the day of the exam. You never know when you are studying the very topic that will be tested the next day.

I can't understand why people study old material. I have attended the CPA exam in Illinois for the last 12 years. Dr. Patrick Delaney, author of *CPA Examination Review*, published by John Wiley & Sons, Inc., and I attend the exam to help our students stay calm, review material, and remain focused. We see candidates studying with textbooks that are 4 to 5 years old. Why are they doing this? Think about it--they are basically saying that topics such as income tax and financial accounting have not changed in 5 years. I want to cry for them as they are starting out with a great disadvantage. They are not being fair to themselves. I realize that money may be a factor. The average cost of a review manual for one exam section is $35 to $40. When you really make passing the exam a priority, you will forgo a few meals at a fast food restaurant and buy the latest book. I have the candidates' best interest in mind here, not my own. I want them to help themselves by giving themselves every possible chance to pass. It breaks my heart to see people setting themselves up to fail.

It is sad when people are prepared before the exam and then, during the exam, let the form of the question scare them into self-doubt. Attack this exam with gusto. Attack with confidence, even if it is your second or third time. Continue to fight for points no matter what you encounter. Whatever you do, don't grade yourself.

When candidates repeat the exam, they begin to think they can determine their grade before they receive it. Don't even try. The last exam you took may have required a different knowledge level. If you feel this exam is tougher than the last exam, it may be true just because you now know more than you did before. Now you are recognizing the real issues. Don't compare the current exam to other exams. Move forward without looking backward. Each exam is its own unique instrument. Perform your best on this exam. Leave the grading to the AICPA.

Persistence does pay off. One of my favorite candidates took the exam 11 times. He took three different review courses and had purchased every supplemental CPA review aid he could find. He joined the Northern Illinois University CPA review upon his eighth attempt. The first time through our review he found that he was still learning new material. So, his eighth attempt was more like a first attempt. He did not pass. Upon his ninth attempt he conditioned two parts. He gained one more section in his tenth attempt. Finally, after 11 exams his tenacity paid off. He was a CPA. He brought four family members to the awards banquet, of which two had flown in from Ireland. I mentioned how wonderful it was that his family members cared so much that they had spent a great deal of money to attend the celebration. He laughed and said it was nothing compared to the $19,683.62 he had spent taking the exam, enrolling in review courses, and purchasing CPA materials. The total astounded me. He was correct--as this is not a cheap affair. Unsuccessful attempts can be costly. Still, I admire him greatly as he stuck with the task. (Two weeks after he found out that he passed the CPA exam his company made major cutbacks. He kept his job because he was a CPA. The money was probably worth his lifelong career investment in time and in the company pension plan!) In my eyes, he will always be a great person. He never gave up and he crossed the finish line to success.

Make some changes to your study routine. Revise your study plan based upon your known weaknesses. One never knows when little changes will make big gains. Adjust and go for a passing score!

23 CONGRATULATIONS--YOU ARE A CPA!

You have patiently waited for almost 3 months and finally you receive the letter stating that you are a CPA! Are you really a CPA? It depends. Some states require an ethics examination. Other states require work experience before they will allow you to use the initials CPA. Although the exam is administered on a national basis, Certified Public Accountant (CPA) is a title conferred by a state or governmental jurisdiction that authorizes the holder to practice as a CPA in that jurisdiction.

COMPLETING AN ETHICS COMPONENT

Be sure you understand the requirements of the state in which you practice. Relax--the difficult part is over. Now you simply follow the rules and pay the necessary licensing fees.

The letter you receive, notifying you that you are a CPA, will include the necessary steps. The ethics component, when required, can be in the form of a course requirement or an open-book examination. If an examination is required, you will receive the rules, be asked to read them, and respond to a list of questions. The only mistakes you could possibly make are reading something incorrectly or missing the deadline for completion. Don't take this step lightly. The jurisdictions that require an ethics component believe a CPA must be knowledgeable not only about technical matters but also about matters that affect a person's integrity.

Make a copy of the examination before you begin. Write your answers on the copy. Complete all of the paperwork on the copy so you are not ruining the real exam. Have a CPA who is a friend or coworker review your answers. After you have proofed and reviewed your responses, carefully copy them over to the actual exam form.

Take the same care with the ethics examination that you did with the initial application to sit for the exam. Prepare a folder entitled "Ethics Examination." Keep a copy of the actual paperwork you sent back to the board. On the folder, list when and where you sent the information. Go to the post office and have the papers weighed and the proper amount of postage affixed. Use a postal method that allows you to track the receipt. Put all information in your folder. Mark the expected response date on your calendar. Call the board when you do not hear from them on a timely basis.

PROOF OF WORK EXPERIENCE

When work experience is a requirement, your employer is often asked to provide the necessary proof. Public accounting firms are very familiar with the paperwork. If you work for a company or firm that is not knowledgeable in the area, your first call should be to the board of accountancy for your jurisdiction. Ask them to provide you with sample letters from previous cases. Your company's auditor could prepare a letter to attest to the type and quality of work that you perform. Again, before you ask an audit team member to do this, consult with the board of accountancy.

Make copies of all forms before you give them to employers to complete. Allow them plenty of time to meet the deadline. Give polite, gentle reminders a few days before the due date. Usually this is not a high priority item for your auditor or employer. Don't take it personally, just give them the time and reminders as needed.

Just as you did for your application and perhaps the ethics examination, keep all of the paperwork in a folder. Note the response dates on your calendar. Follow up on the due dates. Be sure you have affixed the proper amount of postage.

FRAME THAT CERTIFICATE AND UPDATE YOUR RESUME

Get your certificate professionally framed. After all, it is a professional certification that you earned through your hard work. Proudly display it in your office. In fact, I even know of people who framed their letter reporting the scores. Get your business cards and letterhead changed. Update your resume. You never know when a better job might come along. Now that you are a CPA, you will have an advantage over other candidates.

List any and all special accomplishments in the education and professional certification section of your resume, such as the review class you took. If you passed all four sections of the exam upon first attempt, add a line to your resume that says: "Successfully completed all four sections of the *(list the exam month and year)* CPA exam upon first attempt." What a statement you have just made! You have accomplished something that only 12-15% of the nation can do. Be sure to mention it in your job interviews. List any special state award or AICPA medals that you earned. Maybe bragging just isn't your style, but this is the competitive business world. If you don't make your employer aware of your achievements, who will? Go ahead, let your parents or employers submit your name to the local paper. After all, it is a good advertisement for your employer. Notify the accountancy department of your university of this achievement. Passing the exam is a success. Enjoy the rewards and recognition. Attend any special awards or certificate presentations in your state. Take lots of pictures to save and show your grandchildren. People have been trying to pass the CPA exam since 1917. This exam is going to be around for a long time to come. You have met the challenge and now you should enjoy the rewards.

CONTINUING PROFESSIONAL EDUCATION (CPE)

To keep a current CPA license, each jurisdiction requires a set number of continuing professional education (CPE) credits. The number of credits is usually specified in hours and may vary by your type of employment. For example, educators and those CPAs practicing in government and private industry positions may not need as many CPE hours as those CPAs who practice in public accounting. Usually it is up to the CPA to maintain a record of CPE hours and to provide proof only when requested to do so. The best proof of hours would be certificates of attendance which are issued for each course by the sponsor. Where should you go to obtain your CPE hours?

Begin your search for CPE at the American Institute of Certified Public Accountants (AICPA) in New Jersey. In fact, upon passing the exam, you should join two organizations

1.   The AICPA
2.   Your state CPA Society

The AICPA provides quality CPE in a variety of forms such as live lectures, self-study, and interactive on-line programs. Your employer may cover some CPE costs. State CPA societies are very reasonable and involve little travel costs. Don't assume that all lectures and programs with an accounting topic would qualify for CPE credit. The only courses that qualify for CPE credit for licensure purposes are those offered by sponsors approved by your state board. A sponsor that has been approved by another state's regulatory agency for CPE credit in that state may be acceptable in your state. Obtain proof of the sponsor's approval prior to paying for or attending any course by calling your state board.

To maintain membership in the AICPA, CPAs in public practice must earn 120 hours of CPE every 3 years with a minimum of 20 hours taken each year. Note that this requirement applies to CPAs in **public** practice only. CPAs in other than public practice must earn 90 CPE hours every 3 years with a minimum of 15 hours taken every year. CPE hours usually count for both state and AICPA credit. The dues and fees you pay for CPE are deductible to some extent on your income tax return. Let's face it--upon passing the CPA exam you have clearly achieved a professional goal and you should continue to do whatever it takes to remain at a professional level. The accounting profession is undergoing frequent changes. Earning CPE hours will not only help you to stay on top and be informed of changes and new developments, but attending courses provides an opportunity for you to network with other professionals.

NETWORKING

Passing the exam is truly an individual experience. Only you could go into that examination room, sit for 2 days, and answer the questions correctly. Now that you are a CPA, you will find that remaining current is much more of a group experience. Some of your best learning experiences may not occur in a classroom but by interacting with other CPAs. Don't be afraid to volunteer to serve on a committee at your state society or one of its local chapters. Upon passing the CPA exam, you will be the most current and well-studied on all accounting subjects as you ever will be. In the future, you will probably focus on a few select areas such as tax, consulting, audit, or fraud and will no longer be as knowledgeable in all facets of the accounting profession. Volunteer work will help you to meet people, define your preferred area of focus, and reward yourself with new challenges.

SAYING THANK YOU

So your boss wasn't exactly supportive throughout the entire CPA exam-taking experience? Your spouse and/or friends were not behind you 100% of the time? Forgive and forget as you probably had your bad days too. Forget about the negative times and move on with your life. Take the time to thank your boss, colleagues, and family. Tell your friends you couldn't have met the challenge without them. It takes so little to be humble and thankful. The rewards from what you have achieved are many. Share the glory and the recognition. You really couldn't have done it without the support of outsiders. Be a gracious winner.

WHAT'S NEXT?

Your first priority will probably be to catch up on home and work activities that you have ignored during your exam preparation. You should also consider obtaining at least one more additional certification. There are two certifications that relate closely to the CPA exam

1. Certified Internal Auditor (CIA)
2. Certified Management Accountant (CMA)

Both certifications are earned by passing a rigorous examination. Much of the CIA certification tests the auditing knowledge that you learned for the CPA exam. There is content overlap among all three examinations. If you are a CPA, you will be exempt from passing one or more sections of the CIA and CMA exams. Why not use the technical knowledge and examination strategies that you have perfected to the utmost? The organizations that support and administer these examinations are

- CIA--The Institute of Internal Auditors in Altamonte Springs, Florida (www.theiia.org/cia)
- CMA--The Institute of Management Accountants in Montvale, New Jersey (www.rutgers.edu/accounting/raw/ima)

BELIEVE AND ACHIEVE

How does it feel to be so successful? You have accomplished a very important goal in your life. Use your newly acquired certification as a tool to open doors for yourself. Never lose your desire to achieve. Do you remember how the journey to become a CPA began? You started by believing in yourself. You supported that belief with hard work and dedication to the task at hand. The lessons you have learned will benefit you throughout your life. When the task is difficult, believe first in yourself. Continue in life with hope and determination. Congratulations, you are a CPA!

PERSONALLY SPEAKING

Passing the CPA exam will probably rank among your greatest accomplishments. Being a CPA has given me many opportunities. I have traveled worldwide and have always been respected for my integrity and knowledge. I take the title "CPA" seriously. I realize that I am blessed with an ability to analyze technical information. Did you make any promises to yourself when you were studying for the exam? I did. I promised myself that when I passed the exam, I would use my title to gain experience and share my knowledge with people that needed my help. Yes, I do work for pay, but I have also used my status and achievements to help others that are less fortunate by donating time to many organizations. I hope you do too. Here are some suggestions for giving back to the society that has given you so many opportunities:

- Volunteer to do tax returns for the elderly.
- Serve on a not-for-profit board such as a church or community organization.

    HINT: You are very qualified to serve in the treasurer's position.

- Become active in your state society of CPAs. Work your way up to serving on the technical committees where you can influence the standard-setting process of the profession.
- Be a role model for children. Travel to schools and share stories about the commitment that you made. Let them know that the road to success is not an easy one. Remind them the pleasure that you receive from achieving is far greater than the sacrifice it takes to get there.
- Contact government officials about traveling to developing countries to assist them in updating their banking and accounting models.

Remain proud of your achievement. I am so proud to be a CPA that my license plate says, "BE A CPA." I want the whole world to know that I have achieved success. Congratulations--you, too, are successful. Congratulations--**you** are a CPA!

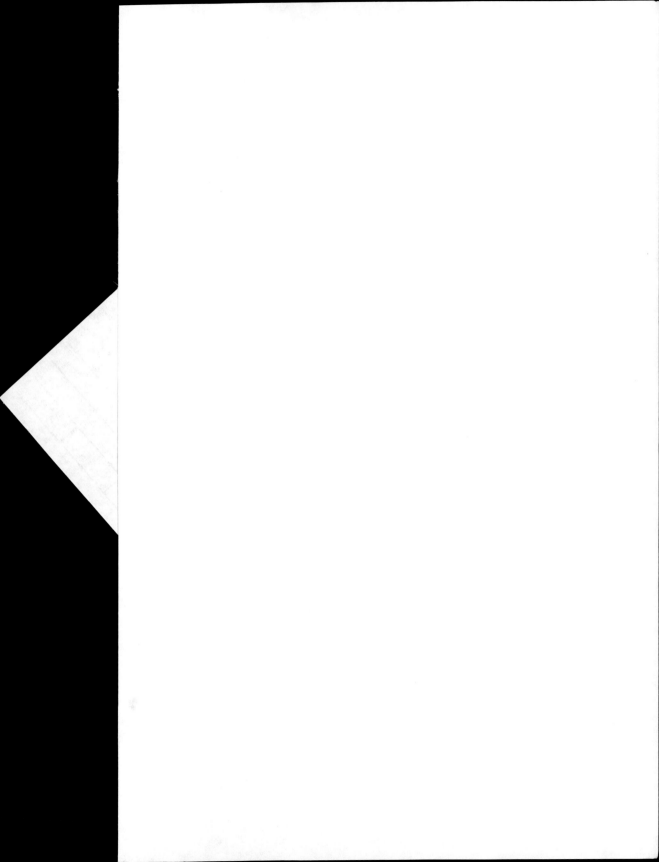

Demco. Inc 38-293